FABRICATED FOODS

other AVI books

Dairy Science and Technology

Food Science and Technology

FABRICATED FOODS

Edited by **GEORGE E. INGLETT, Ph.D.**
Chief, Cereal Properties Laboratory
Northern Regional Research Laboratory
Agricultural Research Service
U.S. Department of Agriculture
Peoria, Illinois

WESTPORT, CONNECTICUT
THE AVI PUBLISHING COMPANY, INC.
1975

Library of Congress Catalog Card Number: 74-33975
ISBN-0-87055-179-5

Printed in the United States of America

Contributors

DR. KERMIT BIRD, Head, Nutrition Programs Group, Nutrition and Technical Services, Food and Nutrition Service, U.S. Department of Agriculture, Washington, D.C.

DR. BENJAMIN BORENSTEIN, Manager, Food Industry, Technical Service Department, Roche Chemical Division, Hoffman-LaRoche, Inc., Nutley, New Jersey

DR. MALCOLM C. BOURNE, Associate Professor, Food Science, New York State Agricultural Experiment Station, Department of Food Science and Technology, Geneva, New York

DR. GEORGE M. BRIGGS, Department of Nutritional Sciences, University of California, Berkeley, California

DR. FELIX FRANKS, Manager, Biophysics Division, Unilever Research, Colworth/Welwyn Laboratory, Unilever Limited, Colworth House, Sharnbrook Bedford, Mk 441LQ England

DR. MARTIN GLICKSMAN, General Foods Corporation, Corporate Research Department, White Plains, New York

MR. JOHN L. HOLAHAN, Vice President/New Product Process Development, General Mills, Inc., Minneapolis, Minnesota

DR. GEORGE E. INGLETT, Chief, Cereal Properties Laboratory, Northern Regional Research Laboratory, ARS, USDA, Peoria, Illinois

DR. OGDEN C. JOHNSON, Corporate Vice President of Scientific Affairs, Hershey Foods Corporation, Hershey, Pennsylvania

DR. I. KATZ, Director of Flavor Research, International Flavors and Fragrances, Inc., Union Beach, New Jersey

DR. CONSTANCE KIES, Professor, Department of Food and Nutrition, The University of Nebraska-Lincoln, Lincoln, Nebraska

DR. S. KURAMOTO, Vice President, Director, Technical Support, International Flavors and Fragrances (U.S.), Flavor Division, New York, New York

MR. N. RICHARD LOCKMILLER, General Manager, Proteins Division, A. E. Staley Manufacturing Co., Decatur, Illinois

DR. DANIEL ROSENFIELD, Director, Nutrition Affairs, Miles Laboratories, Inc., Elkhart, Indiana

MR. JOEL L. SIDEL, Sensory Scientist, Tragon Corporation, P.O. Box 783, Palo Alto, California

MR. OAK B. SMITH, President, Wenger International, Inc., 1807 Federal Reserve Bank Building, Kansas City, Missouri

DR. HERBERT STONE, President, Tragon Corporation, P.O. Box 783, Palo Alto, California

DR. WALTER J. WOLF, Research Leader, Meal Products Research, Northern Regional Research Laboratory, ARS, USDA, Peoria, Illinois

MRS. ANNETTE WOOLSEY, Stanford Research Institute, Life Science Building 100, Menlo Park, California

Preface

This book is comprised of selected papers from a Short Course on Fabricated Foods sponsored by the Agricultural and Food Chemistry Division of the American Chemical Society and held in Las Vegas, Nevada, March 27-29, 1974. Important aspects of Fabricated Foods reviewed at this meeting were: economics, government regulations, strategic considerations, marketing, carbohydrates, soy protein chemistry, extrusion processing, sensory evaluation, texture, flavor, and nutrition.

The contributors to this volume are authorities having a close and continuing acquaintance with some aspect of Fabricated Foods. Both topics and authors were selected by the Editor to cover the broad areas concerned with these rapidly developing food products. Another editor and Short Course organizer could have easily selected differently. The intention was to provide reference material on these foods that would be useful to many people.

The Editor expresses his utmost appreciation to the authors who were willing to meet his challenge, and to their companies, government agencies, and universities who allowed their participation. In addition, the Editor extends his gratitude to the session chairmen; Victor V. Studer, John L. Holahan, Malcolm Bourne, Ogden C. Johnson, and Roy Teranishi. Contributing also in large measure to the success of the Short Course and this book are some of my associates: Wilma J. Bailey, Doris M. Davis, Evelyn F. Edwards, Stanley J. Kazeniac, Richard J. Magee, Rose Marie Pangborn, and Virginia Mae Thomas. Their assistance is duly acknowledged.

Career-service employees of the U.S. Department of Agriculture are expressing their own opinions in their articles, and not those of the United States Government. Mention of companies or products by name does not imply their endorsement by the United States Government over others not cited.

July 30, 1974   GEORGE E. INGLETT

Contents

CHAPTER 1

G. E. Inglett | # Fabricated Foods in Perspective

Foods that have been designed, engineered, or formulated from various ingredients, including additives, will be called fabricated foods in this book. Fabricated foods are made by structuring, shaping, or blending various ingredients into finished food products. These products are rapidly increasing in number in grocery stores. Consumer acceptance of fabricated foods is based largely on their convenience, appearance, sensory values, reproducibility, and economic value.

Many fabricated foods are reproductions of existing foods. A well-known example of a fabricated food is margarine. Despite the long legal, marketing, scientific, and technological hurdles, margarine has become a respectable, highly regarded, and useful food. Many foods are now undergoing a transition from a poor imitation of an existing food to a sophisticated fabricated food.

A spectrum of fabricated dairy-type foods can be seen in Fig. 1.1 These products are illustrated by margarine, imitation ice cream, a nondairy creamer, and a whipped topping mix. In Fig. 1.2, foods containing soy proteins are displayed. Soy proteins provide functional qualities in these products as well as good nutritional values. In the bacon-like product the structure is provided by spun soy protein isolate. The sausage-like product also contains fabricated soy proteins. The ground meat-like products contain textured vegetable protein.

INGREDIENTS OF FABRICATED FOODS

The ingredients used in fabricated foods must be readily available, economical, safe, and must serve a useful function. It is essential that regulations exist to protect the public from any food ingredient, as well as finished food product, which is unfit for human consumption or harmful to health, and to ensure that the consumer is not misled by labeling, advertising, or other claims.

A major breakthrough for the fabricated foods industry was the permission by the USDA (1971) to use textured vegetable protein products in combination with meat in child-feeding programs.

Many fabricated foods have made a major impact on traditional foods and beverages. Margarine, for example, has more than 66% of the tablespread market (USDA 1972). Retail citrus beverage purchases are about 21% of the market. Non-dairy whipped topping has 50% and coffee whiteners 35% of the market. Soy proteins are expected to replace meats

1

FIG. 1.1.   FABRICATED DAIRY-TYPE FOODS

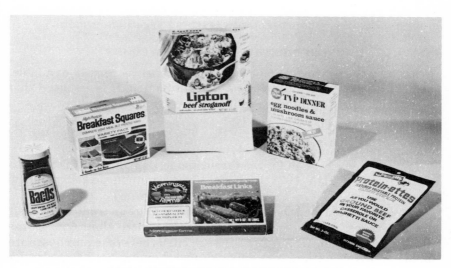

FIG. 1.2.   FABRICATED FOODS CONTAINING SOY PROTEINS

in processed-product formulations, and the impact of this replacement is expected to be large in the near future.

Among some of the other important government regulatory actions, the Food and Drug Administration's Nutrition Labeling proposal (1973) has greatly expanded the need for more complete data on food composition. The Agricultural Research Service of the USDA has been working with the food industry to develop plans for a computerized Nutrient Data Bank, which will be an international repository of analytical data on food and beverage products and their ingredients. It will be used in developing the successor to the USDA's Agricultural Handbook No. 8, "Composition of Foods—Raw, Processed, Prepared." Currently, this Handbook is the major source of food composition data in the U.S. Companies are encouraged to provide analytical data on food composition that they now have or may obtain in the future.

Labeling of fabricated foods is a particularly difficult problem. In Fig. 1.3, you will see a box of fabricated breakfast bars. The ingredients used to prepare this fabricated food are listed in Fig. 1.4. As you will observe on the label, 43 ingredients are utilized in preparing this food. It is particularly difficult for the consumer to relate the value of the listed ingredients to their need in the food product.

FABRICATED FOOD SALES

Sales of fabricated foods were estimated at 13 billion dollars in 1972 and are predicted to grow to 23 billion dollars in 1980 (Anon. 1973).

FIG. 1.3. FABRICATED BREAKFAST BARS

NUTRITION INFORMATION

| Serving Size | 2 bars |
| Servings per Container | 4 |

| Calories | 370 | Carbohydrate, gm | 46 |
| Protein, gm | 12 | Fat, gm | 15 |

PERCENTAGE OF U.S. RECOMMENDED DAILY ALLOWANCES (U.S. RDA)

Protein	25	Vitamin D	25
Vitamin A	25	Vitamin E	25
Vitamin C	25	Vitamin B6	25
Thiamin	25	Folic Acid	25
Riboflavin	25	Vitamin B12	25
Niacin	25	Phosphorus	25
Calcium	25	Iodine	25
Iron	25	Magnesium	25

Ingredients: Sugar, enriched flour (bleached), shortening, water, milk protein, soy protein isolate, cocoa (Chocolate only), glycerine, refiners syrup, peanut oil, peanut butter, soy protein concentrate, mono and diglycerides, starch, dried egg whites, salt, malted milk (chocolate malt only), artificial and natural flavors, leavening, magnesium carbonate, calcium phosphate, sodium caseinate, soy lecithin, dextrose, calcium sulfate, cocoa (Butter Pecan and Cinnamon only), calcium carbonate, sodium ascorbate, vitamin E, cinnamon (Cinnamon only), artificial coloring, vitamin A palmitate, niacin, iron, vitamin B12, vitamin B6, riboflavin, thiamin, vitamin D, folic acid and potassium iodide. Freshness preserved by sodium propionate, BHA, citric acid, BHT, and propyl gallate.

Distributed by
General Mills, Inc.
General Offices
Minneapolis, Minn. 55440

General Mills   Made in U.S.A.
NET WT 340 gms.

Breakfast Squares

Compare these two light breakfasts

Two bars (one serving) give you as much protein, basic vitamins and minerals, and total food energy as one slice of bacon, one medium egg, one slice of buttered toast and ½ cup of blueberries.

NUTRITIONAL COMPARISON

	Two Bars	Bacon, Egg and Fruit Breakfast
Calories	370	300
Protein, gm	12	11
Carbohydrate, gm	46	25
Fat, gm	15	17

Percentage of U.S. Recommended Daily Allowances (U.S. RDA)

Vitamin A	25%	15%
Vitamin C	25%	15%
Thiamin	25%	10%
Riboflavin	25%	15%
Niacin	25%	8%
Calcium	25%	6%
Iron	25%	15%
Vitamin D	25%	6%
Vitamin E	25%	4%
Vitamin B6	25%	6%
Folic Acid	25%	2%
Vitamin B12	25%	15%
Phosphorus	25%	15%
Iodine	25%	15%
Magnesium	25%	4%

FIG. 1.4.   INGREDIENTS IN FABRICATED BREAKFAST BARS

Vegetable protein product sales were forecast to grow from 82 million dollars to 1.5 billion dollars during this period. This predicted increase in sales is based on rising prices and shortages of meat expected by 1980. Current and estimated fabricated food markets from 1972 to 1980 are shown in Table 1.1.

CHALLENGES FACING FABRICATED FOODS

Some of the challenges facing fabricated foods are consumer education, goverment regulations, economics of ingredients, marketing, need for new ingredients, safety of ingredients, quality control, nutritional quality of ingredients and finished foods, and production technology. Better creations of dairy-like and meat-like products still remain a high-priority challenge. Success in these areas, as with all fabricated foods, will be measured by repeat sales to the consumer.

Fabricated foods should be more than just good business: they should represent the very best food in terms of quality, safety, and nutrition. Quality food ingredients can be designed into these foods by reducing or eliminating undesirable substances. A scientific reason for increasing

TABLE 1.1

CURRENT AND ESTIMATED FABRICATED FOOD
MARKETS (1972-1980)

	Millions of Dollars		
	1972	1976	1980
Dairy substitutes	874	994	2,527
Beverages	157	212	274
Snack foods	2,002	2,467	3,066
Prepared desserts	60	82	111
Salad dressings			
Spoonable	314	371	439
Pourable	123	172	238
Vegetable protein products	82	316	1,532
Dietetic foods	39	48	96
Prepared cereals	670	753	848
Cookies and crackers	1,558	1,686	1,825
Cake and roll mixes	230	241	250
Pop tart products	68	86	109
Soft drinks	5,450	7,412	10,100
Pet foods	1,304	1,648	2,081
	12,904	15,588	23,496

Source: Anon. 1973.

interest in fabricated foods is their potential as a means of avoiding the developing threat of environmental contamination of our food resources. As our environment becomes more polluted, increased levels of contaminants are being found in food crops. Among these are heavy metals (particularly mercury, lead, and cadmium), polycyclic aromatic hydrocarbons, polychlorinated biphenyls, pesticides, and mycotoxins. Processing of food crops to give food ingredients with reduced levels of contaminants is highly desirable. Since processed ingredients are the building blocks of fabricated foods, products can be made from ingredients from which any potential hazard has been removed.

CONCLUSION

It is necessary to maintain a sense of proportion about fabricated foods. In relation to the many other hazards of life, the risks arising from the consumption of fabricated foods are very small. The American diet is probably safer than it has ever been. American industry must continue to maintain its high standards of producing not only the world's most abundant food but also the world's safest, most nutritious, and highest-quality food.

BIBLIOGRAPHY

ANON. 1973. Fabricated foods market to exceed $23 billion by 1980. Food Technol. *27*, No. 12, 46.
FDA. 1973. Food labeling. Fed. Regist. *38*, 6950-6975, Washington, D.C., March 14.

USDA. 1971. Textured vegetable protein products (B-1) to be used in combination with meat for use in lunches and suppers served under child feeding programs. FNS Notice 219. Food and Nutrition Serv., Washington, D.C. Feb. 22.

USDA. 1972. Synthetics and Substitutes for Agricultural Products. Projections for 1980. Marketing Research Report No. 947. Econ. Res. Serv., Washington, D.C.

CHAPTER 2

Kermit Bird | # Fabricated Foods in Our Economy

Some of the most important fabricated foods are snacks, cookies and crackers; soft drinks; dairy substitutes; prepared cereals; salad dressings; cake and roll mixes; beverages other than soft drinks; vegetable protein products; prepared desserts; pop tart products; and dietetic foods. Total sales of fabricated foods are expected to climb from 1972's 13 billion dollars to 23 billion dollars in 1980. At present, fabricated foods account for 6.5% of total food sales, and this may increase to 8% by 1980. Fabricated foods that are presently in use or are being submitted for possible acceptance into U.S. Department of Agriculture (USDA) feeding programs will receive primary consideration in this chapter. Using these products as examples in no way means endorsement or approval of them by USDA.

DEFINITION OF TERMS

Fabricated foods are foods that have been taken apart and put together in a new form. Designed, engineered, or formulated from ingredients, they may or may not include additives, vitamins and minerals. Examples are breakfast pop tarts and formulated milk-based drinks that have special application as body builders for undernourished children, and pregnant or lactating women; or they may be old standby foods that have had new ingredients or nutrients added to them. *Formulated* foods and *engineered* foods are the same as fabricated foods.

Restoration is addition of selected nutrients to a food to restore nutrients lost through processing. If enough vitamin C were added to a frozen apple pie to bring the vitamin C back to its original level in the apples, the pie could be called a restored food.

Fortification is addition of selected nutrients not normally present in a particular food. If protein were added to the apple pie mentioned above, protein not being a natural nutrient to pie, this would be called fortification. Another example is adding vitamin D to milk.

Enrichment is addition of nutrients to a food so as to make that food conform to some special standard for that food. Vitamins and minerals added to an ordinary flour to achieve the standard for enriched flour constitute flour enrichment.

Nutrition enhancement is addition of nutrients to a food by fortification, enrichment, or restoration. Nutrification is the same as nutritional enrichment.

Nutritionally modified foods have had nutrients added to them so that

7

they contain food values at least equal to the natural foods they may replace in the diet. Textured vegetable protein has minerals and vitamins added to it so that it has all the nutrients of the meat it replaces in the diet.

Simulated foods are designed to completely replace some other food; they are made to look, taste, and feel like the food they replace. Meat analogs, made from plant proteins, are similar to the real meats they replace. Soy milk is designed to replace cows' milk.

Synthetic foods are those made from materials generally thought of as nonfood sources. An imaginary example might be a product made from corncobs, with minerals and vitamins added for nutrition, and sweetened for taste acceptance. Artifically sweetened soft drinks and fruit drinks are synthetic fruit juices.

Imitation foods are those made to look like and replace a food that has a "standard", but they do not meet the standard requirements. In the meat field, for example, it would be fairly simple to fabricate a sausage-type product, that would look, feel, and taste like a frankfurter. If, however, this product did not meet the standard of composition for frankfurters, as defined by Animal and Plant Health Inspection Service (APHIS) of the U.S. Department of Agriculture, it would be labeled imitation.

Convenience foods require less labor in storing, handling, preparing, serving or eating than the foods they replace. This particular definition of "convenience" keeps changing as the kind and amount of "labor needed" changes its location from one place to another in the marketing system. An example: Several years ago almost all french fries were prepared in the end user's kitchen. Now many fries are prepared in a potato-processing plant that may be several thousand miles away. Since labor is saved in the home or institutional kitchen, these new french fries are thought of as "convenience" foods. A decade from now we will have forgotten that french fries were once prepared in the user's kitchen and they will have lost their image as a "convenience food," much as canned soups and sliced bread have done.

THE "WHY" OF FABRICATED FOODS

Fabricated foods have been defined as "ingredients put together in a new form." But, why would anyone want to take a perfectly good egg out of its natural shell container, add something to it, subtract something from it, process it, put it in a new form, repackage it, freeze it, and market it as a fabricated product? This is now being done! Fabricated foods serve useful purposes, and fill the following needs:

(1). In certain applications, *meal costs can be lowered.* In our school
      lunch program "enriched macroni with fortified protein" lowers
      meal costs even though its price per pound is about the same or
      slightly higher than regular macaroni. This product receives
      credit as a meat alternate, and must be used in the same dish
      with meat, fish, or cheese. The meat/meat alternate entrée com-
      bination costs a school lunch manager less than an all-meat
      entrée would cost, while providing about the same nutrition and
      satiety.

(2). *The nutrition of a meal may be enhanced.* Examples are our
      USDA family feeding program juices. All our fruit and vegetable
      juices must be enriched with vitamin C to our juice specifica-
      tions. Our margarine has to be enriched with vitamin A. Our
      new Women, Infants, and Children Program (WIC) cereals must
      contain specified levels of iron and other nutrients.

(3). *Meals can be made more convenient* with fabricated foods. One
      example is the newly developed combination food used in school
      lunch called the "cup-can." It is simply a specified amount of
      meat and vegetable put together so that school lunch meat and
      vegetable requirement are met, and is used in schools that do not
      have kitchens or cafeterias. As in vending-machine canned en-
      trées, the can itself serves as both the heating and serving con-
      tainer.

      The "CN Pizza", a newly formulated product designed for
      schools, combines bread, margarine, meat and /or cheese, and
      perhaps a vegetable in one frozen, prepared, fabricated food. A
      convenient fortified food is our "formulated grain-fruit break-
      fast" baked item. This fabricated item is convenient because it
      allows omitting the fruit/juice component of the breakfast. Nu-
      trition is built into the baked product. A school can save time,
      labor, and kitchen facilities by serving the "formulated grain-
      fruit breakfast item" and a glass of milk in place of our usual
      breakfast of milk, bread/cereal, and fruit/juice.

(4). Foods can be formulated *to fill special needs.* Example: In the
      "cup-can" meal the required bread and butter meal components
      were inconvenient to serve. A bakery developed a baked product
      combining bread and butter. The resulting "butter-biscuit" filled
      a convenience need, as outlined in Table 2.1

(5). Fabricated foods can provide other meal advantages. They can
      improve the *balance* of a meal, they can increase *palatability,* and
      finally can provide *satiety* and other advantages.

TABLE 2.1

CONVENIENCE OF FABRICATED FOODS

Conventional Meal	"Cup-Can" Meal
Components of Meal	
Meat entrée	Entrée in cup-can
	¼ cup vegetable in
1 vegetable	cup-can
1 fruit (or 2nd vegetable)	1 fruit (or 2nd vegetable)
Bread	Bread in butter-biscuit
	Butter in butter-biscuit
Butter or margarine	Milk
Milk	
Convenience Aspects	
Requires kitchen with full complement of ovens, sinks, refrigerators, dishwashers, etc.	No kitchen needed (heating oven only)
	Limited serving line
Requires serving line	Children can eat at desks, outside or in hallways
Requires cafeteria	
Requires full staff of well-trained workers	Limited staff and may be untrained
Requires cooking utensils, china, cutlery, trays, etc.	All eating and serving items, including trays are disposable. No cooking or serving utensils needed.

PLANT PROTEINS — A SPECIAL CASE

Plant proteins are one of the most interesting areas of growth for fabricated foods. Proteins from plants are not new in terms of food technology: soy flour and wheat gluten have been used for many years. The great development that changed the character of soy products has been the ability to incorporate texture into them. The physical structure of plant proteins is so important to us in the school-feeding programs that in our new Textured Meat Alternate (TMA) Appendix specifications have been written on determination of whether or not a product has texture by putting numerical values on a testing process of hydration, retorting, grinding, and screening. The new TMA specifications show several other changes, as follows: all nutrients are related to a per gram of protein; hydration of the final product is standardized at 18%; and several new nutrients are added. Although the major plant protein ingredient in fabricated food is now soy protein, other sources of plant proteins, such as cottonseed, peanuts, rape, sesame, safflower, sunflower, wheat, corn, and even grasses could be used, as more experience with these plant proteins is attained.

At current meat and soy product prices savings of $5 million per yr are possible to schools. In 1972 the soy products volume was about 9 million lb; it was about 20 million in 1973. Volumes are expected to be about 46 million lb in 1974. Relative to other sources of protein, fabricated plant proteins will be encouraged and accelerated. By 1980 plant protein products may replace about 17% of the meat items in the American diet. They are also becoming increasingly important in the dairy and baking industries.

In addition to plant proteins as ingredients in fabricated foods, other non-conventional protein items will become important fabricated food ingredients. Yeasts and microbial sources will undoubtedly have utility in the far future. In the more immediate future whey protein, fish protein, and similar products will have greater application.

Blends of proteins will be the key to good nutrition in fabricated foods. Soy protein, for example, lacks methionine but has more lysine than is needed for proper nutrition. Blending soy protein with cereal products improves the lysine and methionine balance. Animal protein ingredients, such as casein, whey, and fish protein, can fill an important role in providing amino acid balance. Mixing protein ingredients may have a secondary benefit. Meats are said to provide "unknown micronutrients" not present in vegetable proteins. This is a problem for presently used foods as well as newly fabricated foods derived from plant proteins. The best nutritional defense against this "unknown micronutrients" charge is to strive for greater variety and diversity in our foods and food ingredients. Plant proteins as the primary source of protein in a fabricated food, for example, should be broadened to include proteins from oilseeds, nuts, grains, microbial sources, yeast sources, and, of course, animal sources. Diversity in our fabricated food ingredient list would tend to counteract the present trend toward less variety, and result in more confidence in the ability of the food processing industry to provide good nutrition.

PROBLEMS OF THE FUTURE

An outline of some of the problem areas involving fabricated foods in the future is: (1) The market range for these foods is needed. Is their market related to their use, their ingredients, or the foods they replace? (2) Identification of the products themselves is needed. This might include defining them, setting up standards of composition, and settling on names or labels, which is the greatest problem now facing the industry. (3) In most fabricated foods a satisfactory texture is very difficult to achieve. Texture is just as important as taste, appearance, and nutrition. It appears to be a neglected area of investigation. (4) Creating a favorable image for these foods will be increasingly important in the future. Many consumers now view fabricated foods with suspicion or even alarm. (5) Finally, the problems of nutritional labeling must be solved. Not only is the problem for the label itself, but presents an entirely new area of work to the analytical laboratories.

In spite of the immensity of the challenge ahead, a better-fed population in this country will be the result, not only in terms of nutrition but also in convenience, lower costs, and improved meal balance.

CHAPTER 3

Ogden C. Johnson

Government Regulations
Affecting Fabricated Foods

Interest in fabricated foods has increased in recent years, probably in response to increasing costs of basic food products and as well as to improved technology. In general, the concern of regulatory agencies in relation to fabricated foods has been in terms of correct labeling and the use of ingredients that are generally recognized as safe, or whose safety is based on adequate and appropriate evelution.

More recently the question of imitation foods and the nutritional quality of these foods has been raised by both consumer groups and by the regulatory agencies. The concern of the consumer groups involves both alterations in the nutritional qualities of the product and economic considerations. Frequently an "imitation food" is fabricated from less costly ingredients; yet the consumer may be asked to pay what would appear to be a relatively high price for a product that in the minds of some is considered to be inferior because it is not "natural" food.

The regulatory agencies are concerned with the safety of the product, including its nutritional quality. They are also concerned with the nomenclature used, since many fabricated foods mimic natural foods, and could very easily be given the same common or usual name. Food companies that have spent considerable time and money developing products and going through the necessary legal exercises to establish a Standard of Identity for traditional foods do not want new foods that do not conform to the Standards of Identity to use the established name.

Regulatory agencies have started to develop rules directing what types of special labeling can or must be used on fabricated products. This involves not only nutritional labeling, but labeling for foods for use in special diets such as sodium content, fatty acid composition, special types of fortification, and ingredients. Such labeling can be very useful for promoting some fabricated foods. Since these foods are formulated in many cases from isolated ingredients of known composition, certain of the qualities that make the product particularly attractive to some groups of consumers can be built in, and the label can be used to call these values to their attention.

Rather than discussing each specific fabricated food, it is better to consider the types of regulation that should effect this class of foods. One must remember that the regulatory and consumer concerns will change with time. New technology provides a mechanism for developing fabricated foods that is not covered by existing regulations. However, many of the general regulations already in force can be applied to fabricated foods, even though the original intent of these regulations may not have been to provide a means of controlling new foods.

GENERAL REGULATIONS

General regulations are those which have been part of the Food and Drug Administration's regulations for a considerable period of time. The Standards of Identity make it more difficult to fabricate certain new foods and achieve a place for them in the market, because these regulations restrict the nomenclature that can be associated with some products. However, standards establish parameters in relation to appearance and ingredients.

Development of food standards for some fabricated foods has already occurred. Additional standards or guidelines can be expected as these new foods become "traditional foods" and the industry seeks to provide some of the assumed benefits associated with a food standard.

FOOD ADDITIVE REGULATIONS

Food additive regulations apply to all ingredients used in food, but since many of the fabricated foods require new technology and new chemical components associated with that technology, consideration of food additive regulations is very critical. Consumer concern on the use of food additives has led some companies to seek to fabricate new foods primarily from traditional food components. While this can be achieved in some cases, it is obvious when one looks at the ingredient labeling of many fabricated foods that the properties being sought cannot be achieved without whipping agents, stabilizers, emulsifiers, artificial flavors, and colors—all food additives.

LABELING REGULATIONS

Labeling regulations apply to fabricated foods. Thus, the ingredient listing, correct name, identification of artificial flavors or colors when these have been used, and correct placement and type size must be taken into consideration. While the regulations covering labeling apply to all foods, they frequently result in labels that highlight certain aspects of fabricated foods that the manufacturer would like to de-emphasize. However, these factors—use of numerous food additives, incorporation of artificial flavors, and the use of new ingredients in the product—are of primary concern to consumers. Thus, one can expect regulatory agencies to exert considerable pressure to provide for full disclosure on new fabricated foods.

Special Types of Labeling

Special types of labeling including nutritional labeling, common or usual names, and labeling in relation to the use of foods in special diets offer great opportunity to the manufacturer of fabricated foods. Many of the qualities, such as the nutrient content, are under better control in such fabricated foods than in traditional commodity foods.

Several of the new regulations deserve special consideration. The new regulation dealing with imitation foods permits a manufacturer to establish a new common or usual name even though his product may "imitate" or be an easily recognized substitute for a traditional food. The product must have a nutritional quality equivalent or superior to the traditional food, and it must be appropriately identified so the consumer is not misled. A definition of nutritional equivalency has been built into the regulation, and when fabricated foods that are nutritionally equivalent and have appropriate nutritional labeling are presented to the consumer, it is clear that the product has particular properties, and that these properties are associated with a *new* food.

The labeling of special dietary properties, such as sodium content or fatty acid composition, though they can be applied to traditional foods, are of particular value to the manufacturer desiring to build these special qualities into a fabricated food. The new food may be a reasonable replacement for a traditional food that must be excluded from a modified diet. The ability to label these products and to establish common or usual names can be very useful; and in some instances the statement that the product is an imitation can be another useful method for identifying how it could fit into the diet.

In addition to those regulations dealing with labeling and composition, one must consider controls applied by the Federal Trade Commission in relation to advertising claims. Many fabricated foods have properties that make them unique, but often these properties are promoted in such a way that their uniqueness becomes almost magic. It is becoming obvious that consumer concerns regarding advertising claims and the Federal Trade Commission's responses will result in action in several areas. Manufacturers of fabricated foods should consider how these foods should be promoted in relation to the actions and policy statements of the Federal Trade Commission.

STATE REGULATIONS

A final area that is one of the more difficult to discuss deals with state regulations. Several states have taken very firm positions on the sale of fabricated foods or foods containing fabricated ingredients. In many instances the manufacturer finds that he must make changes in labeling in one state or another, and this can result in increased costs. More consideration as to the alternatives that would be satisfactory within states where the more rigid position is being taken would offer a reasonable starting point. There are instances when compatibility between state and federal regulations cannot be achieved, and the manufacturer may find it necessary to modify his products or to seek relief through the courts. In any case, an evaluation of past actions by state regulatory agencies should be part of the basic evaluation of product labeling, and in some cases, its composition.

MARKETPLACE

The basic requirements of the marketplace to have a product identified for consumers in such a manner that its value is evident is a key factor in relation to all fabricated foods. The regulations will serve to establish uniform product names and may force improvement of nutritional quality, since these are factors that consumers have clearly indicated that they expect.

Some manufacturers appear to feel that the regulatory agencies should establish regulations that will make it easier to promote the products. The promotion of these products cannot be based on acceptable regulations. The manufacturer must accept the fact that in the final analysis, the role of the fabricated food in the diet will be determined by the consumer, as guided by the presentation of the product in advertising and labeling. Failure to provide the "value" expected in a fabricated food may result in regulatory action, if the labeling is false and misleading.

Presentation to the consumer that a fabricated food is more nutritious, more stable, or better than a natural product can be made, if these are in fact true statements, and the consumer will not be misled as to the degree of improvement that has been built into the product. But of far more importance than the regulatory controls will be the consumer response: if a fabricated food is to become an important product in the marketplace, consumers must receive the value they expect. Poor quality, undefined purpose for the food in the diet, or unacceptable comparisons between the fabricated food and a traditional food which become apparent on use, will result in market failure.

CONCLUSION

Manufacturers should not look to regulations such as Standards of Identity or guidelines to protect their image, or to establish the market for fabricated foods in some magic way. Fabricated foods which meet a consumer need and provide acceptable value in terms of taste, texture, usefulness, and nutritional quality can achieve an economically viable place in the market and will be used by the consumer as part of their diet. Fabricated foods that simply are exhibiting an improved technology, but have no readily defined purpose, obviously cannot be sold, and manufacturers will not be able to achieve success on technology alone. Because fabricated foods in the minds of some consumers, particularly those concerned with the safety of the food product, appear to be a threat to good diets, manufacturers should be very careful in their labeling of the product and their presentation of the product in terms of promotion and advertising. The Food and Drug Administration and the U.S. Department of Agriculture can be expected to impose considerable regulatory control on fabricated foods if there appears to be consumer deception. Manufacturers of fabricated foods have the degree of future regulatory control in their own hands at the present time. Failure to exercise control within the industry will result in a more rigid regulatory policy.

CHAPTER 4

John L. Holahan | # Strategic Considerations Behind Fabricated Foods Development

Fabricated foods require processing systems that are as unique as any to be found in the process industries. Twice in the last 5 yr the Kirkpatrick Chemical Engineering Achievement Award has gone to groups who developed unique processes for fabricated foods. In 1969 the award was made to General Mills for its Spun Protein development. In 1973 the award was made to British Petroleum Proteins, Ltd., for the process of making yeast by the fermentation of hydrocarbons.

These awards and many other happenings clearly indicate the accelerating pace of process development for fabricated foods. Companies are willing to commit substantial resources and time to this purpose. Obviously, there would be no need for the development of fabricated foods if there were not a need for them, or if they could not be sold. Why do these products sell? Why is there a demand for them? Why the predictions that this demand will increase? Here may be some answers to these questions.

CONVENIENCE

Since World War II, convenience has provided a major incentive for the purchase of processed foods. This motivation, once it was recognized, has been promoted by marketing people in every conceivable way. This convenience factor has been dubbed "built in maid service." Consider that in my grandmother's day, a woman, especially if she were on a farm, spent most of her waking hours growing food, processing it, cooking it, and cleaning up the attendant messes. In my mother's day, these chores were reduced to 8 hr per day. Today a wife can feed her family as well with about 2 hr per day of her labor. With some 38% of women in the U.S. now working outside the home, and with young homemakers swamped with the chores of attending to children, husbands, pets, and outside activities, there are no large trends back to the more labor-consuming methods of food preparation. We are also aware of the strong interest in convenience foods by women overseas. For example, marketing people in Japan tell us about the many working women among the young married couples and of their desire for foods that are quick and easy to prepare.

SHORTAGES

In addition to the demands for energy, fiber, and minerals created by the affluence of the developed nations, world supplies of food are becoming somewhat scarce because of various crop shortfalls. These shortfalls were not severe in that they were normal variations on the down side of average crop yields. However, with the world's population and food supply in such tight balance, any shortfall becomes disastrous for some people. Because of this tight balance, small variations in food supply are likely to result in wide price swings.

Each commodity, product, and product line requires its own careful analysis. Robert Fischer, president of Soy Pro International, uses the term "extractables" for such products as food extracted from the soil, and for goods manufactured from raw materials extracted from the earth. Grains, oilseeds, fuel, and many scarce minerals are examples. All these extractables, says Fischer, are likely to be in short supply for a long time.

Future planning must take into consideration that the U.S. has to import more than 50% of the following strategic materials: antimony, asbestos, barium, bauxite, bismuth, castor oil, chromium, cobalt, cordage fibers, manganese, mercury, mica, natural rubber, nickel, opium, platinum, quinine, shellac, strontium, vegetable-tanning extracts, tin, titanium, and zinc.

In the food field some people are predicting continued long-term shortages of meat, fish, and dairy products. This situation suggests that fabricated foods might be used to partially replace or extend meat, fish, and dairy products. It should be kept in mind that they will always be price-sensitive. The potential significance of new fabricated foods cannot be minimized. Considering the great advantage of feeding people grains and oilseed products as compared to beef products, several speakers declared at the World Soy Protein Conference (1974) that textured vegetable proteins are one of the great developments of the twentieth century.

TECHNOLOGY'S ROLE

Technology will play the leading role in effecting solutions to the current and long-term supply and demand problems of extractable products. A new emphasis on technology, not unlike that which prevailed immediately before and during World War II, is very likely. America may again be heading into an era where technology leads and marketing follows. For example, when the technologies of World War II were made available to the world at large, development people had a 25-yr lead time to convert these technologies into a wide variety of new consumer products, with marketing people tending to lead the way and technical people adjusting the technologies as required. Perhaps we are near the end of this era and will be entering a new one—prompting once again a new burst of technology.

PROTEIN DESIRE

At the World Soy Protein Conference (1974), immediate and future shortages of food were seen as a protein shortage rather than as a carbohydrate shortage. This was within a framework, not spelled out, of critically needed population control. "Protein desire" emerged as a more descriptive term than "protein shortage." Protein shortages for humans could be wiped out overnight if we did away with our dependence on meat and dairy products—which will not happen. As people earn more, they desire to eat better and are willing to spend more for food. David Terry, a marketing specialist on our James Ford Bell staff, has well-documented figures which show that Americans have traditionally spent 2.5% of their disposable income on beef products. As affluence increases among the developed nations, so too does the desire for up-scale proteins which currently are to be had only in meat, fish, and dairy products. This world-wide protein desire cannot be fully satisfied without new fabricated foods.

At the World Soy Protein Conference (1974), Senator Humphrey defined part of protein desire as a "protein need," especially in the developing nations. He emphasized the nutrition imperative for adequate protein in the diets of pregnant women, babies, and small children. The future well-being of an individual is critically affected by a child's protein intake during the first 5 or 6 yr of life. Over 2 billion lb of PL 480 foods distributed thus far to developing nations have saved millions of people from malnutrition and some from actual starvation; but such foods should be made more palatable for as little extra cost as possible. Palatability represents still another great challenge for fabricated foods development. There has to be more to mass feeding than the mixing together of the right nutritional blend of cheap ingredients.

UNIVERSALITY

Universality signifies that if a fabricated food is to be truly successful, it must have appeal to people in every economic category. The acceptance of textured proteins illustrates this point. Textured proteins received the first large acceptance when allowed as meat extenders in the USDA school lunch program (1971). People in less affluent nations were quick to notice this and said, in effect, "If Americans are willing to feed this to their children, it must be all right." Quite unexpected, however, was the acceptance of extended hamburger by housewives even in affluent suburbs.

Universality goes deeper than this. In comparing the developed nations with the developing nations, experience suggests that the latter are better able to withstand shortages and gross dislocations. This assumption makes us anxious to probe into the eating habits and practices of the people of developing nations. Perhaps they have things to teach us which should be considered in the development of fabricated foods. For example, 5 Calories of energy are required to place 1 Calorie of food on the American table. Contrast this with China where 3 Calories of food are produced from 1 Calorie of energy, because the food chain from field to table and waste disposal occurs within a 30-mile diameter circle.

PRESERVATION

Few American consumers give much thought to the fact that in some developing countries, as much as 50% of the crop is wasted (25% to rodents and insects, and 25% to spoilage). The initial thrust for the processed-foods industry came from a recognition of the need to protect perishable food products from spoilage. Butter and cheese were the first methods conceived for preserving milk. Napoleon Bonaparte was quick to realize that an army moved on its stomach and was the first to utilize canned foods just a few years after their discovery by Nicolas Appert in 1795. The birth of the packaged foods industry can be traced to Adolph Green, founder of the National Biscuit Company. In 1899 he took crackers out of the cracker barrel and put them into the now familiar 1- and 2-lb cartons. A few years later this packaging principle was adopted by the emerging ready-to-eat breakfast food companies founded by Kellogg, Post, and Perky. Add freezing and refrigeration and one now has the spectrum of methods by which the processed-foods industry preserves and stores the crop. When we talk about a 6 to 12 months' shelf-life for foods, we also imply that we have in America a vast and highly fragmented system of storing and preserving our crops and perishable foods. Our system starts with the farms; moves to the elevators; to the processing plants; into a vast variety of bins, containers, cartons, bottles, cans, and bags; into finished-product warehouses; to the supermarkets; and finally to shelves and freezers in the home.

The processed-foods industry has become so expert that food preservation is taken for granted in America. Statistics from the developing nations indicate how tragically far they are from an adequate system of food preservation. Those of us who are developing new processed/fabricated foods regard shelf-life as a key parameter.

PALATABILITY AND NUTRITION

Since fabricated foods require expensive product development efforts and processing systems, they must enjoy substantial sales to pay out. Foods that don't taste good don't sell, so palatability is a necessary consideration. Furthermore, eating is an enjoyable activity. People aren't about to replace meals, formal or informal, with even good-tasting pills. These eating habits have developed over millenia of human existence and are not going to change.

Nutrition must also be considered. People eat not only to enjoy good food, but also to stay alive. Companies in the processed food industry generally must evolve corporate policies which influence the nutritional properties of their fabricated foods. If meal replacement products are developed, policies concerning nutrition must be adopted. Also if meat and dairy product replacements and extenders are developed, their nutrition must be considered. These policies are in the best interest of both the company and the consumer.

SUMMARY

Centuries ago some fabricated foods emerged from the need to preserve crops. Today that need is still urgent. In this century, convenience and built-in maid service has provided an added dimension. Foods must taste good and be compatible with the ways people want to eat to be successful. Eating is too much an imperative social occasion to regard it in any other way. Fabricated foods must be nutritious; and they must be reasonably close in nutrition to the products they replace and extend.

The one-world era, with world markets and competition, provides the current new thrust to fabricated foods development. Since the demand for the affluent foods such as meat, fish, and dairy products cannot be fully met, attractive and tasty replacements and extenders for them are in demand. Food shortages, even with urgently needed population controls, will provide the incentive to develop foods with universal appeal so that food supplies can be more evenly distributed.

These concepts are some of the elements leading to a new era of fabricated food development. It is an era where technology will lead the way in developing many foods yet to be conceived, reduced to practice, and ultimately made available for sale in the world marketplace.

BIBLIOGRAPHY

World Soy Protein Conference. 1974. J. Am. Oil Chem. *51*, 47A-207A.

USDA. 1971. Textured vegetable protein products (B-1) to be used in combination with meat for use in lunches and suppers served under child feeding programs. FNS Notice *219*, Washington, D.C., Feb. 22.

CHAPTER 5

N. R. Lockmiller | Marketing of Fabricated Foods

This chapter will cover broadly the marketing of vegetable protein ingredients, fabricated foods from basic materials, and a brief mention of the use of fabricated foods in the marketplace. An ingredient is a vegetable protein that is obtained by processing of a grain or oilseed. For example, soy flour and grits, vital wheat gluten, cottonseed flour, milk proteins, and many others are considered as ingredients, while the upgraded products from the basic proteins, such as soy protein concentrates, isolates, textured proteins, and blends of basic ingredients processed into textured proteins, are fabricated ingredients. Fabricated ingredients can be used as the source of protein in a finished food as well as providing structural or functional properties. Other less-processed ingredients must also be combined with other components to produce a finished food product.

The primary function of marketing is threefold: (1) to fill a demand, (2) to create a demand, and, most important of all (Drucker 1954), (3) to create a customer.

MARKETING PREMISES

There are several marketing premises that should be discussed at this point with regard to the marketing of fabricated foods. The following requirements and changes must be made before fabricated foods will be accepted to a greater degree.

Educational

In the U.S., meat, fish, and poultry have been in plentiful supply for many years. This situation is changing. The world protein supply is another question, as many countries are deficient in protein. Domestically, proteins in the form of fabricated foods have been used sparingly, and it has been through the USDA, FDA, industry associations, and individual suppliers that the food processor has become better educated in the use of protein ingredients in finished food products. One such industry group is the Food Protein Council, which has, among others, the following objectives: (1) to improve and promote the image of food protein to a level commensurate with the high quality, improved functionality, and economy of today's various food protein products; (2) to assist legislative, regulatory, standard-setting or other bodies to develop practicable standards and tests with regard to food protein, to the end that the public interest will best be served; and (3) to compile and disseminate information to the industry and others which will promote the utilization of members' products.

Changing of Eating Habits

This relates somewhat to the preceding paragraph; however, this change from traditional foods to fabricated foods requires a change in eating habits if the usage of these products is to be increased.

Regulatory Aspects

Local, state, and federal regulations on the use of protein ingredients and fabricated foods have, for the most part, been restrictive. Recent and progressive thinking within the USDA and FDA has resulted in increased interest on the part of the processor and consumer in the use of protein ingredients and fabricated foods. Most notable, within the USDA, a major breakthrough was realized in February, 1971, with the development of the Food and Nutrition Service regulations pertaining to the National School Lunch Program (USDA 1971). Also there has been the FDA's proposed regulation on the part of the consumer for a balanced diet with respect to protein, fat, and carbohydrates.

Other marketing premises, such as protein supply, development of new products to meet consumer demand, and the improvement in the nutrition of fabricated foods, will be covered in subsequent chapters.

As mentioned earlier, it is the function of marketing to fill or create a demand, and certainly to create a customer. To accomplish any or all of these, it is necessary to rely on a well-used marketing tool—"market research". Market research is a broad term which may either be an informal or formal effort within an individual company or organization. Feedback from customers through sales repre_entatives or a more formal approach, where a market researcher contacts potential customers, yield the same benefit. It indicates where the customers' interests are and what kinds of ingredients they are looking for. On the other hand, a researcher may develop an entirely new product that will reverse the marketplace demand equation. Table 5.1 indicates most of the current uses or demands for basic protein ingredients.

With regard to fabricated food ingredients, market research indicates that these products may be used as substitutes, extenders or basic ingredients in processed finished foods. In subsequent discussions, they will be discussed in more detail.

In most companies of international stature, it is important to consider the world supply and demand for food. Fischer (1974) pointed out that there is a new, different world food market situation that affects the

TABLE 5.1

SOY PROTEIN INGREDIENTS

Soy Protein Ingredients	Protein %	Prices $/Lb	1973 Volume of Production in U.S. Million Lb	Current Uses
Flour and grits	40-55	0.14-0.17	450-600	Ingredients for baked goods, dog food, sausages
Concentrates	65-70	0.30	55	Mfg. textured products; ingredients in processed meats, baby foods, health foods
Isolates	90-97	0.55-0.56	50	Mfg. analogs such as meatless ham, bacon, hot dogs, etc.
(1) Modified isolates	90-97	0.92-1.33		Whipping agents
Textured items (1) Extruded (2) Spun	50-55 90+	0.27 & up 0.50 & up	110	Bacon bits, bacon strips and similar food, meat extenders

demand for fabricated foods, particularly those from vegetable proteins. Factors in this situation are the following developments: (1) our capacity to increase production of traditional proteins is becoming limited; (2) the long-standing reserves of surplus grains have been reduced; and (3) there has been an increase in demand for animal protein due to higher per capita incomes in many countries.

Once there has been found or created a need or customer for a product, progress to produce that product according to the demands of the marketplace can proceed. As others have pointed out in this book, several companies are now producing protein ingredients and fabricated foods. A partial list of protein ingredient suppliers is given in Table 5.2.

Marketing represents the full effort in getting the product to the marketplace. Selling is one of the most important aspects of the marketing job. The selling job is broken down into the domestic and international markets.

DOMESTIC MARKETING

Industrial Markets

These markets are the food processors who utilize protein ingredients to fabricate a finished food product. In these areas, proteins or fabricated

TABLE 5.2

PROTEIN INGREDIENT PRODUCERS[1]

Suppliers	Soy Flour and Grits			Concen-trates	Iso-lates	Spun Fibers	Textured Soy Prod.
	Defatted	Low-fat[2]	Full-fat				
A-D-M	x	x	x	-	-	-	x
Anderson-Clayton	-	-	-	-	x	-	-
Cargill	x	x[3]	-	-	-	-	x
Central Soya	x	x	x	x	x	-	-
Far-Mar-Co	x	x	-	x	-	-	x
General Mills	-	-	-	-	x	x	x
Griffith Labs	-	-	-	x	-	-	x
Gurley, Inc.	x	-	-	-	-	-	-
Lauhoff Grain Co.	x	-	-	-	-	-	x
Miles (Worthington)	-	-	-	x	x	x	x
National Protein	-	-	-	-	-	-	x
Ralston Purina	-	-	-	-	x	x	x
A. E. Staley	x	x	-	-	x[4]	-	x
Swift & Company	x	-	-	x	-	-	x

[1]Data supplied in part by Soypro International.
[2]All low-fat flour producers also offer lecithinated flour.
[3]Cargill offers lecithinated but not low-fat flour.
[4]Modified proteins.

foods are used for functionality and nutrition. For functionality, products are generally used at fairly low levels to absorb moisture or fat, emulsify fat, aerate the product, provide flavor, and to some small extent protein. A more important area is provided with the fabricated ingredient, namely, supplementation or extension of red meat, poultry, and fish. Tables 5.3 and 5.4 show the effect on cost of hamburger versus meat patty made with soy protein concentrate and textured protein. This meat, poultry, and fish extension or combination is effective in spaghetti sauce, pizza, meatballs, meatloaf, sloppy joes, casseroles, entrées, Mexican specialities, chicken and fish salads, fish sticks, and fabricated meats. Furthermore, fabricated ingredients are used as complete nutritive replacements for meat, poultry, and fish. This is particularly true where fabricated ingredients are used in scrambled eggs, baked potatoes, salads, skillet dinners, etc., where a flavored product is used as a complete replacement. An example of this would be the bacon-like products offered in the marketplace, as well as various meat, fish, and poultry-flavored spun or thermo-extruded textured proteins.

The industrial market, for the most part, is reached through direct sales representation, although brokers and distributors are used extensively by many. The technical service requirements for servicing this industry are significant and those companies with good technical service seem to enjoy an advantage over those with lesser services. Table 5.1 indicates the volume of ingredients sold in total for the calendar year 1973.

TABLE 5.3

COST BALANCE ON HAMBURGER VERSUS MEAT PATTY
(SOY PROTEIN CONCENTRATES)[1]

	Hamburger	Meat Patty (Soy Protein Concentrate)
Patty weight (lb)	100	129[2]
Ingredient cost ($)	60.00	62.50
Cost of product per lb ($)	0.60	0.485
Savings per lb (%)	0	19
Yield of cooked product (lb)[3]	70.2	98.5
Shrinkage (%)	30	23
Cost of cooked product, per lb ($)	0.85	0.63
Savings per lb (%)	0	26

[1]From Sair and Melcer 1970.
[2]Twenty-nine lb of hydrated soy protein concentrate added to 100 lb of meat.
[3]Protein content of the cooked hamburger 22.8%; cooked meat patty 20.7%.

TABLE 5.4

COST BALANCE ON HAMBURGER VERSUS MEAT PATTY
(TEXTURED SOY PROTEIN)*

		Meat Patty	
	Hamburger	26% Hydrated Textured Soy	40% Hydrated Textured Soy
Cost/100 servings ($) (2 oz each raw basis)	6.50	5.15[1]	4.82[2]
Cost/serving ($)	0.0650	0.0515	0.0482
Savings (%; raw basis)	-	21	26[3]
Weight of 2-oz serving (oz; cooked basis)	1.5	1.65	1.65
Cost/oz ($) (cooked basis)	0.043	0.031	0.029
Savings (%) (cooked basis)	-	28	33

[1]Derivation of cost: per 100 lb of ground beef at $0.52/lb add 12 lb TVP at $0.34/lb plus 24 lb water,
  giving $0.52/lb for the beef and $0.412/lb for the beef + TVP patty.
[2]Derivation of cost: per 100 lb of ground beef at $0.52/lb add 22 lb Temptein (Spun Soy Protein Nuggets,
  Miles Laboratories) at $0.55/lb plus 44 lb water, giving $0.386/lb for the beef + Temptein patty; at a
  26% meat replacement the cost is $0.431/lb.
[3]At 26% meat replacement this savings is 17%.
*Source: Horan 1974.

Institutional Markets

Sales of products to this important area, which includes schools, restaurants, hospitals, government agencies, etc., constitute a major market segment for those wanting to utilize protein ingredients in fabricated foods. The use of textured proteins, in particular, has given a tremendous boost to the sales of these products to this important market segment. Sales are handled through individual food service or institutional sales groups, working mostly through brokers, and in the case of the School Lunch Program, working with brokers or directly with school systems on a bid basis. Many of the food-service customers demand smaller package sizes.

Retail

Finished food products using fabricated ingredients are sold through normal distribution channels; however, it is interesting to note here that much effort is put behind retail products containing fabricated ingredients. Davidheiser (1970) indicated that: (1) consumers cannot detect fabricated foods in prepared meats; (2) the quality of products containing fabricated foods was highly rated on all major quality factors; (3) consumers feel that fabricated foods improve product quality; and (4) price was a major factor in selecting a particular brand of meat products.

Several producers of totally vegetable-based fabricated foods are shown in Table 5.5. Another aspect of retail marketing is the trend toward extended ground beef or the packaged fabricated food designed to extend ground beef. The retail ground beef market has been extensive, products being offered by Kroger (Burger Pro), Red Owl (Juicy Burger II), and others from Safeway and other major chains. Several companies have offered packaged products to extend ground beef, including Burger Bonus (Staley), Burger Builder (General Mills), Burger Plus (Cargill), Plus Meat (Central Soya), and Quick Chef Plus Burger (Jewel). Other products are being offered in the retail shelf which are predominantly fabricated proteins, including Red Skillet TVP Dinners (Gooch Foods, Inc.) and Protein-ettes (Creamette Co.).

INTERNATIONAL MARKETING

In many of the more developed countries, fabricated proteins are being used in combination with meat. England (British Soy Protein, Spillers), Japan (Kikkoman, Nisshin), Israel (Shefa Products), Sweden (Strange-Cullinar), and South Africa (Tiger Oats Ltd.) are the most active in the production of textured protein products.

In many of the developing countries, a deficiency of protein exists; it is compensated by importation of fabricated proteins, and local production is being considered. Major help in assisting and relieving the protein deficiencies in many developing nations is provided through AID donation programs. Table 5.6 indicates the volume of fortified foods supplied for 1973.

FUTURE MARKETING

It appears that the future for protein ingredients and fabricated proteins is promising. A number of factors dictate that protein ingredients

TABLE 5.5

PRINCIPAL PRODUCERS: SOY PROTEIN FOODS (FINISHED PRODUCTS)

	Dietary Foods	Convenience & General Foods	Soy Milk	Roasted Soybeans
Edible Soy Products, Inc.	-	-	-	x
El Molino	x	-	x	-
Fearn Soya	x	-	x	x
Flavor Tree Foods, Inc.	-	-	-	x
General Mills	-	x	-	-
Loma Linda Foods	x	x	x	-
Miles (Worthington)	x	x	x	-
Miles (Nutritional International)	x	-	x	-

TABLE 5.6

QUANTITIES OF SOY-FORTIFIED FOODS DISTRIBUTED IN U.S. OVERSEAS ASSISTANCE PROGRAMS (JULY 1, 1972-JUNE 30, 1973)

Food	Quantity Million Lb
Soy-fortified bulgur	296.6
Wheat-soy blend (WSB)	111.7
Sweentened WSB	55.4
Corn-soy-milk (CSM)	277.4
Instant CSM	64.1
Instant sweetened CSM	101.1
Soy-fortified corn meal	22.3
Soy-fortified rolled oats	21.8
Soy-fortified bread flour	52.1
Total	1002.5

and fabricated proteins should be utilized in increasing quantity: (1) reduced availability of animal protein (see Table 5.7, which shows the conversion rate of various animal proteins); (2) relative cost of fabricated vegetable proteins (Table 5.8 shows the relative protein products to 1 acre of land); (3) further increase in the use of convenience foods; (4) ability of the fabricated food processor to provide products that have good uniformity and the capability of being fortified as required; and (5) change in dietary requirements. It is probable that domestic and world diets may need to be reduced in fat and cholesterol content in order to achieve control over such diseases as heart disease, obesity, etc.

The future market for fabricated foods and protein ingredients has been well outlined by Hammonds and Call (1970), who reached the following major conclusions: (1) the current maximum market potential

TABLE 5.7

CONVERSION OF VEGETABLE PROTEIN INTO ANIMAL PROTEIN[1]

Class	Production Level	Annual Crude Protein Yield (Lb)	Annual Crude Protein Consumed (Lb)	Efficiency (%)
Cow	1500 gal at 3.25% protein	490	1290	38
Hen	320 eggs at 13% protein	5	16	31
Broiler	6 crops at 4 lb wt	2.5	8	31
Fish	One acre carp, warm pond	1500	7500	20
Rabbit	4 litters of 10 at 3 lb carcass	18	105	17
Porker	2¼ litters of 12 at 90 lb carcass	270	1850	15
Lamb	2 litters of 3 at 35 lb carcass	24	275	9
Steer	650 lb carcass	75	1250	6

[1]Wilson 1968.

TABLE 5.8

PROTEIN PRODUCTION FROM 1 ACRE OF LAND[1]

Source of Protein Supply	Satisfying Man's Protein Requirements (Days)
Soybeans	2,224
Wheat flour (whole)	887
Corn meal	773
Rice (brown)	772
Milk	236
Poultry	185
Swine	129
Beef cattle	77

[1]Catron 1967.

for protein ingredients is approximately 3.1 billion lb yearly, with a 2.0 to 2.2-billion lb untapped protein market which can be satisfied, at least in part, with fabricated proteins; (2) products must be produced with good or little flavor; and (3) the meat industry offers great potential, and Hammonds and Call indicate that extenders and analogs combined will reach 10% of all domestic meat consumption by 1985. Proteins or fabricated proteins could be as much as 2.45 billion lb.

The evidence is that there is greater movement toward fabricated foods in the marketplace. However, it will take the combined efforts and ingenuity of the researcher, the engineer, and the marketer to ensure that the transition to fabricated foods is orderly and productive.

BIBLIOGRAPHY

CATRON, D. V. 1967. Impact of nutrition and food science on animal agriculture. Soybean Dig. *27*, No. 12, pp. 71-74.

DAVIDHEISER, E. 1970. Are consumers ready for soy products? Soybean Dig. *31*, No. 1 pp. 12-13.

DRUCKER, P. F. 1954. The Practice of Management. Harper & Row, New York.

FISCHER, R. W. 1974. Future of soy protein foods in the marketplace. J. Am. Oil Chem. Soc. *51*, No. 1, pp. 178A-180A.

HAMMONDS, T.M., and CALL, D. L. 1970. Utilization of protein ingredients in the U.S. food industry. Part II. The future market for protein ingredients. A. E. Res. 431 (Revised). Department of Agricultural Economics, Cornell University, Agricultural Experiment Station, Ithaca, New York. August.

HORAN, F. E. 1974. New Protein Foods, Vol. Al, Technology. A. M. Altschul (Editor). Academic Press, Inc., New York and London.

SAIR, L., and MELCER, I. 1970. Carbohydrate and protein additives to meat products. Proc. Joint Symp. Carbohydrate Protein Interactions. Am. Assoc. Cereal Chem., St. Paul, Minn.

USDA. 1971. Textured vegetable protein products. FNS Notice 219. Food and Nutrition Service, USDA, Washington, D.C. Feb. 22.

WILSON, P. N. 1968. Biological ceilings and economic efficiencies for the production of animal protein AD 2000. Chem. Ind., July 6, pp. 899-902.

CHAPTER 6

F. Franks | # Physical-Chemical Principles of Food Fabrication

Historically food technology has developed along lines indicated by the *origin* of products, e.g. vegetable, meat, fish, milk, fat. In terms of research, therefore, the emphasis has usually been on achieving an understanding of the product system as such, but the scientific background data necessary for such an approach on a rigorous basis are as yet largely non-existent. Such progress as has been made, and often quite successfully, has relied on empiricism coupled with experience and inspired hunch.

The economic trends shown in Fig. 6.1 make a reappraisal of the utilization of our food resources a matter of some urgency, and this may give an impetus to fabrication technology. As other chapters of this book cover adequately the social and economic aspects of the problem, this chapter will be based on the assumption that food restructuring and fabrication are here to stay. If it is accepted, therefore, that food production will increasingly rely on fabrication, based on the manipulation of natural raw materials, then a different classification of nutrients, one more familiar to the chemist, will become of greater relevance, i.e., protein, carbohydrate, lipid, water, flavors, preservatives, vitamins, rather than meat, fruit, milk, etc. At present we know little about the structures (molecular and supermolecular) of, or interactions between, the basic components which give rise to the various attributes of food products; therefore, it is difficult to design products with predictable compositions, textures, flavors, and storage properties starting from the molecular raw materials. On the other hand, a considerable technological folklore exists concerning the function of various complex combinations of nutrients in the performance of food products during processing by the manufacturer and by the consumer.

The food industry has much to learn from the history of the plastics and polymer Industries. Some of the methods and theories developed so successfully by synthetic polymer chemists can and will be employed in due course by food scientists. In fabrication the aim is to achieve uniformity, i.e., absence of variability, in the raw materials, and thus a high degree of predictability in product attributes. The similarity between natural and synthetic polymers was realized by Carothers, who in 1931 commented: "The idea that natural high polymers involve some principle of molecular structure peculiar to themselves and are not capable of being simulated by synthetic materials is too strongly

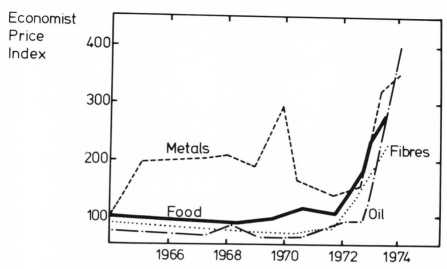

FIG. 6.1. COMMODITY PRICE TRENDS, BASED ON THE COST OF FOOD IN 1964
From the London Sunday Times, December 1973.

suggestive of the vital hypothesis which preceded the dawn of organic chemistry, to be seriously considered." My proposition is that we might now turn the tables and learn about natural polymers from the behavior of synthetic polymers. There are of course several additional features to be taken into account, e.g., peculiar "native" conformations, complicated solvent interactions, and a high degree of specificity in some of the reactions; but on the other hand modern experimental techniques are much more highly developed than those available to Baekeland, Carothers, and Staudinger in the earlier part of this century.

MOLECULAR STRUCTURE AND INTERACTIONS

The food scientist is more limited than the chemist in the chemical and physical treatments he may employ in the design and manufacture of a product. Thus any treatment which is likely to produce chemical changes, i.e., changes in the covalent structure, may have to be followed by costly and exhaustive safety testing. For this and other reasons the physical chemistry of food fabrication is based mainly on non-bonded interactions, i.e., hydrogen bonding, electrostatic, van der Waals, and hydrophobic interactions. This presents a major problem, because these weak interactions are much less rigorously characterized than covalent bonding.

Fig. 6.2 shows schematically a variety of structures and interactions which determine the properties of the finished product, together with

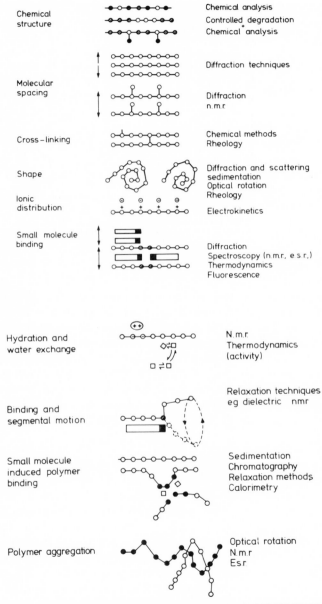

Chemical structure		Chemical analysis Controlled degradation Chemical analysis
Molecular spacing		Diffraction techniques
		Diffraction n.m.r.
Cross-linking		Chemical methods Rheology
Shape		Diffraction and scattering sedimentation Optical rotation Rheology
Ionic distribution		Electrokinetics
Small molecule binding		Diffraction Spectroscopy (n.m.r., e.s.r.) Thermodynamics Fluorescence
Hydration and water exchange		N.m.r. Thermodynamics (activity)
Binding and segmental motion		Relaxation techniques eg dielectric nmr
Small molecule induced polymer binding		Sedimentation Chromatography Relaxation methods Calorimetry
Polymer aggregation		Optical rotation N.m.r. E.s.r.

FIG. 6.2.   MOLECULAR STRUCTURES, INTERACTIONS AND DYNAMIC PROCESSES
WHICH DETERMINE THE PROPERTIES OF POLYMERIC SYSTEMS

Relevant experimental techniques are indicated.

the relevant experimental techniques which might be used to study the particular problem. Apart from the gross monomer composition of a polymer, which can be obtained by degradation followed by chemical analysis, it may be important to know in the case of polysaccharides, whether the polymer is a block or random copolymer. Thus in alginates, derived from seaweed, where the two monomers are guluronic acid and mannuronic acid, the mechanical and thermal properties of gels with a poly-G content differ markedly from those with poly-M blocks and those with extensive M-G regions (McDowell 1961; Smidsrød 1974). Furthermore, the presence of chemical crosslinks (such as disulfide bonds in proteins) or side chains, as in pectins, are likely to affect the textural and thermal stability of products.

Long-range structures or overall shapes can be studied by scattering or diffraction methods and they play an important part in rendering fabricated products anisotropic. Where the macromolecule is a polyelectrolyte, such internal conformations can be markedly influenced by alterations of the total charge distribution, i.e. adjustment of pH and/or type and amount of electrolyte. Chemists often express the effects of electrolytes in terms of ionic strength, but with substances of natural origin this is at best a very rough approximation. It is well known that certain ions interact very specifically with given proteins or polysaccharides.

The interaction of biopolymers falls into several classes: (1) with solvent—hydration—responsible for observed solubility behavior and the stability of "native" states; (2) with non-polymeric species, such as with lipids in egg yolk; (3) with other polymeric species, e.g., protein-carbohydrate, or different types of protein; and (4) with themselves, giving rise to aggregation which may be ordered, as in fibers, or random, as in gels.

Molecular interactions can usually be studied by a variety of spectroscopic techniques. These have to be carefully chosen depending on the particular molecule or segment of a molecule under study and the type of interaction involved. The spectroscopic parameters of importance are frequency, intensity, band shape, and polarization/depolarization characteristics.

DYNAMICS

The rates of motion (diffusion) of molecules or molecular segments and the rates of recovery of equilibrium after the application of an external field (relaxation) may play an important part in the performance of macromolecular aggregates such as food products. These properties are frequently studied by pulse spectroscopic techniques, i.e., a pulse of radiation is applied to the sample and the recovery behavior is noted. The frequency and type of radiation are determined by the nature of the relaxation process under study. Molecular exchange is another feature of complex systems which can affect overall bulk attributes. Thus the existence of a well-defined structure or complex, such as a protein-lipid complex or lipoprotein, does not necessarily mean that any protein molecule is permanently associated with a given number of phospholipid, glyceride, or cholesterol molecules. The lipid molecules may be engaged in fast exchange processes between different complexes, but over a time average there is a high concentration of the complex. The actual exchange processes can be studied by means of appropriate techniques, the choice being governed by the exchange rate. Fig. 6.3 shows the time scales of various molecular dynamic processes and the experimental techniques capable of monitoring such processes.

In the design of a fabricated product an important question is whether the final system should constitute an equilibrium state, and if not, what kinetic controls can be built into the system to prevent attainment of equilibrium during normal processing, shelf-life, and storage conditions. This is shown in diagrammatic form in Fig. 6.4: one or several intermediate states can, in principle, be "stabilized" by providing for a kinetic barrier. In the case of disperse systems, such as emulsions, this is often achieved by raising the viscosity of the continuous phase or by incorporating absorbed layers of proteinaceous materials, which act as a

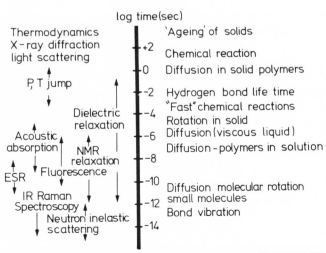

FIG. 6.3. TIME SCALE OF MOLECULAR DYNAMIC PROCESSES AND RANGES OF PHYSICAL TECHNIQUES COMMONLY USED FOR MONITORING SUCH PROCESSES

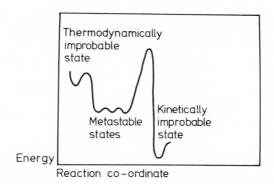

FIG. 6.4. DIAGRAMMATIC REPRESENTATION OF EQUILIBRIUM AND NON-
EQUILIBRIUM STATES

The shallow energy minima correspond to metastable states
which are readily interconvertible.

barrier to coalescence of the disperse particles. In the following examples describing various physico-chemical aspects of fabrication the importance of equilibrium versus kinetic processes will become more apparent.

PHYSICO-CHEMICAL PROBLEMS ASSOCIATED WITH MARGARINE

Probably one of the best-established fabricated foods is margarine, the
most important consumer attribute of which is "consistency". Let us
examine the various physico-chemical parameters which play a part in
determining "consistency". Historically margarine was developed as a
cheap butter substitue and for this reason it was, like butter, based on a
water-in-oil (W/O) emulsion. It has since been found that the consistency is in no way related to the fact that margarine is an emulsion.
Identical consistencies can be achieved in the absence of water. However, legislation (based on the butter substitute) now demands that
margarine shall contain at least 16% water.

Margarine consists of a mixture of 300 to 500 glycerides, of which
some 200 are solid at room temperature (Hilditch and Williams 1964;
Jurriens 1968). The crystalline material is mainly responsible for the
consistency of the product. The composition is chosen according to the
criterion of "dilatation", which in turn is a measure of the volume
change associated with the melting of the solid glycerides. Fig. 6.5
shows two types of dilatation curves, the shapes of which depend
primarily on the glyceride composition (Bailey 1950). On a process basis
the dilatation is usually equated with the amount of solid phase present.
A steep dilatation curve indicates that over a very small temperature

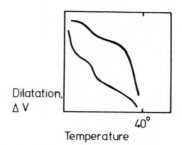

FIG. 6.5. TYPICAL DILATATION CURVES OF FAT MIXTURES

Product demands are that at 40° the mixture should be completely melted.

range a large amount of solid melts and, since this is associated with the
latent heat of fusion, a steep dilatation line is associated with a "cool"
mouth feel, which is also characteristic of butter and cocoa butter.

Since the total amount of solid phase at a given temperature can be
obtained from a knowledge of the glyceride equilibrium phase diagrams, it should be possible to design products with predictable consistencies. However, more detailed studies have shown that, apart from
the amount of solid phase, the consistency, and therefore the dilatation,
depend critically on the rate of crystallization, the crystal size distribution, and the type of crystal formed. Fig. 6.6 shows in diagrammatic
form the phase behavior of a binary glyceride mixture. If a liquid of
composition A is cooled to A' under equilibrium conditions, then crystals of the beta-polymorph separate out. The entropy of fusion is large
and crystallization is slow, resulting in few, well-formed crystals. If the
mixture corresponding to A is cooled rapidly to A'', crystallization will
be rapid, with separation of small crystals of the α-polymorph. Thus the

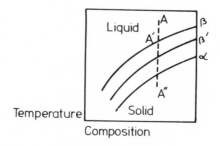

FIG. 6.6. SOLID-LIQUID PHASE DIAGRAM OF A SIMPLE GLYCERIDE MIXTURE IN
WHICH THREE POLYMORPHIC SOLID STATES CAN EXIST

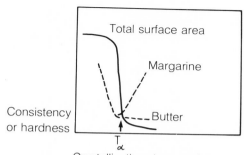

FIG. 6.7.   CONSISTENCY (HARDNESS) AND TOTAL SURFACE AREA AS FUNCTIONS
OF THE SOLIDIFICATION TEMPERATURE

rate of cooling determines the polymorphic form which crystallizes, and also the crystal size (Rossell 1967).

The relation between crystal size, consistency, and crystallization temperature is shown for butter and margarine in Fig. 6.7 on the assumption that the two substances are simple fat mixtures. The inference is that at low temperatures small crystals (large total surface area) are formed—$T\alpha$ is the melting point of the α -polymorph—whereas at high temperatures the behavior of margarine reflects the presence of large crystals. If margarine is subjected to mechanical work, however, its consistency approaches that of butter. The basic difference between the mechanical properties of the products becomes quite clear by reference to Fig. 6.8, which shows the deformation under applied stress. This shows butter to have the properties of a plastic solid, i.e., low yield stress and high viscosity, whereas margarine is brittle with a high yield stress. Since margarine is processed under non-equilibrium conditions, the changes on storage must also be considered and compared with those observed for butter. Both products contain fat crystals which promote W/O emulsions (Larsson 1967; Krog and Larsson 1968). The partial wetting of the crystals, necessary for emulsification, is achieved by incorporation of small amounts of monoglyceride.

In any disperse system the large drops (or crystals) grow at the expense of the small ones. Since the aqueous phase contains water-soluble solutes such as flavors, its chemical potential is eventually lowered to such a point that the excess pressure of the small droplets will be offset with a subsequent stabilization in the droplet size distribution. The driving force for the disproportionation of bubbles or crystals is given by $2\sigma/R^2$ where σ is the surface tension and R the radius of the bubble or crystal. Therefore the process of disproportionation stops when

$$\frac{\partial}{\partial R} \frac{2\sigma}{R} > 0$$

i.e.
$$-\frac{2\sigma}{R^2} + \frac{2}{R} \frac{\partial \sigma}{\partial P} > 0$$

This can be written as
$$-\sigma + 2\Sigma \geqslant 0$$

where Σ, the surface modulus, is given by $A\partial\sigma/\partial A$, where A is the surface area.

Thus the condition for quasi-equilibrium is

$$\Sigma > \frac{1}{2}\sigma$$

and this can be achieved by means of an adsorbed surface film with a long relaxation time. In practice proteins fulfil such a function. The long-term recrystallization, i.e., a $\longrightarrow$ ß transformations and the formation of larger crystals (Knoester, de Bruijne, and van den Tempel 1968), does not actually occur in butter, and the reasons for this are not yet understood. It may be that the process is subject to low rates or that large crystals are prevented from forming by "poisoning" of the crystal growth sites. In any case some natural phenomenon interferes with the processes which are governed by the above inequalities.

In summary we can see how the technology of margarine production depends on complex interrelationships of several aspects of physical chemistry, such as solid-liquid phase equilibria, multicomponent solubility behavior polymorphism, nucleation and crystal growth, wetting and emulsification, stability of disperse phases, and mechanical properties of crystal assemblies.

Although margarine has been chosen as an illustrative example, a similar line of reasoning can be applied to other food composites which rely for their consumer attributes on crystallization and disperse particle size distributions, e.g., ice cream and confectionery products.

SHAPE AND FUNCTION OF NATURAL POLYMERS

As another example of the physico-chemical basis of fabrication, carbohydrates were selected whose function in natural systems is to provide mechanical strength and texture. The carbohydrate polymers in question are chemically relatively simple in that they consist of a

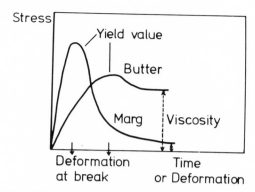

FIG. 6.8. RHEOLOGICAL CHARACTERISTICS OF BUTTER AND MARGARINE

limited number of monomers (usually two). These can be simple hexose sugars of their derivatives, e.g., acids or esters. Fig. 6.9 shows the chemical composition of members of the carrageenan/agarose family of polysaccharides. They are based on a recurring sequence of galactoseanhydrogalactose repeat units, i.e., the polymer has the composition $(A\text{-}B)_n$. Agarose is the nonelectrolyte modification, whereas carrageenans are the corresponding sulfates differing in their degree of substitution. The conformation of the sugar residues with respect to one another is measured in terms of the angles of rotation of the residues about the glycosidic linkages. Potential energy calculations have shown that the freedom of rotation about these bonds depends on steric factors,

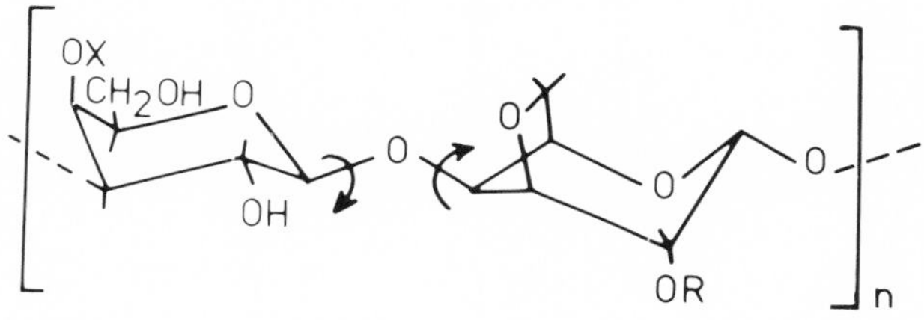

Agarose: X , R = H

κ−Carrageenan: X = SO_3^- , R = H

ι−Carrageenan X , R = SO_3^-

FIG. 6.9. BASIC "MONOMER" UNIT (A - B) OF AGAROSE AND CARRAGEENAN POLYSACCHARIDES

electrostatic repulsion, and van der Waals interactions between neighboring residues. These factors in turn depend on the type of sugar residue and the nature of the glycosidic linkage. Various polysaccharide structures can be identified, some of them illustrated in Fig. 6.10 (Rees A, in press). From a combination of fiber X-ray diffraction methods, molecular model building and potential energy minimization calculations, it has become apparent that some polysaccharides can adopt certain ordered conformations which depend for their stability on various electrostatic and hydrogen-bonding interactions; even hydrophobic interactions cannot be ruled out as a stabilizing factor. Since all these interactions are relatively weak, the observed stability of the ordered systems relies on a high degree of cooperativity, i.e., many coordinated processes take place simultaneously. Fig. 6.11 summarizes the types of conformation which can exist (Rees B, in press). If the polymers were completely regular in their chemical composition and if the ordering processes were completely cooperative, then the whole molecule would be involved in a disorder→order transformation (as is indeed the case with DNA). Actually, natural polysaccarides contain small numbers of sugar residues which, by virtue of their linkages, are incapable of perpetuating the cooperative process (Rees and Wight 1971). The composition of the polymer shown in Fig. 6.9 is therefore $(A - B)_n - C -$

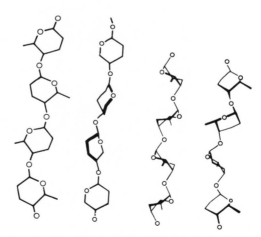

FIG. 6.10. SOME POSSIBLE CONFIGURATIONS OF CARBOHYDRATE HOMOPOLYMERS

(1) Cellulose (flat ribbon), (2) ß-1, 4-xylan (twisted ribbon), (3) poly(guluronic acid) (buckled ribbon), and (4) sodium polygalacturonate (twisted, buckled ribbon).

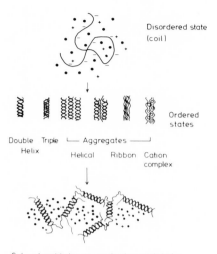

Disordered state
(coil)

Ordered states

Double Triple └── Aggregates ──┘
Helix   Helical   Ribbon   Cation
                                complex

Gel ordered linkages randomly orientated

FIG. 6.11.   SOME OF THE ORDERED STRUCTURES AND AGGREGATES WHICH CAN
BE ACHIEVED FROM SIMPLE PERIODIC POLYSACCHARIDES

Random orientations of ordered regions give rise to gels.
Water molecules are denoted by ● and ions by +.

$(A - B)_m$. The dramatic effect of such a C site on the propagation of order is shown in Fig. 6.12. As a result of these nuclei of disorder, the polymer chains associate to form limited sequences of ordered structures which in turn make up a random network (see Fig. 6.11) and give rise to gels of different strength, textures, and thermal stabilities. The molecular characteristics of the gelling polysaccharides have now been studied in such detail that bulk properties of gels can be predicted with a reasonable degree of confidence (Smidsrød 1974). This is turn enables the food technologist to choose suitable raw materials on the basis of their chemical composition.

ADSORBED PROTEIN FILMS AT LIQUID SURFACES

As a rule, complex food products are highly heterogeneous, disperse systems and are therefore metastable. They are usually stabilized by "edible surfactants", i.e., proteins, and the nature of the interfacial layers plays an important part in determining the properties of the product.

The technological folklore states, and it is widely accepted, that at a liquid interface proteins are completely denatured. (Neurath and Bull

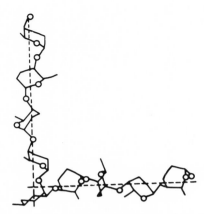

FIG. 6.12.   THE EFFECT OF A "FOREIGN" SUGAR (IN THIS CASE: RHAMNOSE) RE-
SIDUE ON THE PROPAGATION OF DIRECTIONAL ORDER OF A POLYSACCHARIDE
CHAIN (GALACTURONAN)

1938). To test this and also to obtain an insight into the relationships between molecular structure and surface properties of proteins three proteins of widely differing structural integrities, namely lysozyme (globular and rigid), bovine serum albumin, BSA (globular and flexible), and β-casein (flexible coil) were chosen. By monitoring the adsorption process with various surface-chemical techniques (force/area and surface concentration measurements) it has been established that polymer flexibility and hydrophobicity give rise to rapid adsorption followed by a subsequent partial desorption, as the polymer molecules slowly rearrange themselves and try to achieve the equilibrium configuration. On the other hand, the highly structured globular protein lysozyme is adsorbed slowly to form a monolayer of "native" protein, and this process is followed by the gradual build-up of multilayers. The adsorption kinetics of lysozyme and casein are compared in Fig. 6.13, and the differences are striking (Phillips and Graham). BSA exhibits an intermediate behavior, but if lysozyme or BSA are first heat-denatured, they behave like flexible, unstructured β-casein.

A study of the rheological behavior of the adsorbed protein films reveals a close correlation with the molecular structure (Graham and Phillips 1974). Thus β-casein films are liquid-like, but BSA and lysozyme films exhibit a marked viscoelasticity which is very sensitive to concentration and appears to reach maximum values at concentrations corresponding to monolayer coverage. The surface rheology in turn can be related directly to the ability of the proteins to stabilize

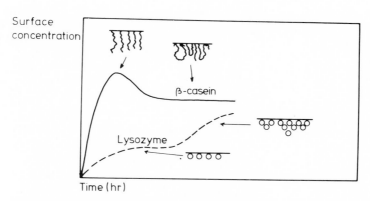

FIG. 6.13.   THE KINETICS OF ADSORPTION OF β-CASEIN AND LYSOZYME AT AN AIR-
WATER SURFACE

The nature of the surface films at different stages of the process are
shown in diagrammatic form.

foams and emulsions. The unique property possessed by proteins, and
not of course by synthetic polymers used as stabilizers, is their ability to
unfold to different degrees. These partly or wholly unfolded states
markedly affect the mechanical behavior of surface films. Current
studies at our laboratories on the aggregation and solution behavior of
β-casein have implicated individual amino acid residues with observed
bulk phenomena. A very detailed understanding of molecular structure
and conformation can thus help the processer to achieve some degree of
control over the interactions of complex polymeric raw materials.

THE STRUCTURE AND FUNCTIONAL PROPERTIES OF EGG YOLK

As a complex food system which is not yet amenable to sound
physico-chemical investigation the egg provides a good example. The
structure and function of yolk are of particular importance. Usually the
technology of fabrication will use as a starting point a well-known
natural system and, in the case of egg, large numbers of fabricated
substitutes are on the market. They are able with varying degrees of
success to perform some of the functional roles of egg yolk in processed
food products.

A particularly rigorous test for an egg substitute is its performance in
cake baking. According to the literature the egg functions in a dual role:
the egg white provides a heat-setting protein, while the yolk and phospholipid act as emulsifiers for the oil-soluble batter constituents (Mac-
Donnell *et al.* 1955).

Like other naturally occurring lipoproteins, egg yolk contains different types of lipoproteins which are classified according to their composition. Thus low-density lipoprotein (LDL) is rich in lipid (up to 90% by weight) while high-density lipoprotein complexes are rich in protein. It has been established that the LDL fraction is of primary importance in cake-baking processes. The chemical composition, which is well established, does not appear to be the crucial factor in the performance of egg yolk LDL. Thus the dissociation of the LDL into protein, phospholipid, glyceride and cholesterol and incorporation of a mixture of these constituents into a cake batter does not give rise to cake textures with the required specific volume. Clearly, therefore, the function of yolk LDL depends on the manner in which the constituents are organized in the intact LDL complex (Schultz and Forsythe 1967).

Over the past 10 yr much effort has been devoted to the study of blood serum lipoprotein structures, and the established techniques can readily be applied to egg lipoprotein. Thus small-angle X-ray scattering suggests a spherical LDL particle of mean diameter 24 to 27 nm, which has a center of low electron density surrounded by an annulus, ~2 nm thick of high electron density. This is consistent with a lipid core surrounded by a polar layer. Nuclear magnetic resonance studies of lipids indicate that the glyceride and phospholipid alkyl chains are mobile and in a liquid-like environment, fast exchange taking place, whereas the polar head groups (the phosphate derivatives) are interacting with the protein, probably by dipole and/or hydrogen-bonding forces (Kamat and Lawrence 1972).

The combination of the structural information with the detailed dynamics of the various molecules involved, the sedimentation behavior of the intact complex and the known chemical composition, allows us to suggest the structure shown in Fig. 6.14. Rather than the mixture of the various constituent species, it is this integral structure which is responsible for the functional properties of egg yolk. This conclusion is confirmed by the fact that blood plasma LDL, which has the same general properties as egg LDL, is an excellent egg substitute. It is therefore unlikely that fabricated egg substitutes based on protein/lipid mixtures will be very successful.

CONCLUSIONS

If food fabrication is to be taken seriously, investigations of the structures and interactions of the various food components in simplified, yet realistic model situations, may well make it possible to relate molecular details to bulk product attributes. Such an approach might advantage-

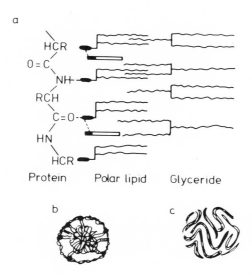

FIG. 6.14. PROTEIN, POLAR LIPID, GLYCERIDE

(a) The molecular organization of the egg yolk LDL particle showing the nonpolar care and the polar periphery; (b) A cross section view of the particle; and (3) The schematic representation of the surface of the particle showing that the complex does not contain sufficient protein for complete surface coverage.

ously be modeled on the methodology which has been developed over the past 50 yr by polymer physicists and chemists and which has led to many spectacular industrial successes, e.g., the development of stereospecific polymers.

The slow development of this type of approach to the study of food systems may be due to two basic problems: (1) the food industry is still firmly rooted in its agricultural past, so that the "chemical" approach to food processing is viewed with suspicion by both manufacturer and consumer and (2) a sound scientific investigation of the complex structures and interactions involved must of necessity combine the techniques of physics, chemistry, and biology, but truly integrated multidisciplinary research efforts are still a rarity in the general scientific environment.

In the end, however, the economic trends as illustrated in Fig. 6.1 may force food processers to treat the basic problems underlying fabrication from molecular raw materials with greater urgency, if only to avoid the wasteful under-utilization of our natural resources.

ACKNOWLEDGEMENTS

Much of the work discussed in this paper originated from the various Unilever Research Laboratories and I wish to record my gratitude to my colleagues, D.E. Graham, V.B. Kamat, M. C. Phillips, D.A. Rees and M. van den Tempel for many helpful discussions.

BIBLIOGRAPHY

BAILEY, A. E. 1950. Melting and Solidification of Fats. Interscience Publishers, Inc., New York.

GRAHAM, D. E., and PHILLIPS, M. C. (to be published). The Conformation of Proteins at Interfaces and their Role in Stabilizing Emulsions. *In* Symposium on Theory and Practice of Emulsion Technology, Brunel Univ. Sept. 1974, A. L. Smith (Editor). Academic Press, London.

HILDITCH, T. P., and WILLIAMS, P. N. 1964. The Chemical Constitution of Natural Fats. Chapman and Hall, London.

JURRIENS, G. 1968. Analysis of Glycerides and Composition of Natural Oils and Fats. *In* Analysis and Characterization of Oils, Fats and Fat Products, H.A. Boekenoogen (Editor). Vol. 2, Interscience Publishers, New York.

KAMAT, V. B., and LAWRENCE, G. A. 1972. Physical studies of egg yolk low density lipoprotein. Chem. Phys. Lipids *9*, 1-25.

KNOESTER, M., DE BRUIJNE, P., and VAN DEN TEMPEL, M. 1968. Crystallization of triglycerides at low supercooling. J. Cryst. Growth *3, 4,* 776-780.

KROG, N., and LARSSON, K. 1968. Phase behavior and rheological properties of aqueous systems of industrial distilled monoglycerides. Chem. Phys. Lipids *2*, 129-143.

LARSSON, K. 1967. The structure of mesomorphic phases and micelles in aqueous glyceride systems. Z. Phys. Chem. N. F. *56* 173-198.

MACDONNELL, L. R., FEENEY, R. E., HANSON, H. L., CAMPBELL, A., and SUGIHARA, T. F. 1955. The functional properties of the egg-white proteins. Food Technol. *9*, 49-53.

MCDOWELL, R. H. 1961. Properties of Alginates. Alginate Industries, Ltd., London.

NEURATH, H. and BULL, H. B. 1938. The surface activity of proteins. Chem. Rev. *23*, 391-435.

PHILLIPS, M. C. and GRAHAM, D. E. unpublished results.

REES, D. A. (A, in press). Carbohydrates. *In* MTP International Review of Science: Organic Chemistry Series One, G. O. Aspinall (Editor), Vol. 7, Butterworths, London.

REES, D. A. (B, in press). The Biochemistry of Carbohydrates. *In* MTP International Review of Science: Biochem. Series One, W. J. Whelan (Editor), Vol. 5, Butterworths, London.

REES, D. A., and WIGHT, A. W. 1971. Polysaccharide conformation. Part VI. Model building computations for α-1, 4-galacturonan and the kinking function of L-rhamnose residues in pectin substances. J. Chem. Soc. B 1366-1372.

ROSSELL, J. B. 1967. Phase diagrams of triglyceride systems. Adv. Lipid Res. *5*, 353-408.

SCHULTZ, J. R., and FORSYTHE, R. H. 1967. The influence of egg yolk lipoprotein—carbohydrate interactions of baking performance. Bakers Dig. *41*, 56-62.

SMIDSRØD, O. 1974. The molecular basis for some physical properties of alginates in the gel state. Disc. Faraday Div. Chem. Soc. *57*, in press.

CHAPTER 7

W.J. Wolf

Soy Proteins for Fabricated Foods

Fabricated foods are made by combining the 3 basic components of foods—carbohydrates, fats, and proteins—in ways that provide convenience, texture, flavor, and other desirable characteristics. For many years soybeans have supplied oil as the major component for margarine, a well-known fabricated food. Of the more than 8 billion lb of soybean oil now produced annually in the U.S., over 6 billion lb go into domestic food products including 1.5 billion lb converted into margarine (Soybean Digest 1974). In the past few years, traditional animal protein sources such as milk, eggs, and meat have risen sharply in price, and per capita beef consumption has dropped from 116 lb in 1972 to 109 lb in 1973. Similarly pork consumption dipped from 67 lb to 61.5 lb. Protein ingredients, such as nonfat dry milk and sodium caseinate, likewise have become more expensive and supplies uncertain. Consequently, soybeans are now becoming an important source for an additional food component, namely, protein. Although there is now a short supply of some of the soy protein products, this is expected to be only temporary while industry is increasing plant capacity. There is no shortage of raw material for these products. At present most of the defatted soybean meal is fed to animals, and only about 1% of the total U.S. soybean crop is used domestically for edible protein products.

Soy proteins are available in a variety of forms designed for incorporation into traditional and new fabricated foods. After describing conversion of soybeans into their diverse protein forms, I shall review their physical, chemical, and functional properties which are important in incorporating them into foods. For more detailed discussions of these subjects, the reader is referred to Wolf and Cowan (1971) and Smith and Circle (1972).

SOYBEAN STRUCTURE AND COMPOSITION

Soybeans are legumes which consist of about 8% seed coat, 2% hypocotyl, and 90% cotyledons. Composition of whole beans and the seed parts are given in Table 7.1. Two-thirds of the cotyledons consist of oil and protein but little, if any, starch is present. The oil is stored in numerous small inclusions (0.2 to 0.3 μ in diameter) called spherosomes, whereas the bulk of the protein is found in larger storage sites (2 to 20 μ in diameter) called protein bodies or aleurone grains (Fig. 7.1). Protein bodies are 98% protein plus small amounts of lipid and phytic acid (Tombs 1967).

TABLE 7.1

COMPOSITION OF SOYBEANS AND SEED PARTS[1]

Fraction	Protein (N X 6.25), %	Fat, %	Carbohydrate, %	Ash, %
Whole bean	40	21	34	4.9
Cotyledon	43	23	29	5.0
Hull	8.8	1	86	4.3
Hypocotyl	41	11	43	4.4

[1]Average values for nine varieties on a moisture-free basis.
Kawamura 1967.

SOY PROTEIN FORMS

The orderly arrangement within the cotyledon cells must be disrupted by processing to separate the food components of soybeans. Three general classes of soy protein products are presently manufactured as food ingredients and classified according to protein content: (1) grits and flours; (2) protein concentrates; and (3) protein isolates. Composition and yields of these products are shown schematically in Fig. 7.2.

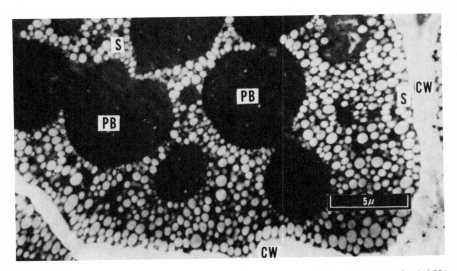

Courtesy of Saio and Watanabe (1968)

FIG. 7.1. TRANSMISSION ELECTRON MICROGRAPH OF SECTION OF MATURE SOYBEAN COTYLEDON

Structures labeled are protein bodies, PB; spherosomes, S; and cell wall, CW.

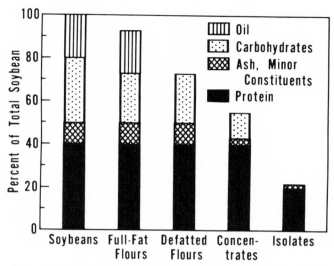

FIG. 7.2. PROXIMATE COMPOSITIONS (DRY BASIS) AND YIELDS OF PROTEIN
FORMS PROCESSED FROM SOYBEANS

Grits and Flours

Full-Fat Flours.—Grits and flours have minimum protein contents of 40-50% depending on fat content and typical compositions are given in Table 7.2. The simplest product of this type used in foods is full-fat flour. It is made by steaming beans to debitter them[1] and to inactivate fat-oxidizing enzymes. The hulls, which are mainly carbohydrates (Table 7.1) such as cellulose and other polysaccharides, are removed and the dehulled beans are then ground to yield full-fat flour. Soy flours are defined as having particles of 100 mesh or less, whereas grits have particles greater than 100 mesh. Because only minor fractionation occurs in making full-fat flour, its composition (Table 7.2) is essentially the same as that of the cotyledon (Table 7.1).

Defatted Flours.—The majority of flours and grits prepared are of the defatted type. The first steps in manufacturing defatted flours and grits consist of cracking and dehulling beans and tempering the cracked meats to about 11% moisture. The tempered meats are then passed through smooth rolls to form thin flakes which are extracted with hexane to remove the oil. The bulk of the defatted flakes produced today

---

[1]Some workers claim that beany and bitter flavors form enzymatically when the seed is crushed; hence the heat treatment may in reality be preventing bitterness from developing rather than removing it (Nelson *et al.* 1971).

TABLE 7.2

PROXIMATE ANALYSES OF COMMERCIAL SOYBEAN FLOURS AND GRITS [1]

	Full-fat %	Defatted %	Low-fat %	Lecithinated %
Moisture	5.0	5.0	5.5	5.5
Protein (N X 6.25)	41.5	53.0	46.0	45.2
Fat	21.0	0.9	6.5	16.4
Crude fiber	2.1	2.9	3.0	2.4
Ash	5.2	6.0	5.5	5.3

[1]As-is basis (Meyer 1970A).

is used for animal feeds and is processed in a desolventizer-toaster which recovers the hexane and also toasts (cooking with steam) the flakes to inactivate factors responsible for poor nutritional qualities of raw (untoasted) flakes.

Soy proteins are sensitive to moist heat treatment and are rapidly insolubilized during steaming (Fig. 7.3). Two tests are used to measure

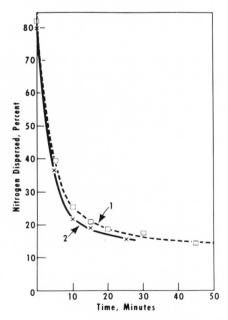

Courtesy of Belter and Smith 1952

FIG. 7.3. EFFECT OF STEAMING TIME AT ATMOSPHERIC PRESSURE ON WATER DISPERSIBILITY OF NITROGENOUS CONSTITUENTS OF (1) DEFATTED AND (2) FULL-FAT FLAKES

extent of heat treatment given to flours and grits. The first is nitrogen solubility index (NSI) which measures the percent of total Kjeldahl nitrogen that is extracted with water. The other frequently used test is the protein dispersibility index (PDI) and is expressed as the percent of total protein that is extractable with water. In principle both tests measure the same property but results do not agree because the water extracts are prepared under different conditions (American Oil Chemists' Society 1973). Edible grits and flours are prepared with a range of NSI or PDI values to give products that vary in enzyme activity, flavor, color, and nutritional quality as well as in protein solubility. Smith and Circle (1972) give the following range of NSI values for varying degrees of heat treatment:

Extent of Heating	NSI
Minimum	85-90
Light	40-60
Moderate	20-40
Fully toasted	10-20

The desolventizer-toaster yields only the fully toasted product, hence other desolventizing methods summarized in Table 7.3 are used to prepare edible flakes and grits (Becker 1971; Milligan and Suriano 1974). After desolventizing, the flakes are ground and screened into flours or grits as desired.

TABLE 7.3

PROCESSES USED TO DESOLVENTIZE SOYBEAN FLAKES FOR EDIBLE PRODUCTS

Process	Method of Hexane Vaporization	PDI Range of Flakes[1]
Schneckens	Steam jacketed conveyer with steam sparge[2]	40-50
Flash desolventizer-deodorizer	Super-heated hexane followed by inert purge gas	70-90[3]
Vapor desolventizer-deodorizer	Super-heated hexane followed by steam sparge under vacuum or pressure	10-90

[1]Becker 1971. PDI = protein dispersibility index.
[2]Newer versions of this system use hollow screw conveyers with heat transfer agents circulating through them to increase heat transfer efficiency.
[3]When flakes with lower PDI values are desired, the flash desolventizer is followed by a meal stripping and cooking operation (Milligan and Suriano 1974).

Defatted flours contain a minimum of 50% protein by definition and typically will analyze somewhat higher (Table 7.2). Flours of fat content between those of full-fat and defatted flours are also available and are made by adding oil to defatted flour to the desired fat level. Lecithinated flours are another type available; they are made by adding up to 15% lecithin to defatted flour and are used where additional emulsifying properties are desired as in baked goods. Typical uses of soy flours of varying heat treatment are as follows:

NSI	Uses
>75	Bleaching of wheat flour by lipoxygenase
50-60	Breads, cakes, cookies, doughnuts, marcaroni
25-35	Beverages, pancakes, waffles, infant foods
15-25	Beverages, crackers, cookies, cereals, infant foods

Protein Concentrates

Defatted soy flakes can be upgraded in protein content by further fractionation to remove about one-half of the carbohydrates and some of the minor constituents. The resulting products are protein concentrates (Fig. 7.2) which have a minimum protein content of 70%. Three processes are employed to make protein concentrates (Fig. 7.4). In the first process aqueous alcohol is used to leach out the soluble sugars

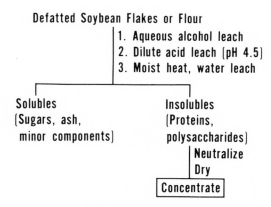

FIG. 7.4.   OUTLINE OF THREE PROCESSES FOR MANUFACTURING SOY PROTEIN CONCENTRATES

Processes differ in the initial extraction step as described in text.

(sucrose, raffinose, and stachyose) plus some of the ash and other low-molecular-weight components. The proteins and polysaccharides remain insoluble and are desolventized to yield the concentrate (Mustakas *et al.* 1962). A recent variation of this first process includes extraction of the defatted meal with hexane: ethanol to remove residual lipids before treatment with aqueous alcohol (Hayes and Simms 1973). In the second process the proteins are insolubilized by leaching meal with dilute acid at pH 4.5 (the isoelectric point of the major soy proteins). The polysaccharide-protein mixture is then neutralized and dried (Sair 1959). The third process insolubilizes the proteins by steaming, and the low-molecular-weight constituents are then washed out with water (McAnelly 1964).

Chemically there is little difference between the various protein concentrates, but they differ in their physical properties (Table 7.4). Water solubility of the proteins in the alcohol-leached and moist-heat, water-leached concentrates is very low, but is much higher in the acid-leached concentrate. Particle size and shape of the different concentrates also vary significantly (Wolf and Baker 1975).

Protein Isolates

The third class of soy protein products manufactured is the isolates, which are the most highly refined form (Meyer 1970B, 1971). The isolation process is based on the differences in solubility of soybean proteins as pH is varied (Fig. 7.5). This solubility behavior is typical of the class of proteins called globulins. When soybean meal with a high PDI is suspended in distilled water, the resulting pH is about 6.5 and high protein solubility is obtained. In contrast, very little protein ex-

TABLE 7.4

COMPOSITIONS AND PROPERTIES OF SOY PROTEIN CONCENTRATES
MADE BY DIFFERENT PROCESSES [1]

	Process		
	Alchohol Leach	Acid Leach	Moist Heat, Water Leach
Protein (N X 6.25), %	66	67	70
Moisture, %	6.7	5.2	3.1
Fat (petroleum ether extractable), %	0.3	0.3	1.2
Crude fiber, %	3.5	3.4	4.4
Ash, %	5.6	4.8	3.7
NSI[2]	5	69	3
pH of 1:10 aqueous dispersion	6.9	6.6	6.9

[1]As-is basis (Meyer 1971).
[2]NSI = nitrogen solubility index.

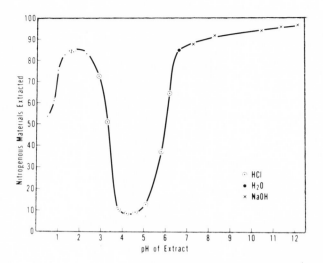

Courtesy of Smith and Circle (1938)

FIG. 7.5.   EXTRACTIBILITY OF DEFATTED SOYBEAN MEAL PROTEINS AS A FUNC-
TION OF pH

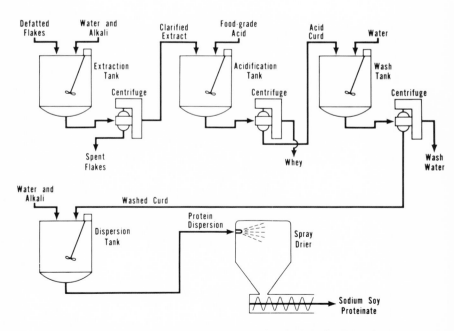

FIG. 7.6.   SCHEME FOR COMMERCIAL PREPARATION OF ISOLATED SOYBEAN PROTEIN

tracts at pH 4 to 5 which is the isoelectric region of the major proteins. Isolates are therefore prepared (Fig. 7.6) by extracting undenatured defatted flakes or meal with dilute alkali at pH 7 to 9 and centrifuging out the insoluble polysaccharide residue. The clarified extract is then acidified to pH 4.5 thereby precipitating the major proteins as a white curd. The protein curd is separated from the soluble fraction (whey) by centrifuging. After washing, the curd can be slurried in water and spray-dried in the isoelectric condition. In the usual procedure, however, the curd is neutralized with sodium hydroxide to resolubilize it and then spray-dried to give the sodium proteinate. The spray-dried proteinates are spheres or partially collapsed spheres (Fig. 7.7). Potassium and calcium proteinates are also made commercially.

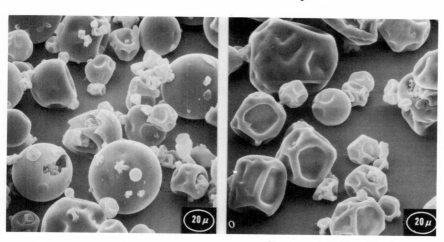

Courtesy of Wolf and Baker (1975)

FIG. 7.7. SCANNING ELECTRON MICROGRAPHS OF TWO COMMERCIAL SOY PROTEIN SAMPLES

(A) Spherical particles and (B) Partially collapsed spheres.

TABLE 7.5

COMPOSITIONS AND PROPERTIES OF FOUR COMMERCIAL
PROTEIN ISOLATES[1]

	A	B	C	D
Moisture, %	4.7	6.4	7.6	3.7
Protein (N X 6.25), %	92.8	92.2	92.9	94.7
Crude fiber, %	0.2	0.1	0.1	0.2
Ash, %	3.8	3.5	2.0	2.7
NSI	85	95	—	
pH of 1:10 aqueous dispersion	7.1	6.8	5.2	5.5

[1]As-is basis (Meyer 1971).

Isolates supplied by different manufacturers do not differ greatly in composition (Table 7.5) but can vary significantly in physical properties. Processing conditions are varied to change properties such as gelation, solubility, molecular weight distribution and viscosity. It is recommended that all sources of supply be evaluated for a given food application.

PHYSICAL AND CHEMICAL PROPERTIES

Amino Acid Composition

Contents of essential amino acids in the three major soy protein forms are listed in Table 7.6. Fractionation of proteins occurs during preparation of acid-leached concentrates, moist heat, water-leached concentrates and isolates. Consequently these products have slightly different amino acid contents than defatted flours. For example, methionine and cystine are found in somewhat lower amounts in isolates than in soybean meal and are of particular concern because they are the first limiting amino acids. The high lysine content of soy proteins makes them useful for supplementing cereal proteins which are deficient in this amino acid.

Solubility

The relationship between solubility and pH for soy proteins was discussed earlier (Fig. 7.5). This property is important in food systems of pH 3.5 to 6.5 if solubility is required or if a curdled protein is undesirable (e.g., coffee whitener). Insolubility in the isoelectric region can be

TABLE 7.6

ESSENTIAL AMINO ACID CONTENTS OF
COMMERCIAL SOY PROTEIN FORMS[1]

Amino Acid	Defatted Flour	Protein Concentrate	Protein Isolate
Isoleucine	4.6	4.9	4.8
Leucine	7.7	8.0	7.8
Lysine	6.2	6.2	6.0
Methionine	1.3	1.3	1.0
Cystine	1.2	1.6	1.0
Phenylalanine	5.3	5.3	5.5
Threonine	4.2	4.3	3.7
Tryptophan	1.4	1.4	1.3
Valine	4.9	5.0	4.8

[1]Grams amino acid per 16 gm nitrogen (Meyer 1971).

abolished by extensive enzymatic modification such as digestion by pepsin. Such products are used primarily as whipping agents.

Solubility such as depicted in Fig. 7.5 is typical only of flakes or flours prepared with a minimum of heat treatment during extraction of the oil. As pointed out earlier, moist heat rapidly insolubilizes soy proteins (Fig. 7.3).

Commercial isolates vary in solubility because of processing variations (Nash and Wolf 1967). Part of the insolubility of isolates arises during the isoelectric precipitation step (Nash et al. 1971; Anderson et al. 1973). One reaction responsible for insolubility appears to be the formation of disulfide-linked protein polymers. When the isolates are treated with sulfhydryl compounds such as cysteine or mercaptoethanol, depolymerization occurs and partial solubility is regained. A portion of the isolates, however, remains insoluble even with added sulfhydryl compound (Nash et al. 1971).

Molecular Size Distribution

Undenatured soy proteins are a complex mixture of molecules that differ in size, charge, and structure. The distribution in molecular weight ranges from 8000 to about 600,000 as demonstrated by ultracentrifugation (Fig. 7.8) or by gel filtration (Hasegawa et al. 1963). In the ultracentrifuge the water-extractable proteins of defatted meal separate into 4 fractions, with sedimentation coefficients of about 2, 7, 11, and 15S. Relative amounts of the fractions and molecular weights of various proteins that have been isolated and characterized are summarized in Table 7.7. The 7S and 11S fractions comprise more than 60% of the total protein, and about 80% of the proteins have molecular weights of 100,000 and higher.

The 2S fraction contains the low-molecular-weight proteins: several trypsin inhibitors, cytochrome c, allantoinase, and 2 partially characterized globulins.

The 7S fraction constitutes more than one-third of the total protein but at least 4 different kinds of proteins are present: beta-amylase, hemagglutinins, lipoxygenases, and 7S globulin. The first three of these proteins are probably minor constituents. Gel filtration separates the 7S fraction into 4 subfractions (Hasegawa et al. 1963). Gel electrophoresis reveals 3 major bands in the 7S ultracentrifugal fraction isolated by sucrose density gradient centrifugation (Hill and Breidenbach 1974).

About one-third of the total protein is found in the 11S fraction. Thus far only one protein called the 11S globulin or glycinin has been found in this sedimenting fraction. The 15S fraction makes up the remainder of

2 7 11 15

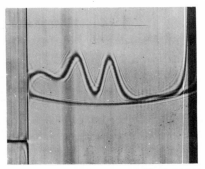

Courtesy of Wolf (1970)

FIG. 7.8. ULTRACENTRIFUGAL PATTERN FOR WATER-EXTRACTABLE SOY PRO-
TEINS AT pH 7.6, 0.5 IONIC STRENGTH IN 0.01 M MERCAPTOETHANOL

Sedimentation is from left to right and numbers are approximate sedimentation coefficients in Svedberg units.

the protein; little is known about this fraction and some workers have
suggested that it is a polymer of the 11S protein.

When the water-extractable soybean proteins are adjusted to pH 4.5
during the preparation of isolates, only relatively small portions of the
2S and 7S fractions remain soluble whereas the other fractions precipitate quantitatively. An unmodified protein isolate, therefore, has a
molecular size distribution similar to that shown in Fig. 7.8 (Nash and
Wolf 1967).

TABLE 7.7

SOYBEAN PROTEIN FRACTIONS OBTAINED BY ULTRACENTRIFUGATION[1]

Fraction	Percentage of Total	Components	Mol Wt
2S	22	Trypsin inhibitors	8,000
			21,500
		Cytochrome c	12,000
		2.3S Globulin	18,200
		2.8S Globulin	32,000
		Allantoinase	50,000
7S	37	Beta-amylase	61,700
		Hemagglutinins	110,000
		Lipoxygenases	108,000
		7S Globulin	186,000-210,000
11S	31	11S Globulin	350,000
15S	11	—	~600,000

[1]From Wolf 1972A.

Association-Dissociation Reactions

The 7S and 11S globulins undergo rapid and reversible association-dissociation reactions under mild changes in ionic environment. The 7S globulin at pH 7.6, 0.5 ionic strength has a mol wt of 180,000 to 200,000 but when the ionic strength is lowered to 0.1, the protein dimerizes to a 370,000 mol wt species (Koshiyama 1968A). When the water extractable proteins of defatted meal are analyzed in the ultracentrifuge at 0.1 ionic strength, about 60% of the 7S fraction observed at 0.5 ionic strength is converted into the 9S or dimer form (Wolf 1969). Recent studies, however, show that the 7S fraction contains at least 3 electrophoretically distinguishable proteins capable of forming dimers at 0.1 ionic strength (Hill and Breidenbach 1974).

The 11S globulin also forms a faster sedimenting form when ionic strength is changed from 0.5 to 0.1 but extent of association is low (Naismith 1955). When ionic strength is reduced still more, to 0.01, the 11S protein dissociates into smaller units that sediment as 7S and 2 to 3S entities (Wolf and Briggs 1958).

Subunit Structure

An added complexity of the 7S and 11S globulins is their subunit structure. Both molecules are built up of smaller units that interact very specifically to form the parent globulins.

The 7S globulin contains 9 amino-terminal residues, a fact that indicates that the molecule contains at least 9 polypeptide chains (Koshiyama 1968B). Reagents capable of dissociating proteins into subunits disrupt the 7S structure. When the protein is dissolved in $8M$ urea or $4 M$ guanidine hydrochloride, the mol wt decreases from 180,000 for the native structure to 22,500 to 24,000—about one-ninth of the original molecular weight (Koshiyama 1971). Dissociation into subunits also occurs on treatment with the anionic detergent sodium dodecyl sulfate.

In acid solutions at low salt concentrations, the 7S globulin is converted into 2S and 5S species. Conversion of the 7S globulin into the slower sedimenting forms is inhibited by salts and the conversion is reversed when the protein is dialyzed against pH 7.6, 0.5 ionic strength buffer (Koshiyama 1968A).

The 11S globulin at pH 7.6, 0.5 ionic strength, has a quaternary structure made up of 12 subunits with the following amino-terminal residues: 8 glycines, 2 phenylalanines, and either 2 leucines or 2 isoleucines (Catsimpoolas et al. 1967). Isoelectric focusing of the 11S protein in urea-mercaptoethanol solution separates only 6 subunits.

Apparently the 350,000 mol wt unit is a dimer of 2 identical "monomers" which in turn each contain 6 subunits (Catsimpoolas 1969). Although the 11S protein has an isoelectric point of about pH 5, three of the subunits are acidic with isoelectric points of pH 4.75, 5.15, and 5.40, and 3 subunits are basic with isoelectric points at pH 8.00, 8.25, and 8.50. Molecular weights of acidic and basic subunits are 37,200 and 22,300, respectively (Catsimpoolas et al. 1971). Stability of the 11S molecule may depend on interactions between the acidic and basic subunits.

Electron microscopic studies suggest 2 structures for the 11S molecule. The first consists of 2 doughnut-like rings stacked one on top of the other (Catsimpoolas 1969). The second structure is proposed to be two split-rings facing each other (Saio et al. 1970). Both models, however, include a hole in the center of the molecule. The quaternary structure of the 11S molecule is disrupted under various conditions, including low ionic strength, high or low pH, high concentrations of urea, detergents, and temperatures above 80°C (Wolf 1972B). For reasons still unknown, the 11S globulin is more susceptible to irreversible changes in conformation than the 7S globulin.

A good example of a food system in which the quaternary structures of the 7S and 11S globulins are disrupted is the spinning of fibers from protein isolates. The first step in the spinning operation involves dissolving the protein in alkali with subsequent breakdown into smaller units and unfolding of the subunits. When the alkaline solution is pumped through spinnerettes into an acid-salt bath, the proteins coagulate into continuous filaments. The fibers are only slightly soluble in solvents which will dissolve the original isolated protein. Apparently the unfolded protein subunits interact nonspecifically to form the insoluble filaments rather than refold and reassemble into the quaternary structures found in the native proteins (Kelley and Pressey 1966).

Denaturation

Because of their complex structures the major soybean proteins are sensitive to many of the agents that cause denaturation—heat, extremes of pH, high concentrations of alcohols, urea or guanidine hydrochloride, and detergents. Of these agents, heat is one of the most important because of its widespread use in food processing.

As discussed earlier (Fig. 7.3), the most obvious change observed when soybean proteins are heated is a loss of solubility. The physical and chemical effects that occur at the molecular level when the proteins are heated are poorly understood. About three-fourths of the proteins in steamed soybean meal are soluble in pH 8.6 buffer containing 0.1 M mercaptoethanol plus 8 M urea whereas mercaptoethanol in buffer dissolves only about one-fourth of the denatured proteins (Shibasaki *et al.* 1969). Hydrogen and hydrophobic bonds are believed to be broken by 8 *M* urea; hence these bonds are likely to be major factors causing insolubility of heated meal proteins. Insolubilization of proteins also occurs during the moist heat treatment involved in extrusion of defatted meal to prepare the textured materials now used as meat extenders. Gel electrophoresis of the proteins that remain soluble after extrusion shows that some proteins decrease in solubility and new bands appear as extrusion temperature is increased (Cumming *et al.* 1973).

A denaturation phenomenon of importance in food systems is gelation. When protein isolates in concentrations of 7% or higher are heated, viscosity increases and gels are formed (Circle *et al.* 1964). In the temperature range of 70 to 100°C, gels form within 10 to 30 min. Disulfide bond-breaking agents, such as cysteine and sodium sulfite, help solubilize the unheated isolates, lower viscosities of unheated and heated isolate dispersions, and inhibit gelation.

Catsimpoolas and Meyer (1970) propose the following steps in the gelling of soy isolates:

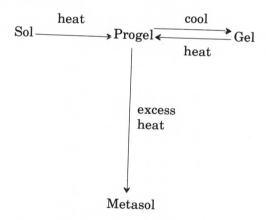

First, the protein dispersion (sol) is irreversibly converted to a high-viscosity solution or progel, which upon cooling becomes more viscous and then gels. Reheating "melts" the gel and restores the progel state. Excessive heat (125°C), however, converts the progel to a metasol that no longer gels upon cooling. The metasol is also formed when disulfide bonds are broken. Effects of lipids on gelation have also been reported (Catsimpoolas and Meyer 1971).

Gelation does not occur at low protein concentrations. When 0.8% solutions of the water-extractable proteins of defatted meal are heated,

the 11S and 15S fractions plus part of the 7S fraction are aggregated
(Watanabe and Nakayama 1962; Saio *et al.* 1968). Heating 0.5% solutions of 11S protein at 100°C causes a rapid increase in turbidity followed by precipitation of protein (Wolf and Tamura 1969). Ultracentrifugation showed that the 11S protein disappears in less than 5 min of
heating and a fast sedimenting aggregate (90 to 100S) forms. On further
heating, the soluble aggregate grows larger in size and precipitates
completely in 7 min. As the 11S component disappears a slow sedimenting fraction of 3-4S also appears. This fraction is about one-half of the
total protein and surprisingly shows no further changes on heating up to
30 min. When the 11S protein was heated in 0.1 to 0.5 M mercaptoethanol, the precipitation step was accelerated and the intermediate
soluble aggregate was undetected. In contrast, when the 11S protein
was heated with N-ethylmaleimide (a sulfhydryl group blocking agent)
present, the 3 to 4S fraction and soluble aggregate appeared but the
latter did not precipitate. The following reaction sequence was pos-
tulated:

$$11S \xrightarrow{\quad(a)\quad} \text{A-subunits} + [\text{B-subunits}]$$
$$\downarrow (b)$$
$$\text{Soluble aggregates}$$
$$\downarrow (c)$$
$$\text{Insoluble aggregates}$$

Presumably heat disrupts the quaternary structure of the 11S protein
and releases the two types of subunits: A-subunits (3 to 4S fraction) that
remain soluble and B-subunits that aggregate very rapidly. Reaction b
is very rapid because the B-subunits are not detected in a slow sedimenting state. Precipitation as a result of reaction c is catalyzed by sulfhydryl compounds but inhibited by N-ethylmaleimide. Hydrophobic bonding appears to be the major factor in forming the insoluble aggregates.

FUNCTIONAL PROPTERTIES

Soybean proteins in their various forms are often used at low levels (1
to 2%) in fabricated foods to impart desirable characteristics or functional properties either in handling during processing or in the finished
product. At higher levels the soy ingredient can serve as a source of
dietary protein as well as provide functionality, e.g., blending of textured soy flour with ground meats. Some of the functional properties
attributed to soy proteins are summarized in Table 7.8 and discussed in
greater detail elsewhere (Wolf 1970). Clear documentation of claims for
a given functional property is often difficult to find. Likewise, mean-

TABLE 7.8

FUNCTIONAL PROPERTIES OF SOYBEAN PROTEINS[1]

Property	Food System
Emulsification	Processed meats, baked goods, whipped toppings
Fat absorption	Processed and simulated meats, baked goods
Water absorption	Baked goods, confections, meat patties
Texture	Processed and simulated meats, baked goods
Film formation	Processed meats
Bleaching[2]	Bread
Browning	Baked goods
Aeration	Whipped toppings, chiffon mixes, confections

[1]Wolf 1970.
[2]Use of soy flour containing lipoxygenase activity.

ingful tests for measuring functional properties often do not exist (Wolf and Cowan 1971). Because food systems are generally complex mixtures of water, fats, proteins, and carbohydrates, it is difficult to determine the influence of an additional ingredient by simple tests. It is therefore imperative that soy protein products be tested by incorporation into the product formulation and evaluated in the finished food before drawing conclusions about the usefulness of a given protein product.

BIBLIOGRAPHY

AMERICAN OIL CHEMISTS' SOCIETY. 1973. Official and Tentative Methods, 3rd Ed., Methods Ba 10-65 and Ba 11-65, Champaign, Ill.

ANDERSON, R. L., WOLF, W. J., and GLOVER, D. 1973. Extraction of soybean meal proteins with salt solutions at pH 4.5. J. Agr. Food Chem. 21, 251-254.

BECKER, K. W. 1971. Processing of oilseeds to meal and protein flakes. J. Amer. Oil Chem. Soc. 48, 299-304.

BELTER, P. A., and SMITH, A. K. 1952. Protein denaturation in soybean meal during processing. J. Am. Oil Chem. Soc. 29, 170-174.

CATSIMPOOLAS, N. 1969. Isolation of glycinin subunits by isoelectric focusing in urea-mercaptoethanol. Fed. Eur. Biochem. Soc. Lett. 4, 259-261.

CATSIMPOOLAS, N., KENNEY, J. A., MEYER, E. W., and SZUHAJ, B. F. 1971. Molecular weight and amino acid composition of glycinin subunits. J. Sci. Food Agr. 22, 448-450.

CATSIMPOOLAS, N., and MEYER, E. W. 1970. Gelation phenomena of soybean globulins. I. Protein-protein interactions, Cereal Chem. 47, 559-570.

CATSIMPOOLAS, N., and MEYER, E. W. 1971. Gelation phenomena of soybean globulins. III. Protein-lipid interactions. Cereal Chem. 48, 159-167.

CATSIMPOOLAS, N., ROGERS, D. A., CIRCLE, S. J., and MEYER, E. W. 1967. Purification and structural studies of the 11S component of soybean proteins. Cereal Chem. 44, 631-637.

CIRCLE, S. J., MEYER, E. W., and WHITNEY, R. W. 1964. Rheology of soy protein dispersions. Effect of heat and other factors on gelation. Cereal Chem. 41, 157-172.

CUMMING, D. B., STANLEY, D. W., and DEMAN, J. M. 1973. Fate of water soluble soy protein during thermoplastic extrusion. J. Food Sci. 38, 320-323.

HASEGAWA, K., KUSANO, T., and MITSUDA, H. 1963. Fractionation of soybean proteins by gel filtration. Agr. Biol. Chem. (Tokyo) 27, 878-880.

HAYES, L. P., and SIMMS, R. P. 1973. Defatted soybean fractionation by solvent extraction. U.S. Pat. 3,734,901. May 22.

HILL, J. E., and BREIDENBACH, R. W. 1974. Proteins of soybean seeds. I. Isolation and characterization of the major components. Plant Physiol. 53, 742-746.

KAWAMURA, S. 1967. Quantitative paper chromatography of sugars of the cotyledon, hull and hypocotyl of soybeans of selected varieties. Kagawa Univ. Fac. Tech. Bull. 18, 117-131.

KELLEY, J. J., and PRESSEY, R. 1966. Studies with soybean protein and fiber formation. Cereal Chem. 43, 195-206.

KOSHIYAMA, I. 1968A. Factors influencing conformation changes in a 7S protein of soybean globulins by ultracentrifugal investigations. Agr. Biol. Chem. (Tokyo) 32, 879-887.

KOSHIYAMA, I. 1968B. Chemical and physical properties of a 7S protein in soybean globulins. Cereal Chem. 45, 394-404.

KOSHIYAMA, I. 1971. Some aspects of subunit structure of a 7S protein in soybean globulins. Agr. Biol. Chem. (Tokyo) 35, 385-392.

McANELLY, J. K. 1964. Method for producing a soybean protein product and the resulting product. U.S. Pat. 3,142,571. July 28.

MEYER, E. W. 1970A. Soybean flours and grits. Food Sci. Technol. Proc. Int. Congr., 3rd, 1970, 235-241.

MEYER, E. W. 1970B. Soya protein isolates for food. In Proteins As Human Food. R. A. Lawrie (Editor). Avi Publishing Co., Westport, Conn.

MEYER, E. W. 1971. Oilseed protein concentrates and isolates. J. Am. Oil Chem. Soc. 48, 484-488.

MILLIGAN, E. D., and SURIANO, J. F. 1974. System for production of high and low protein dispersibility index edible extracted soybean flakes. J. Am. Oil Chem. Soc. 51, 158-161.

MUSTAKAS, G. C., KIRK, L. D., and GRIFFIN, E. L., JR. 1962. Flash desolventizing defatted soybean meals washed with aqueous alcohols to yield a high-protein product. J. Am. Oil Chem. Soc. 39, 222-226.

NAISMITH, W. E. F. 1955. Ultracentrifuge studies on soya bean protein. Biochim. Biophys. Acta 16, 203-210.

NASH, A. M., KWOLEK, W. F., and WOLF, W. J. 1971. Denaturation of soybean proteins by isoelectric precipitation. Cereal Chem. 48, 360-368.

NASH, A. M., and WOLF, W. J. 1967. Solubility and ultracentrifugal studies on soybean globulins. Cereal Chem. 44, 183-192.

NELSON, A. I., WEI, L. S., and STEINBERG, M. P. 1971. Food products from whole soybeans. Soybean Dig. 31, No. 3, 32-34.

SAIO, K., MATSUO, T., and WATANABE, T. 1970. Preliminary electron microscopic investigation on soybean 11S protein. Agr. Biol. Chem. (Tokyo) 34, 1851-1854.

SAIO, K., WAKABAYASHI, A., and WATANABE, T. 1968. Effects of heating on soybean meal proteins. Nippon Nogei Kagaku Kaishi 42, 90-96.

SAIO, K., and WATANABE, T. 1968. Observation of soybean foods under electron microscope, Nippon Shokuhin Kogyo Gakkai-Shi 15, 290-296.

SAIR, L. 1959. Proteinaceous soy composition and method of preparing. U.S. Pat. 2,881,076. April 7.

SHIBASAKI, K., OKUBO, K., and ONO, T. 1969. Food chemical studies on soybean proteins. On the insoluble protein components of defatted soybean heated by steaming. Nippon Shokuhin Kogyo Gakkai-Shi *16,* 22-26.

SMITH, A. K., and CIRCLE, S. J. 1938. Peptization of soybean proteins. Extraction of nitrogenous constituents from oil-free meals by acids and bases with and without added salts. Ind. Eng. Chem. *30,* 1414-1418.

SMITH, A. K., and CIRCLE, S. J. 1972. Soybeans: Chemistry and Technology, Vol. 1, Proteins. Avi Publishing Co., Westport, Conn.

SOYBEAN DIGEST. 1974. Blue Book Issue *34,* No. 6, 67.

TOMBS, M. P. 1967. Protein bodies of the soybean. Plant Physiol. *42,* 797-813.

WATANABE, T., and NAKAYAMA, O. 1962. Study of water-extracted protein of soybean. Nippon Nogei Kagaku Kaishi *36,* 890-895.

WOLF, W. J. 1969. Soybean protein nomenclature: a progress report. Cereal Sci. Today *14,* 75-76, 78, 129.

WOLF, W. J. 1970. Soybean proteins: their functional, chemical and physical properties. J. Agr. Food Chem. *18,* 969-976.

WOLF, W. J. 1972A. What is soy protein? Food Technol. *26,* No. 5, 44-45, 48, 50, 52-54.

WOLF, W. J. 1972B. Purification and properties of the proteins. *In* Soybeans: Chemistry and Technology, Volume 1, Proteins. A. K. Smith and S. J. Circle (Editors). Avi Publishing Co., Westport, Conn.

WOLF, W. J., and F. L. BAKER. 1975. Scanning electron microscopy of soybeans, soy flours, protein concentrates, and protein isolates. Cereal Chem. In press.

WOLF, W. J., and BRIGGS, D. R. 1958. Studies on the cold-insoluble fraction of the water-extractable soybean proteins. II. Factors influencing conformation changes in the 11S component. Arch. Biochem. Biophys. *76,* 377-393.

WOLF, W. J., and COWAN, J. C. 1971. Soybeans as a food source. CRC Press, Cleveland, Ohio.

WOLF, W. J., and TAMURA, T. 1969. Heat denaturation of soybean 11S protein. Cereal Chem. *46,* 331-344.

CHAPTER 8

Martin Glicksman | Carbohydrates for Fabricated Foods

Fabricated foods are foods designed and built according to plan from individual components, to yield products having specified physical, chemical, and functional properties (Glicksman 1971).

Although fabricated foods are discussed as if they were a new concept, they actually have been part of our society since the beginning of recorded history. The earliest known fabricated food is the staff of life itself—bread. Bread *per se* does not exist in nature, and, while nature made wheat, corn, rye and other cereal grains, it was man who took the harvest and formed it into a food with texture, shape, and flavor that made it a joy to eat. Historically, fabricated foods were developed initially not to titillate the palate, but to use available ingredients in a convenient and utilitarian manner.

Another purpose of fabricating food is to fill both dietary and economic needs. Foods are fabricated to make better use of available raw materials and to make foods with higher nutritional values.

Fabricated foods are formulated and prepared from carefully selected ingredients to yield products with specified properties. There are two basic types of fabricated foods: those designed to simulate natural counterparts currently referred to as "analogs", such as meat and dairy analogs, and those which have no counterpart in nature but are prepared to give variety and spice to the diet. One of the most common and most popular examples of the latter is Jell-O gelatin dessert. Another popular and universal product is ice cream, designed to please the palate hundreds of years ago and still probably the most widely consumed fabricated food in the world. Many types of fabricated food products are now available, all aimed at filling consumer needs. Some of the more important categories are illustrated in Table 8.1.

ROLE OF CARBOHYDRATES

In the emerging era of fabricated foods, attention must be focused on the three basic building blocks of all food products—proteins, fats, and carbohydrates. Carbohydrates in fabricated foods are not included primarily for their nutritional values. In fact, in many applications, such as low-calorie foods, efforts are deliberately made to restrict or minimize their carbohydrate content. Carbohydrates are used largely for functional reasons in fabricated foods. The highly soluble common sugars, like sucrose, dextrose, and corn syrup, are used mainly as bodying and sweetening agents. Thus they contribute such bodying

TABLE 8.1

TYPES OF FABRICATED FOODS

Meat analogs (texturized protein foods)
Dairy analogs (formulated non-dairy products)
Soft moist (intermediate moisture foods)
Novelty foods (imitation caviar, French-fried molded onion rings, etc.)
Low calorie foods
Special-purpose dietary foods (low cholesterol, low sodium, low fat, sugar-free, etc.)
Convenience foods (snack packs, TV dinners, etc.)
Baby foods
Geriatric foods
Snack foods

attributes as viscosity, texture, density, and mouthfeel, among others, while also imparting sweetness and flavor to the organoleptic and sensory aspects of the food. When utilized, they are used at substantial levels and generally constitute a major proportion of the food (Katz 1973; Murray and Luft 1973).

Carbohydrate polymers, more commonly known as gums and starches (hydrocolloids), are used strictly for their functional properties. With the exception of the starches, carbohydrate polymers are used at very low levels, generally under 1% of the foodstuff. Typical use-levels are listed in Table 8.2. These materials are important because of their multi-faceted functional characteristics which can give functional effects achievable in no other way and at very low concentrations. For example, these materials can tie up 500 parts of water in a rigid gel or produce tremendous viscosity changes at concentrations as low as 0.1%, and lower in some situations.

Functional Properties of Hydrocolloids

Hydrocolloids have many functional properties and are classified as shown in Table 8.3. The common gums used in food applications are classified into three categories depending on their source or origin. These are the natural gums and starches, derived from plants; the modified natural products; and, finally, the completely synthetic gums.

TABLE 8.2

PERCENTAGE USE LEVELS OF GUMS IN TYPICAL FOODS

Gelatin Desserts	1.0 - 2.0
Salad dressings	0.1 - 0.5
Ice cream, frozen desserts	0.1 - 0.5
Beverages and beverage mixes	0.05 - 0.5
Baked goods	0.1 - 0.5
Toppings, sauces, gravies	0.05 - 1.0
Cheese, cheese spreads	0.1 - 0.75

TABLE 8.3

CLASSIFICATION OF HYDROCOLLOIDS

Natural	Modified Natural	Synthetic
Plant exudates	Cellulose derivatives	Polyvinylpyrrolidone (PVP)
Arabic	Carboxymethylcellulose	Carboxyvinyl polymers (Carbopol)
Tragacanth	Methylcellulose	Polyethylene oxide polymers (Polyox)
Karaya	Hydroxyethylcellulose	
Ghatti	Hydroxypropylcellulose	
Seaweed extracts	Hydroxypropylmethylcellulose	
Agar	Other derivatives	
Alginates	Modified starches	
Carrageenans	Low methoxyl pectin	
Furcellaran	Propylene glycol alginate	
Plant Seed Gums		
Guar		
Locust Bean		
Psyllium		
Quince		
Tamarind		
Cereal Gums		
Starches		
Corn Hull Gum		
Plant Extracts		
Pectin		
Arabinogalactan		
Fermentation Gums		
Dextran		
Xanthan		
Curdlan		
Animal Derived		
Gelatin		
Albumens		
Caseinates		

These long-chain polymers have many diverse functional properties, but the one major property common to all gums is that of viscosity in an aqueous medium. All gums will dissolve or disperse in water to give a thickening or bodying effect. While the degree of thickening and the quality or rheology of the viscosity effect differs widely among gums, the phenomenon is distinctive and noticeable. In addition, it only requires small amounts of these materials, usually a fraction of 1%, to produce a substantial change in viscosity.

The second major property exhibited by a selected few hydrocolloids is that of gelling. Gelation is the phenomenon involving the association or cross-linking of the polymer chains to form a 3-dimensional continuous network which traps or immobilizes the water within it to form a firm, rigid structure that is resistant to flow under pressure. Only a comparatively few gums form gels, as indicated in Table 8.4. These vary so widely in gel character and texture that they are used only for specific food applications, and only a few of them can be interchanged in certain applications.

TABLE 8.4

HYDROCOLLOID GELLING SYSTEMS IN FOODS

Hydrocolloid	Major Food Gel Application
Agar	Canned meat, bakery icings, glazes
Alginate	Gelled water desserts, milk puddings
Carrageenan	Milk puddings, dessert gels, aspics
Furcellaran	Milk puddings
Pectin	Jams, jellies, preserves
Starch	Milk puddings, confections
Xanthan-locust bean	Milk puddings, dessert gels

In addition to thickening and gelling, gums have many secondary functional properties that are useful in food processing and development. As shown in Table 8.5, these properties range from adhesiveness to whippability. In many applications, more than one of these functional properties come into play, and the versatility and uniqueness of these ingredients is sometimes solely responsible for the feasibility of fabricating specific food products.

TABLE 8.5

FUNCTIONS OF HYDROCOLLOIDS IN FOOD PRODUCTS

Function	Example
Adhesive	Bakery glaze
Binding agent	Sausages
Calorie control agent	Dietetic foods
Crystallization inhibitor	Ice cream, sugar syrups
Clarifying agent (fining)	Beer, wine
Cloud agent	Fruit juice
Coating agent	Confectionery
Emulsifier	Salad dressings
Encapsulating agent	Powdered flavors
Film former	Sausage casings, protective coatings
Flocculating agent	Wine
Foam stabilizer	Whipped toppings, beer
Gelling agent	Puddings, desserts, aspics
Molding	Gum drops, jelly candies
Protective colloid	Flavor emulsions
Stabilizer	Beer, mayonnaise
Suspending agent	Chocolate milk
Swelling agent	Processed meats
Syneresis inhibitor	Cheese, frozen foods
Thickening agent	Jams, pie fillings, sauces
Whipping agent	Toppings, icings

MEAT ANALOGS

One of the most important and exciting areas of development is that of meat analogs. With the skyrocketing prices of meat and the development of new protein sources, the technology needed for converting vegetable proteins into acceptable meat analogs is a challenge accepted by every major food company.

Pyke (1971) has written that "the problem of presenting synthetic protein as a food-stuff or food ingredient with some sort of recognizable and acceptable structure and appearance may be quite difficult. Meat and many protein foods have a recognizable structural anatomy or 'grain'. The structure of meat which gives it one of the culinary qualities for which it is esteemed is due to the orderly arrangement of muscle fibers of which it is composed. In order for synthetic or isolated proteins to compete with meat, they will need to be fabricated into something not entirely dissimilar to meat."

Giddey (1965) reasoned that the first step in synthesizing a meat product would be to transform vegetable proteins into fibers which could then be compacted into meat-like masses. Also, since most organized meat structures depend on insoluble, highly hydrated proteins, it would be desirable for artificial protein structures from vegetable proteins to have the same properties in order to be an acceptable simulated food.

Many ways have been developed for texturizing protein as shown in Table 8.6, and the more important ones will be reviewed. (Circle and Smith 1972; Smith and Circle 1972).

Fiber Spinning

Basic Spinning Processes.—Pioneering work on the experimental production of protein fibers was published by Boyer in 1940 and was directed at textile applications. It was 14 years later that he applied his new technology of spinning protein fibers to the preparation of edible meat-like structures (Boyer 1940, 1954). The process was based on changing the protein configuration by solubilizing the protein, unfold-

TABLE 8.6

METHODS FOR TEXTURIZING PROTEINS

Fiber spinning
Extrusion
Chewy gel formation
Autoclaving coagulation
Pressure variation sponge formation
Non-spinning fiber formation
pH treatment of granules

ing the protein chains, and reforming them in roughly parallel fashion, thus simulating muscle protein fibers. The basic steps of the Boyer process are listed in Table 8.7. This process made possible for the first time the fabrication of meat-like products according to predetermined or designated levels of protein, fat, and carbohydrate. In addition, colors, flavors, vitamins, minerals, amino acids, and other constituents could be added as desired. The Boyer process is still the basis for commerical manufacture of such products. A typical modern process is described in Table 8.8. (Burke 1971; Rosenfield and Hartman 1973; Gutcho 1973).

During processing, other textural properties can be imparted to the prepared fibers. Varying pressures in assembling the final extruded fibers can alter the density and texture. Toughness or tenderness can be controlled to a certain degree by the amount of stretch applied to the fibers during the initial spinning step. Major textural effects can also be produced by additives. These can be incorporated within the fibers by addition prior to spinning, or by various methods of coating the fibers and/or impregnating them after spinning.

TABLE 8.7

BOYER PROTEIN SPINNING PROCESS

1. Preparation of an oil-free meal.
2. Production of a washed and dried protein curd.
3. Preparation of a carefully controlled viscous protein solution.
4. Extrusion of viscous protein solution through spinnerettes into acid coagulating bath.
5. Collecting and stretching the extruded filaments on reels.

TABLE 8.8

MODERN FIBER SPINNING PROCESS

1. Raw material protein isolate (90% protein) is obtained from solvent defatted oilseed meal.
2. Protein isolate is dissolved in sodium hydroxide solution at pH, 10.5 - 12.5 to give solids concentration of 10 - 30%.
3. Dope solution is aged for few minutes until viscosity increases from 25 to 300 poises.
4. Dope is forced through spinnerette (3″ diam., 1000 - 1600 orifices of 0.002″ - 0.006″ diam.) into acid/salt bath.
5. Coagulated fibers are stretched 50 - 400% on pickup reels and collected in bundles (¼″ diam.) which are then assembled in tows (3 - 4″ thick).
6. Fiber tows are squeezed between rollers to remove excess moisture and then passed through neutralizing bath.
7. Fiber tows are then processed further depending on end use, or cut and stored for subsequent treatment.

Some of the more effective additives are the various carbohydrate gums and starches. When incorporated within the fibers, these materials affect: chewability, stretchability, elasticity, cohesiveness, adhesiveness, moisture retention, hydratability (or rehydratability), freeze-thaw stability, and water activity (stability).

When the additives are applied to the exterior surfaces of the fibers, many of the same functional effects can be achieved; and, in addition, a binding effect is obtained. A binder is necessary to hold the fibers and fiber tows together and to impart desirable textural properties to groups of fibers (Noyes 1969; Boyer 1954). The binder may function by holding the filaments together adhesively, by retaining them as in a matrix, and by physically binding them together. Thus, the binder may consist of a casing, such as an edible sausage casing, which is filled with the fiber filaments by well-known procedures. The binder may also be constituted of edible fibers, filaments, or sheets, by means of which the filaments are physically tied together. These materials may be ingredients such as starches, dextrins, cereal flour, and gums, which perform their binding function adhesively, or as a matrix in which the fibrous filaments are embedded (Noyes 1969).

These edible binders may be applied in powder form by a suitable dusting appartus, or the filaments can be passed through a bath of the binder solution. After this procedure, the filaments may be passed through a bath of melted fat. They also may be treated with solid fat by including a ribbon of fat in the tow.

Finally, the groups of filaments are assembled by pressing together to form a tow and are cut into suitable lengths for handling. The importance of a good binder was shown by Horrocks (1972). Protein foods similar to cooked muscle meat in appearance and texture were prepared by impregnating commercial spun protein fibers with homogenized creamy emulsions containing proteins, salts, oil, and flavor precursors. The oriented fibers were heated with a solution of a colloidal binding material, such as agar or carrageenan, providing a protective coating which made the product stable to cooking.

Carbohydrate texturizing materials in these conventional spun fiber processes are used in the following ways: (1) impregnated on the surface of the fiber by physical absorption; (2) incorporated within the fiber, usually being added to the dope; and (3) as a binder for uniting groups of fibers into cohesive matrices.

The most important use of carbohydrates may still depend on future developments. For example, in spun soy protein processes, the starting material is typically a functionally active protein isolate, containing at least 90% protein, which can be unfolded in solution, oriented along parallel axes, and fixed in a new physical realignment.

However, what about denatured proteins that cannot be so manipulated? What about the "funny powders", such as fish protein concentrates or single-cell proteins that have the nutrition but not the activity of undenatured proteins? What about the less expensive proteins that cannot be separated as 90% isolates but are available as flours or concentrates containing substantial proportions of good nutritious protein? What about the protein by-products or wastes which can be collected as nutritious, inactive powders? Many of these materials can be utilized to form textured foods, if they can be processed with an active, carbohydrate texturizing base material. Some of this work has already been done and much more will certainly be accomplished in the future. This concept can be best illustrated by the use of alginates to form alginate-protein fibers.

Alginate Fibers.—Sodium alginate is a carbohydrate polymer extracted commercially from certain species of seaweed where it occurs as a mixture of mannuronic and guluronic acids. The sodium salt is very soluble in water and has the unique property of reacting instantaneously with calcium salts to form insoluble calcium alginate. This property is used in making alginate fibers, which is not a new technique (Glicksman 1969). The earliest description of spinning fibers from sodium alginate solution was in 1912. Later during World War II some attempts were made to produce alginate yarns in Great Britain for use as camouflage netting. Regular production of calcium alginate yarn did not become established until after the war when Courtaulds, Ltd. in England developed this technology for textile applications.

The alginate fibers were made by the wet spinning method using a solution of sodium alginate which passes into a bath of calcium chloride solution. The filaments of calcium alginate were insoluble in water but could be easily dissolved by dilute solutions of sodium carbonate and by solutions of calcium-sequestering phosphates. Calcium alginate yarn found use as an auxiliary or temporary fiber in the construction stages of textile articles where it could be removed as desired by passing the item through a solubilizing bath (Ciba 1969).

In medicine, alginate fibers which have good haemostatic properties have been used as first aid dressings. The dressings are made with a liner of non-irritant alginate fabric which comes into direct contact with the damaged and irritated tissues. It soaks up body fluids, swells, becoming gelatinous in character, and controls seepage from the wound. The moist, soft, and non-tacky alginate layer ensures painless and trouble-free release when the dressing is removed. In addition to fabric, alginate wool similar to cotton wool is also used by surgeons and dentists for haemostatic purposes.

By using this process and incorporating protein into the alginate solution before spinning, protein fibers can be formed from denatured, inactive, non-functional protein materials. This technique has been used successfully and is described in a patent assigned to General Foods (Ishler *et al*. 1963). This process describes the use of sodium alginate or low methoxyl pectin in combination with various protein meals which is extruded into a calcium acetate bath to form alginate-protein fibers. By incorporating aluminum salts before spinning the alginate-protein fibers, the protein fibers are modified so that they can withstand boiling in salt water (Atkinson 1969).

A further modification makes use of a mixture of alginate, carrageenan, peroxide, and soy flour to yield a modified spun protein fiber when extruded into an aqueous calcium chloride bath (Atkinson 1972).

Although the term alginates, as used broadly in the literature, pertains to fiber-forming systems, there are several other carbohydrate systems that have been and can be used for this purpose. Starches, for example, in combination with proteins, yield novel textured, puffed spun fibers.

Puffed Spun Fibers.—Puffed fibrous food products are prepared by: (1) forming a spinning solution containing both protein and starch; (2) extruding the spinning solution into an aqueous acid coagulating bath to form fibers; (3) adjusting the pH of the fibers where necessary to 4.0 to 8.0; (4) drying the fibers to a moisture content of about 8.0 to 35.0% by weight; and (5) puffing the dried fibers (Pyne 1970).

All types of starches or flours can be used, but it is preferred to use cornstarch or corn flour. A preferred product described by Pyne (1970) is made with Col-Flo 67, a cross-linked cornstarch consisting entirely of amylopectin chains cross-linked with acetyl groups. It is easily and quickly dispersed in cold water; when gelatinized, it is smooth, short-textured and bland, and is resistant to breakdown under low pH conditions (Pyne 1970).

Simulated Spun Fiber Formation.—To avoid the difficult and expensive spinning procedure, efforts have been directed towards making fibers without spinning. These simulated spun fibers were made using the alginate-calcium salt reaction as shown in Table 8.9 (Arima and Harada 1971).

TABLE 8.9

NON-SPINNING FIBER FORMATION

1. Prepare aqueous suspension of protein containing 10 to 60% by weight of soluble alginate salt.
2. Coagulate suspension by adding aqueous solution of calcium salt while stirring in blendor.
3. Continue stirring to slice soft curd with rapidly rotating blades to form soft fibers of random short length in flake form.
4. Modify texture by adjusting processing variables—pH, calcium content, temperature, time, etc.

A recent patent describes a similar carbohydrate system to form fibers without spinning (Mullen and Nivens 1974). In this system, carboxymethyl guar or locust bean gum solutions are reacted with solutions of calcium salts to form large sac-like precipitates which are subjected to vigorous mixing and agitation. This action ruptures or severs the sac-like precipitates to form fibrous gel-like masses resembling crabmeat in texture and appearance. This fibrous material can be formulated into a variety of foods where a texture is desired that is similar to breakfast sausage, hamburger, crabmeat salad, or chicken loaf. While these fibrous sacs are essentially composed of nonnutritive carbohydrate polymers, there is no reason why proteinaceous materials cannot be incorporated in the gum solutions before reacting with calcium salts to form the same type of fibrous masses for use as a texturized protein material.

Extrusion

Basic Process.—Another major technique for fabricating textured vegetable proteins is by extrusion of protein compositions under heat and pressure. This is a simple process compared with spinning and requires much less equipment and technology. It does not produce well-defined fibers but gives fibrous particulates that have good mouthfeel and chewiness similar to meat.

The protein in aqueous dispersion is subjected to heat and pressure which causes some realignment of the protein molecules as it is extruded from the high-pressure area into the atmosphere, creating a rapid expansion of the product with a rapid flashing off of the water.

A major advantage is that the raw material does not have to be a 90% protein isolate but can be a meal or flour containing much less protein. The raw material commonly used is solvent-extracted, defatted oilseed meal containing 40 to 70% protein and up to 35% carbohydrate. This material can also be mixed with other texturizing additives prior to extrusion to further modify the processed product. The mixture is sub-jected to a pressure above 1000 psi and temperatures of 240 to 350°F during processing (Burke 1971).

The equipment is similar to that used for processing thermoplastic resin products, i.e., continuous extrusion cookers. Depending upon the type and condition of the starting material and other factors, the ex-truded particles may be compacted or expanded. The expanded form is generally preferred.

A typical extrusion apparatus, such as the Wenger Extruder, consists of a jacketed chamber housing a screw. At one end of the chamber is a pressure plate with a restricted orifice leading to a narrow tube, at the end of which there is a nozzle. The plastic mass is forced through the extruder by the screw while being heated by steam passing through the jacket and by the pressure in the tube built up by the screw (Rakosky 1971; Sanderude and Ziemba 1968; and Chapter 9).

Mechanical agitation of the screw causes partial orientation of the protein molecules, and the narrow tube aligns the molecules prior to expansion. While in the tube, the structure of the plastic mass changes and it takes on a fibrous texture. On extrusion through the nozzle, the plastic mass expands to give a continuous, ropy stream of puffed, fibr-ous, textured protein which is cut into strips, chunks, or ground into powder or granules.

Protein flour, water, color, flavor, and other functional ingredients are mixed and fed to a cooker extruder. Under pressure and heat, the mixture is extruded and expands. The size and shape of the texturized extrudate is controlled by configuration of the dies and the speed of the cutting knife.

Jet-Cooking Extrusion.—One novel extrusion method uses starch carbohydrates as a texturizing base to form various types of novel fabricated products. This process is based on the fact that certain starches of the high-amylose variety have the unique ability to bind other materials into stable extruded shapes. When combined with pro-tein and other nutrients, high-amylose starch-based compositions can be pressure-cooked to give firm textured gels having a chewy, meat-like texture.

The process consists of mixing starch, soy isolate, nutrients, color, and flavoring with water to give a 30% solids dispersion with a protein to starch ratio of about 3 to 1. The mixture is jet-cooked, and, as it comes out of the jet, it can be either cast into blocks or sheets or extruded into cold water, where it sets into fibers or fibrous-like materials. The final gelled material does not disintegrate in either cold or boiling water so that the products can be processed to resemble pieces of meat. The products have textures similar to hamburger or meat loaf and can be used as meat analogs (Anon. 1972; Hullinger *et al.* 1973).

Jet pressure cooked combinations of high-amylose starch plus other ingredients will give cheese-like textures which can be combined with process cheese to give a cheese product with unusual properties. The mixture can be sliced, cubed, and fat-fried while retaining its shape without melting or deforming (Hullinger *et al.* 1973).

High-Moisture Extrusions.—By modification of the water content and the use of hydrocolloid binders and texturizing agents, various types of fabricated meat products can be made by upgrading left-overs, by-products and other lower-grade natural raw materials. An extrusion process has been developed to produce a high-moisture class of foods from low-cost meat, fish, poultry or even vegetable ingredients. In this process the inexpensive, lower-grade ingredients are diced, chopped, and mixed with alginates or other suitable gum compositions and extruded in characteristic shapes resembling onion rings, potato strips, or shrimp semicircles. The extruded pieces are then breaded and fried to yield tender, juicy fabricated foods. The process is being used for fabricating shrimp-shaped products from diced or chopped shrimp pieces. The meat/seafood base material makes 51 to 60% of the final product weight. Studies on formed fish indicate that the "sawdust" from cutting frozen fish blocks could be used to make up as much as 30% of the total fish content, thus providing a good method for utilizing a nutritional, but ordinarily wasted, by-product (Anon. 1974).

Hydroxypropylcellulose Thermoforming.—An effective way of utilizing carbohydrates as a base for making texturized protein food products is described by Ganz (1973). This process utilizes a thermoplastic polymer, hydroxypropylcellulose, which is mixed with other food ingredients or protein sources. The mixture is extruded and shaped under temperature and pressure sufficient to cause the admixture to soften and flow into a desired shape. The extruded product, it is claimed, exhibits improvement over the food material component *per se*, particularly in respect to chewing properties, rehydration properties, self-stability, and physical integrity. It is stable during storage and handling but readily softens or disintegrates under chewing or cooking conditions.

The key to this technique is the use of a carbohydrate polymer, hydroxpropylcellulose, commercially known as Klucel, which has several unique properties. It is cold water-soluble, thermoplastic, and is a good binder as well as being compatible with most food materials and ingredients.

Various texturized products can be made by this process. Some that

were reported include (Ganz 1973): (1) a ground beef or hamburger
extender made by extruding hydroxypropylcellulose under specified
conditions of concentration, pressure and temperature, with non-fat
milk solids, soy protein, wheat gluten or even ground cooked beef;
(2) breakfast cereal flakes or pieces made by co-extruding hydroxypropylcellulose with non-fat milk solids or wheat gluten; (3) a novel
candy bar confection made by extruding a combination of hydroxypropylcellulose, sugar, chocolate, salt, and fat; (4) a dry soup mix component made with hydroxypropylcellulose and dehydrated carrot powder,
while improved bouillon cubes were formed from the polymer plus a
bouillon soup dry mix powder; and (5) novelty products made from, e.g.,
broken pecan pieces plus hydroxypropylcellulose to give restructured
nut pieces, or dehydrated peach powder plus the gum to give peach
chunks or pieces suitable for bakery, confectionery, or similar applications.

Chewy Gel Formation

A third type of process for creating textured protein foods was developed by Anson and Pader (1957, 1958 A, B, 1959) about 15 yr ago.
This was a method of making what was called a "chewy gel", essentially
a protein-water system of colloidal dimensions. These "chewy gel"
chunks, when chewed, had the physical properties of resilience, elasticity, and resistance to shear. In addition, they had the property of heat
stability, i.e., retaining their firmness when subjected to heat, particularly in products which are to be subjected to heat processing or normal
cooking conditions prior to eating.

These "chewy gels" are prepared under special conditions of pH,
protein concentration, water content, and heat as shown in Table 8.10.
The resultant gel has a smooth, uniform, hydrated structure that is
pleasantly moist in the mouth and yet has enough textural firmness to
give proper resistance to bite.

Texture and mouthfeel can be modified by incorporating other hydrocolloids into the gel or by coating them on the gel particles. The
incorporation of carbohydrate additives makes the gel weaker and less

TABLE 8.10

CHEWY GEL FORMATION

1.	Adjust concentration of protein-water system.
2.	Adjust pH of protein dispersion.
3.	Controlled heating to form discrete gel particulates.
4.	Shape gel into desired form with or without additives.

gelatinous. The addition of gums, such as, locust bean gum, reduces the rubberiness of the gel and makes it softer. Alginates, seaweed extracts, and locust bean gum facilitates extrusion and gives products with smoother textural characteristics. Because of their water absorption characteristics, gums may also be used to modify and control the rehydration properties of a dehydrated gel.

Soft Moist (Intermediate Moisture) Foods

One area of fabricated foods where carbohydrates must be used at high levels is in the area of "soft moist", "intermediate moisture", or "shelf-stable" products. These are high-moisture products (20 to 40%) which are processed to resist microbial spoilage without the need of refrigeration.

In such products, the water is bound, which reduces the water activity to a point where it will not support microbial growth. This is usually done by incorporating high levels of soluble solids. For food products, this must, of course, be compatible with the flavor, texture, and general organoleptic properties of the food, which has been difficult to achieve except for pet foods. There are no important commercial human foods of this type on the market, although many have been described in the literature.

A typical ham loaf analog described in a recent patent (Katz 1973) has the composition revealed in Table 8.11. As shown in this formulation, the added corn syrup solids and gelatinized starch contributes over 17% carbohydrates to the product and are very important factors to the acceptability of the product to the consumer. In meat products, where

TABLE 8.11

HAM LOAF ANALOG

Component	Amount, %
Water	37.04
Compressed textured soy flour	15.13
Hydrogenated vegetable oil	14.00
Corn syrup solids (28 D.E.)	13.70
Flavored extruded texturized soy protein	8.50
Gelatinized starch	3.50
Salt	3.00
Glycerol	1.75
Smoke flavor	1.70
Ham flavor	0.90
Lactic acid	0.70
Artificial color	0.04
Potassium sorbate	0.04
	100.00

Aw = < 0.95 (Ham Loaf Analog)　　　Aw = > 0.98 (Fresh Cooked Meat)

sweetness obviously is inappropriate, high levels of corn syrup solids can be included by using the lower-D.E. materials. The lower the D.E., the less is the sweetness. Corn syrup solids are available in D.E.'s ranging from 5 to 65. The lower ones, 5 to about 15, have very little or almost no sweetness and can be used effectively in the above applications.

DAIRY ANALOGS

Types of Dairy Analogs

The forerunner of all simulated dairy products is, of course, margarine, which has been available for well over 100 years. After long technological and legal battles margarine has finally achieved the outstanding success that it enjoys today. More recently, concurrent with the advent of aerosol packaging, has come the development of non-dairy vegetable fat-based whipped toppings—first in dry mix powders, then in aerosol cans, and now in frozen, ready-to-use form.

Many types of dairy product analogs or substitutes are being marketed; the major ones are listed in Table 8.12. Typical formulations and processing methods for such imitation dairy products are readily available in the literature. Such products include soft-serve dessert, coffee whitener, frozen dessert, milk shake mix, iced vegetable dairy product, filled milk, chocolate filled milk, imitation milk, and whipped topping. The basic ingredients—proteins, fats, and carbohydrates—may be modified to provide them with specific performance properties. For low-

TABLE 8.12

SIMULATED DAIRY PRODUCTS

Natural Food	Food Analog
Butter	Margarine
Coffee cream	Coffee whitener, coffee lighteners
Whipped cream	Non-dairy whipped topping, imitation whipped topping
Milk	Filled milk, imitation milk
Milk shake	Non-dairy shake, imitation milk shake
Ice cream	Mellorine, imitation ice cream
Sour cream	Imitation sour cream
Buttermilk	Imitation buttermilk
Evaporated/ condensed milk	Imitation milk concentrates
Snack dips	Non-dairy snack dips
Cheese	Imitation cheese

sodium products, the potassium-salt form of the caseinates can be used. Modified vegetable proteins, such as soy, can replace the caseinates. Stabilizers, fats and fillers are modified or selected to give the desired functions in the final product (Arenson 1969).

Whipped Toppings

Although simulated whipped toppings were known for many years, it was only within the last decade that these types of products have gained significant consumer acceptance. The reasons for this lie in the several advantages of the simulated products over the natural products. These are: lower cost, uniformity of whip, non-dairy base, longer shelf-life, versatility of product type (powder, liquid, aerosol), and convenience. The type and variety of ingredients, plus the processing methods and conditions, play an important part in the preparation of good quality products. A typical product formulation for such whipped topping is shown in Table 8.13 (Knightly 1968).

TABLE 8.13

TYPICAL WHIPPED TOPPING FORMULATION

Ingredient	Level (%)	Function
Fat (m.p.94 to 98°F)	30	Provides richness, body, and texture
Protein (sodium caseinate)	2	Acts as film former to entrap aerating gases. Also aids in emulsification, imparts body, and improves flavor.
Sucrose	7	Provides sweetness and body
Corn syrup solids	3 - 5	Imparts additional body with much less sweetness
Emulsifier	0.35 - 1.0	Induces formation of stable emulsion and improves rate and amount of total aeration.
Stabilizer	0.3 - 0.5	Improves body, texture, and gas retention. Stabilizes overrun and prevents syneresis.
Stabilizing salts	q.s	Improves protein solubility and minimizes "wheying off"
Flavor and color	q.s.	
Water	to 100	

Coffee Whiteners

Coffee whiteners have become of increasing importance in recent years to the food industry. While the primary purpose of a coffee whitener is the development of a desirable color change, it also imparts a desirable cream-like flavor and body to the beverage or food to which it is added. Coffee whiteners are available in three forms—powder, liquid, and frozen liquid. All these products are basically oil-in-water emulsions which are dried or carefully concentrated, and which are capable of forming an emulsion when added to an aqueous medium such as coffee.

The stability and functionality of these emulsions depend primarily upon the degree and type of emulsion. Contributing factors are the types and concentrations of the various ingredients and the homogenization procedure. A typical formulation for these types of products is listed in Table 8.14 and illustrates the functions of the carbohydrate ingredients (Knightly 1969).

Imitation Cheese

Cheese products have also been recent targets for innovators. Imitation processed cheese and cheese products have been developed experi-

TABLE 8.14

TYPICAL COFFEE WHITENER POWDER

Ingredient	Level (%)	Function
Vegetable fat	10.0	Provides whitening power, body and viscosity
Protein	2.0	Provides emulsifying properties, some whitening power, imparts body, and improves flavor
Sucrose	2.5	Imparts sweetness, improves body, and reduces freezing point of the emulsion
Corn syrup solids	2.5	Imparts less sweetness but more body and viscosity
Emulsifier	0.5	Stabilizes emulsion, improves dispersibility, and improves rate of solution
Stabilizer	0.15	Improves colloidal solubility of the protein and controls body and viscosity
Stabilizing salts	0.15	Improves colloidal solubility of protein and reduces tendency towards syneresis
Flavor and color	q.s	
Water	to 100	

mentally and are typically based on vegetable fats, protein, hydrolyzed cereal solids, buffer salts, color, and flavor. The texture, viscosity, and mouthfeel of soft, processed cheeses and spreads, as well as hard cheeses and grated cheeses, have been reproduced (Horn 1970).

Sour Cream

Imitation sour cream, in regular, powdered and canned form, is usually composed of vegetable fat, protein (such as non-fat milk solids or sodium caseinate), mono- and diglycerides, buffer salts (phosphates), modified starches or gums, citric or lactic acid, and flavor.

For dry powder products, mixtures of these ingredients are usually blended, homogenized, and spray-dried to yield a powder that can easily be reconstituted with water. Formulations can be varied to suit individual requirements for viscosity, body and texture by adjusting and selecting the type and amount of filler, usually hydrolyzed cereal solids (Horn 1970).

NOVEL FABRICATED FOODS

The one area where the author believes the largest use of carbohydrates will be is in the area of specialized, novel foods. Many unique food systems and concepts have been developed by the creative application of carbohydrate polymer technology. To indicate what is possible, it would be helpful to explore further the alginate gelling system. This system has been selected for several reasons. First of all it has been available for a long time; it is unique and functional in a broad variety of applications; and much of its practical applications are described thoroughly in the literature.

Table 8.15 lists a broad spectrum of suggested and accomplished product applications, of which "imitation caviar" is timely. Recently a great deal of publicity was generated about a Russian process for making a fabricated caviar out of proteins and gelatin (Nesmeyanov *et al.* 1971). In the U.S. synthetic caviar was made with alginates about 18 or 20 yr ago using a much simpler process.

The Russian caviar is a complex system consisting basically of a protein solution or suspension encapsulated by a physical membrane made up mainly of gelatin and vegetable-tanning agents. The process consists of making an aqueous alkaline solution or suspension of the protein, to which is added a gel-forming agent, such as gelatin. Other texture-modifying ingredients are also added, such as glycerol, vegetable oil and starch.

The mixture is then formed into granules by adding it in a drop-wise stream to an immiscible-medium bath, such as oil, which has an upper

TABLE 8.15

ALGINATE-BASED FOOD CONCEPTS

Gelatinized beer
Artificial caviar
Fabricated cherries and blueberries
Imitation low calorie spaghetti & spaghetti sauce
Fabricated meatballs
Fabricated shrimp
Soft drink gels
Extruded onion rings
Fabricated potato chips
Fabricated vegetables
Meat and gravy loaves (sloppy joe, barbecue)
Fabricated sausage casings

layer heated above the gelling temperature of the mix (15 to 40°C) and a lower layer cooled to temperatures below gel melting (0 to 20°C). The granules are washed and tanned by immersion in a solution such as tea extract. They can also be colored by soaking them in food-dye baths.

The American alginate system consists of a very simple procedure. It is basically an extrusion of droplets of sodium alginate solution containing color, flavor, salt, and several texture modifying ingredients, into a calcium salt bath. The droplets react instantaneously with calcium to form an insoluble skin or membrane around the droplet, thus giving a caviar-like appearance and texture. By varying the types and concentrations of alginate and calcium salts and by varying the size of the droplets and the soaking time, many textural modifications can be obtained. This system has never been commercialized in this country probably because most Americans do not like expensive fish eggs.

This chapter has reviewed the current status of carbohydrate utilization in the field of fabricated foods. Technology stands on the threshold of a great new era of food product development and a great deal of creative advances will be accomplished with the application of functional carbohydrate ingredients.

BIBLIOGRAPHY

ANON. 1972. Low-cost textured protein process using starch offers functional flexibility. Foods of tomorrow, Summer 1972, p. F 4, Food Processing *33*.
ANON. 1974. Moist extrusions taking shape. Foods of Tomorrow, Food Proc. 35(1), 30.
ANSON, M. L., and PADER, M. 1957. Protein food product and process, U.S. Patent 2,802,737.

ANSON, M. L., and PADER , M. 1958A. Protein food products and method of making same, U.S. Patent 2,830,902.

ANSON, M. L., and PADER, M. 1958B. Method of making protein food product, U.S. Patent 2,833,651.

ANSON, M. L., and PADER, M. 1959. Methods for preparing a meat-like product, U.S. Patent 2,879,163.

ARENSON, S. W. 1969. Imitation dairy products: their formulation, processing, quality control, Food Eng. 41(4), 76.

ARIMA, T., and HARADA, Y. 1971. Method of producing proteinaceous fibers, U.S. Patent 3,627,536.

ATKINSON, W. T. 1969. Aluminum modified alginate fiber, U.S. Patent 3,455,697.

ATKINSON, W. T. 1972. Spun protein, U.S. Patent 3,645,746.

BOYER, R. A. 1940. Soybean protein fibers: experimental production. Ind. Eng. Chem. 32(12), 1549.

BOYER, R. A. 1954. High protein food product and process for its preparation, U.S. Patent 2,682,466.

BURKE, C. S. 1971. Manufactured Meat Products—Meat Analogues, Repts. Prog. Applied Chem. 56, 649-654.

CIBA, LTD. 1969. Alginates, Ciba Review, 1969/1, Ciba, Ltd., Basel, Switzerland.

CIRCLE, S. J., and SMITH, A. K. 1972. Functional properties of commercial edible soybean products. In Symposium: Seed Proteins. G.E. Inglett (Editor), Avi Publishing Co., Westport, Conn., pp. 242-254.

GANZ, A. J. 1973. Method of making a thermoplastic food product, U.S. Patent 3, 769, 029.

GIDDEY, C. 1965. Artificial edible structure from non-animal proteins, Cereal Sci. Today 10(4), 56.

GLICKSMAN, M. 1969. Gum Technology in the Food Industry, Academic Press, New York, N.Y.

GLICKSMAN, M. 1971. Fabricated Foods, Crit. Rev. Food Technol. 2(1), 21-43.

GUTCHO, M. 1973. Textured Foods and Allied Products, Noyes Data Corp., Park Ridge, N.J.

HORN, H. E. 1970. Will imitation cheese be next? Food Prod. Develop. 4(5), 32, 34, 36.

HORROCKS, D., BUCKLEY, K., and BOOTH, P. 1972. Meat-like protein food. Ger. Offen. 2,201,160 (C.A. 77, 138595).

HULLINGER, C. H.,VAN PATTEN, E., and FRECK, J. A. 1973. Food applications of high amylose starches, Food Technol. 27(3), 22-24.

ISHLER, N. H., MACALLISTER, R.V., SZCZESNIAK, A. S., and ENGEL, E. 1963. Gelled fibers from polymeric carboyhydrate gel precursor containing farinaceous or proteinaceous material. U.S. Patent 3,093,483.

KATZ, M. H. 1973. Meat analogs resistant to microbial spoilage, U.S. Patent 3,736,148.

KNIGHTLY, W. H. 1968. The role of ingredients in the formulation of whipped toppings, Food Technol. 22(6), 731.

KNIGHTLY, W. H. 1969. The role of ingredients in the formulation of coffee whiteners, Food Technol. 23(2), 37.

MULLEN, J. D., and NIVENS, M. P. 1974. Textured base materials or products from certain carboxyalkyl ethers of polygalactomannans and process of preparing same. U.S. Patent 3,782,962.

MURRAY, D. G., and LUFT, L. R. 1973. Low D. E. corn starch hydrolysates, Food Technol. 27(3), 32-33, 36, 38, 40.

NESMEYANOV, A. N., ROGOSHIN, S. V., SLONIMSKY, G. L., TOLSTOGUZOV, V. B., and ERSHOVA, V. A. 1971. Synthetic caviar, U.S. Patent 3,589,910.

NOYES, R. 1969. Protein Food Supplements, Noyes Development Corp., Park Ridge, N.J.

PYNE, A. W. 1970. Puffed fibrous snack food from protein-starch fiber. U.S. Patent 3,493,386.

PYKE, M. 1971. Synthetic Food, St. Martin's Press, New York, N.Y.

RAKOSKY, J. 1971. Vegetable protein-meat mixture, National Provisioner, Jan. 16.

ROSENFIELD, D., and HARTMAN, W. E. 1973. Spun-Fiber Textured Products, World Soy Protein Conference, Munich, Germany, Nov. 11-14.

RUSCH, D. T. 1971. Vegetable based dairy substitutes, Food Technol. *25*(5), 32, 34, 36.
SANDERUDE, K. G., and ZIEMBA, J. V. 1968. New products come easy with extrusion
    cooking, Food Eng. *40* (8), 84-87.
SMITH, A. K., and CIRCLE, S. J. 1972. Protein products as food ingredients. In Soybeans:
    Chemistry and Technology. A.K. Smith (Editor), Avi Publishing Co., Inc., Westport,
    Conn., pp. 339-88.

CHAPTER 9

Oak B. Smith | # Textures by Extrusion Processing

Many fabricated foods are cooked industrially and are given desired textures, shapes, density, and rehydration characteristics by an extrusion-cooking process. This relatively new process is used in the preparation of "engineered" convenience foods: textured vegetable proteins, breakfast cereals, snacks, infant foods, dry soup mixes, breadings, poultry stuffings, croutons, pasta products, beverage powders, and hot breakfast gruels.

First developed as an economical method of gelatinizing starches, extrusion-cookers have been modified during the intervening years to process an ever-widening group of foods, industrial and animal feed products, at ever-increasing capacities, and with production costs per pound which have steadily decreased, as compared with other industrial methods of cooking.

Modifications have been made in the extrusion-cooker which enable it to destroy the growth inhibitors present in soy proteins and in certain pulse proteins (Jiminez *et al.* 1963; Mustakas *et al.* 1964; DeMaeyer 1965). This has led to the protein fortification of extrusion-cooked cereal based foods. However, it took a decade of evaluation of biological performance to learn what could be done and what must not be done in thermal processing of cereals with proteins, vitamins, and amino acids. All fortifying nutrients could be harmed by improper thermal treatments. Protein-enriched breakfast cereals, snacks, infant foods, and instantized beverage powders have quickly developed. A method has been devised to make full-fat soy flours from extrusion-cooked soybeans.

Extrusion-cooked textured soy protein is produced from defatted soy flour or soy concentrates, with or without pH modification of the protein. Used principally as a meat extender, such products are also ingredients in a new range of fabricated protein foods which will be referred to here as the third generation of textured plant protein foods. This chronology considers the meat analog prepared from spun protein isolates as the first generation of textured plant protein foods, and extrusion-cooked meat extenders prepared from defatted soy flours or concentrates as the second generation of such foods. This third generation of textured foods utilizes textured soy protein extenders (extrusion-cooked from defatted soy flours or concentrates) plus isolated soy proteins, unsaturated vegetable oils, egg albumens, and a bit of cereal flour to create this new third generation of textured products in the form of breakfast sausages, slices, patties, roulades, and shrimps.

Extrusion-cooking has the capability of controlling product textures and mouthfeel to a surprising extent through a wide range of product densities and rehydration characteristics. It also acts as a product pasteurizer, producing end products of excellent bacteriological status and shelf-life, without any appreciable contribution to ecological problems.

Extrusion-cooking may be defined as the process by which moistened, expansile, starchy and/or proteinaceous material(s) are plasticized in a tube by a combination of pressure, heat, and mechanical shear. This results in elevated product temperatures within the tube, gelatinization of starchy components, denaturation of proteins, the stretching or restructuring of tractile components, the shaping of the end product, and exothermic expansion of the extrudate.

Extrusion-cooked foods are foods engineered to meet a specific need or group of needs. These include: (1) the need for convenience foods "engineered" to meet specific food requirements; (2) the need for nutritional balance, and for upgrading the biological utilization of foods; (3) the need to pasteurize foods for improved shelf-life; (4) the need to reduce the nutrient losses often encountered in thermal processing of foods; (5) a need to lower production costs; (6) a need for specific textures or functional characteristic(s) of foods or ingredients used in the preparation of foods; and (7) a need for versatility in the line of products to be produced.

This chapter will attempt to explain the capabilities and limitations of extrusion-cooking to meet these needs. Additionally, it will outline some of the methods used to meet specific processing objectives; describe methods developed to control or effect rheological properties of the foods produced; and discuss some of the things we believe can be produced by extrusion-cooking in the future.

METHODOLOGY OF HIGH-TEMPERATURE, SHORT-TIME EXTRUSION-COOKERS

These cookers include a method of steam preconditioning at modest and carefully controlled temperatures (65° to 100°C) at atmospheric pressures; a method of uniform application of moisture; an extruder assembly designed to work the moisturized oilseed or cereal into a dough at moderate temperatures (85° to 110°C); a means of elevating the temperature of the dough in the extruder in a coned nose section of extruder to a desired higher temperature (115 to 175°C) during a very short period of time (12 to 20 sec); a method of forming the dough into the desired shape by use of a final die; and a means of cutting the expanding dough into segments of desired length.

Certain extrusion-cooked products (textured soy proteins or bread-ings, for example) are run through a wet-milling device after extrusion-cooking but before drying and cooling.

Flaked breakfast cereals are made by cutting an extrusion-cooked and cooled extrudate into pea-sized balls which are flaked in a water-jacketed roller mill while the extrudate is still moist and pliable, before drying.

Some products do not benefit by preconditioning with steam, in which case the preconditioner acts only as a feeding device for process mate-rials.

After extrusion-processing, all products are passed through a tunnel type dryer and cooler, sometimes followed by a flavor application reel by means of which liquid flavors or dry-powder flavors are applied exter-nally to the extrudate from a suitable flour-feeding device. Flavors in liquid form (solution or emulsion) are sometimes suspended in a vegeta-ble oil carrier. Alternative techniques have been developed to sugar-coat breakfast cereals or snacks.

Most extrusion-cooked products may be reduced to a precooked flour or granule by impact milling or roller-milling of the dried extrudate.

Extrusion-cookers are built in several configurations—as steam-pressure cookers which discharge into a forming extruder, or as a simpler, long-barreled extruder which gradually builds pressures and temperatures while feed materials are advanced through the barrel, into which steam is injected. The high-temperature/short-time (HT/ST) extrusion-cooker, such as is illustrated in Fig. 9.1, is the only one to be discussed in this chapter.

Such extrusion-cookers are efficient converters of electrical energy to thermal energy and are thermodynamically efficient. They have the ability to entrain moisture and heat; make doughs; gelatinize starches; denature and debitter proteins; control heat-labile growth inhibitors; histologically restructure process materials; and retexture, shape, ex-pand, size, and partially dry the expanded products themselves. Since there is no industry-wide agreement on the meaning of some terms which are basic to this discussion, definitions for these terms are as follows:

Denaturation of protein is the thermal processing of protein which lowers protein solubility, renders the protein digestible, and destroys the biological activity of enzymes and of toxic proteins.

Growth inhibitors may be defined as any substance in foods which exert a deleterious physiological effect on man or animals as revealed by growth or metabolism studies.

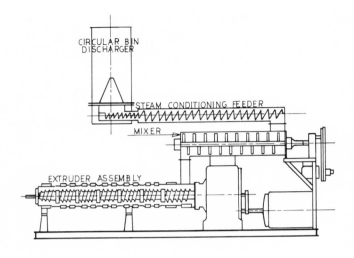

CUTAWAY VIEW OF LARGE CAPACITY
EXTRUSION COOKER

FIG. 9.1.   TYPICAL ARRANGEMENT OF LIVE BIN FEEDER, PRECONDITIONER, AND
EXTRUSION-COOKER

Gelatinization may be defined as the complete rupture of the starch granule, brought about by a combination of moisture, heat, pressure and (in some instances) mechanical shear.

More precise terminology and measurement tools are needed for starch conversion, since gelatinization as defined above, covers only the basic rupture of the starch granule. Starch conversions are much more complex, and occupy several plateaus between the basic rupture of the starch granule and the dextrinization of starches. Precise industry definitions and rapid methods of measurement are needed for each level of starch conversion. Kansas State University scientists have developed a method of measuring levels of starch conversion which uses beta-amylase enzymes to hydrolyze damaged starches, as evidenced and measured by maltose conversion (Anstaett *et al* 1969). This method may have good utility in such measurements.

CAPACITY OF EXTRUSION-COOKERS

Dry expanded pet foods, for example, can be processed at capacities up to 20,000 lb/hr, and textured soy protein up to 3000 and 4000 lb/hr. Snacks are produced in somewhat smaller machines at capacities of 700 lb/hr, and breakfast cereals weighing only 3 lb/cu ft can now be produced on a single machine at upwards of 2800 lb/hr. Breakfast cereal flakes can be prepared at capacities of up to 2000 lb/hr using a combination of cooking and forming extruder arranged as in Fig. 9.2.

ADVANTAGES OF EXTRUSION-COOKING

(1) Gelatinization of cereals or starches results in great uptake of water and improves digestibility and caloric availability. Additionally, gelatinized starches have improved functional characteristics—better extensibility, gas-holding properties, and pasting characteristics. Starches gelatinized by extrusion-cooking bind with added proteins and microingredients (vitamins, minerals, food colors, flavors, etc.) uniformly and irreversibly throughout the extrudate. This assures that a reasonably even distribution of such additives will reach the consumer in every mouthful of food, no matter what the particle size may be. Also, the solubility and textural characteristics of an extrusion-cooked carbohydrate can be adjusted over a wide range, so that it can be produced with product solubility equal to that of a drum-dried infant food, or as

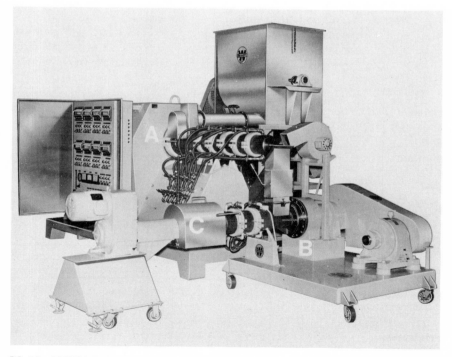

FIG. 9.2. COOKING EXTRUDER (A) AND COOLING AND FORMING EXTRUDER (B) PLUS VARIABLE SPEED KNIFE (C)

chewy as the most dense breakfast cereal. The material also could be given an intermediate density or textural characteristic. It is practical also to extrusion-cook cereal flours or starches which have been modified in pH (within reasonable limits) for desired textural changes.

(2) The inactivation of growth inhibitors and the thermal elimination of anti-palatability factors is important in processing soybeans or pulses. The temperature required to destroy growth inhibitors present in uncooked soy proteins and in certain pulse proteins is uniquely high, but the shortest period at that temperature peak is preferred. The brevity of the cooking period at high temperatures is the major reason for the excellent biological performance of HT/ST extrusion-cooked foods. It is practical to extrusion-cook concomitantly for control of heat-labile growth inhibitors, to gelatinize cereal flours, and to provide desired textural properties to the precooked protein enriched food of good biological feeding value (Table 9.1).

(3) Labor costs and processing costs per ton are lower in extrusion-cooking systems than in any other industrial cooking method known. Processing costs per ton have steadily declined with increasing capacity per horsepower and per man-hour. Investment costs per ton of production capacity are lower for the large-capacity HT/ST extrusion-cookers than investment costs per ton of production capacity in other cooking methods. One possible arrangement of processing equipment is shown in Fig. 9.3.

(4) Extrusion-cookers, dryers, and coolers built as part of the system are designed to be quickly and easily disassembled for clean-out. Total bacterial plate counts are very low, and no insects, larvae, pathogens or *Salmonella* have been known to survive the process, where recommended sanitation procedures have been followed. Fig. 9.4 shows large

TABLE 9.1

PROTEIN UTILIZATION OF TYPICAL EXTRUSION-COOKED MIXTURES OF CEREALS AND OILSEED PROTEINS

Ingredients	Per Values Mixtures	Casein	Net Protein Utilization
Degerminated corn, full fat soy, sugar, Ca_3PO_4	2.40	2.50	74
Full fat soy, full fat peanut, rice flour	2.32	2.50	60
Full fat soy, full fat cottonseed, corn	2.30	3.00	63
Wheat flour, peanut flour, milk	1.68	2.50	54
Rice, full fat soy, defatted soy	2.49	3.00	65
Full fat soy	2.44	3.00	66
Degerminated corn, full fat soy, milk sugar	2.51	3.00	58
Cassava flour, full fat soy	2.51	3.00	57
Expeller cottonseed, defatted soy, sugar corn	2.19	3.00	58

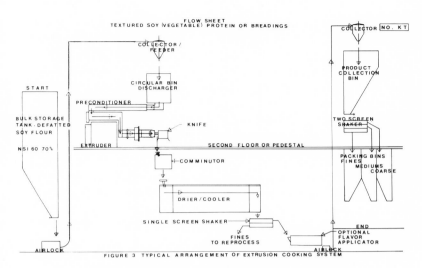

FLOW SHEET
TEXTURED SOY (VEGETABLE) PROTEIN OR BREADINGS

FIGURE 3 TYPICAL ARRANGEMENT OF EXTRUSION COOKING SYSTEM

FIG. 9.3. FLOW SHEET FOR TEXTURED SOY PROTEINS OR BREADINGS

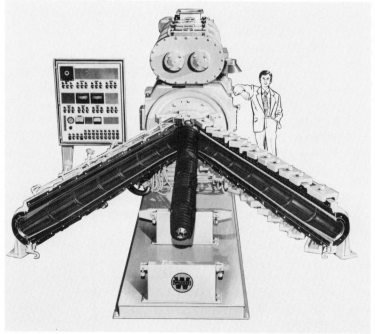

FIG. 9.4. LARGEST HT/ST EXTRUSION-COOKER WITH EXTRUDER OPENED FOR EASE OF CLEANUP, SANITATION OR CHANGEOVER TO ANOTHER END PRODUCT

model of HT/ST extrusion-cooker with hinged extruder jaws for ease of clean-up.

(5)   The shelf-life of extrusion-cooked products seems extraordinarily good without refrigeration, if reasonable sanitation procedures have been followed. Fat-splitting enzymes are essentially deactivated during the extrusion-cooking process, improving the oxidative stability of the lipids in the process. One additional possibility seems to offer a reasonable explanation of the unexpectedly good shelf-life. British workers (Daniels *et al*. 1970) showed that high-energy mixing of a dough in the absence of air results in a marked increase in lipid binding in the dough. When such doughs were freeze-dried and powdered, they showed no sign of rancidity in storage, unlike air-mixed doughs, which released the greater part of their lipid in the free form and quickly developed rancid off-odors. Daniels *et al*. (1970) showed that bound lipids protect against peroxidation and lipid peroxides formed exclusively in the *free* lipids of the doughs. Aerobic mixing of doughs results in the release of lipids which were bound in the early stages of dough hydration. They found also that aerobic mixing of the dough, under various work levels, while increasing the amount of air available to the dough, led to a decrease in the lipid binding after mixing. Moreover, as the work load increased, the effect of air on lipid binding became more pronounced.

By anaerobic mixing, on the other hand, Daniels and his colleagues were able to increase the work level greatly, while actually increasing the percentage of bound lipids. The aerobic mixing work was performed in the presence of normal amounts of air, while the anaerobic mixing was performed under nitrogen or under vacuum. Extrusion-cooking cannot be considered as anaerobic mixing. Nonetheless, the conversion of moistened granular materials to a colloidal dough occurs in HT/ST extrusion-cookers inside the extruder barrel itself, at which point there is a starving effect, as far as air is concerned, which helps explain the unusual shelf-life of HT/ST extrusion-cooked products.

(6)   Extrusion-cookers are very versatile. The same HT/ST extrusion-cooker can produce any one of a whole range of normal or protein-enriched food products. The basic equipment is designed in extruder configuration to produce the specific food or foods which are desired at the outset. However, should some other extrusion-cooked product be desired at a later date, interchangeable extruder components are produced (to such extent that it is necessary to exchange an existing extruder screw, head, or die for another) to produce the new product or products. It is also possible to lengthen or shorten the extruder assembly where needed to produce some new product. Flexibility of product line is perhaps the most important capability of extrusion-cookers.

(7) They require only a small amount of labor and a small amount of floor space per ton of production capacity. Careful positioning of system components will further reduce labor requirements.

(8) Extrusion-cookers can produce a wide range of product shapes, textures, sizes, densities, rehydration ratios, and rehydration characteristics. Individual ingredients or mixtures may be cooked. They can gelatinize starches while simultaneously cooking for control of growth inhibitors.

(9) HT/ST extrusion-cookers can cook vegetable proteins with practically no harm to protein quality and with only minimal drop in vitamin content, when microencapsulated vitamins are used.

(10) They histologically modify and restructure all foods processed by them. It is possible to control the texture of the cooked product within reasonable limits.

(11) They can cook a wide range of ingredients—all the cereal flours, oilseed and pulse proteins, wet-milled starches, dehydrated flours of root carbohydrates, defatted vegetable proteins (soy, peanut, linseed, copra, etc.). Egg proteins, fish proteins, or meat proteins can be blended into any of the above, in dry or slurry form, prior to extrusion-cooking. Synthetic amino acids blended into cereals show only modest losses (Howe *et al*. 1965) during HT/ST extrusion-cooking of the mixtures. Milk proteins can be blended into such mixtures, but special precautions must be exercised when cooking mixtures which include milk proteins. Many flavors are sufficiently stable to stand HT/ST extrusion-cooking, but others are so volatile that they should be applied after extrusion and after drying, perhaps in an oil emulsion.

(12) Engineered convenience foods have been the fastest-developing foods of industrialized societies. Many wives and mothers work today at jobs outside the home, or are involved with other time-consuming activities—from P.T.A. to women's lib, from bridge to golf, from bowling to politics, or simply in chauffeuring children to a host of extracurricular activities. All such demands on the housewife's time have combined to bring a host of new convenience foods to the family table. Occasionally these foods are so well engineered and flavored or are of such economic importance that they earn a permanent place in the diets of a nation. No more versatile tool exists for the "engineering" of convenience foods than extrusion-cooking systems.

(13) Extrusion-cookers produce almost no effluent or other ecological hazard.

(14) HT/ST extrusion-cookers consume less total energy per ton of production capacity than any other cooking method known and are thermodynamically efficient.

Professor Hawthorn of the University of Strathclyde (1973) has reported a theory that the world needs to examine the production of foodstuffs from the standpoint of energy consumed in *all* aspects of getting that food on the table. Generally, manufacturers of foods examine the processing costs per ton, but we must look much further—to the energy input in producing fertilizer and pesticides plus the energy subsidy needed in preparing the soil, fertilizing, irrigating, cultivating, harvesting, drying, processing, particle sizing, packaging, storage, refrigeration, shipment, distribution, preparation in the home, and (presumably) the treatment and disposition of effluents. Slesser (1973) points out that "energy utilization to power the human race is just as subject to the laws of thermodynamics as is the energy utilization to power an internal combustion engine." Berry (1972) has shown that thermodynamic analysis is a realistic way to assess the ultimate value of an economic process because it does so in terms of the only commodity in the world in ultimate limitation—thermodynamic potential. "If the economists in the marketplace were to determine their shortages by looking further and further into the future, these estimates would come closer and closer to the estimates made by their colleagues, the thermodynamicists."

When food costs are examined in the light of total energy subsidy plus the total labor costs, and related to 100 gm of utilizable protein, or to 100 cal of metabolizable energy, we may find that many of our food patterns should indeed be changed.

(15)   Extrusion-cookers have the ability to modify greatly the texture, mouthfeel, and utility of every product which is extrusion-cooked, be it breakfast cereal, snacks, breadings, or textured soy protein.

The last of these is probably as good an illustration as can be found to explain the steps through which desired textural changes are produced. The raw material normally used in the production of textured vegetable protein is defatted soy flour (min. 50% protein; max 3% fiber; max 1% fat, and preferred NSI of 50 to 70). Fig. 9.5 is a microphotograph of uncooked solvent-extracted soy flour, which is the major raw material for the production of textured soy protein. Soy protein concentrates or other vegetable proteins high in protein content also may be used in the preparation of such chewy protein gels. The nitrogen solubility of *unprocessed* vegetable proteins is quite high. However, during extrusion-cooking the proteins are denatured, the major evidence of which is a great reduction in their solubility. As defatted vegetable proteins are denatured, the protein strands are rendered stretchable and become good encapsulators of gases, yet retain the characteristics of rapid firming of the cell structure after extrusion through the final die plate. The reduction in solubility of the proteins, plus their characteristic of

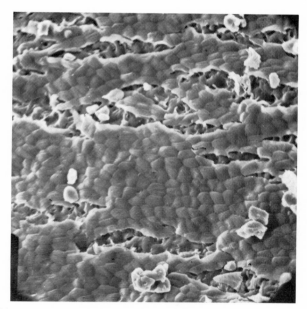

FIG. 9.5.   ELECTRON SCAN MICROPHOTOGRAPH OF UNCOOKED SOLVENT EX-
TRACTED SOY FLOUR (MAGNIFICATION × 400)
Individual cells containing protein bodies are each enshrouded in
a capsule of cellulose. Being uncooked, the cells are distinct,
similar, intact and easily identified. Orientation of the lower layer
is tangential to orientation of the upper layer.

becoming stretchable, act concomitantly to make these denatured proteins capable of reorientation into certain desired structures.

In this way, defatted soy flours or concentrates are made into chewy
textured soy proteins by an extrusion-cooking process which ac-
complishes all of the following steps: (1) moistening and heating of the
protein flour (pH adjustment for changed textural characteristics is
possible, but not necessary); (2) effective destruction of residual growth
inhibitors; (3) denaturation of protein, which makes the protein
stretchable; (4) rupture of the cellulose sac which surrounds each protein body; (5) joining of these liberated protein bodies into rivulets of
protein, which subsequently are twisted together into protein strands;
and (6) the stretching and twisting of these protein strands and the
uniform, systematic layering of these strands one over another produces
a structure quite similar to the structure of muscle tissue. This gives
textured soy protein its chewy, meat-like characteristic and its laminar
structure, as illustrated in Fig. 9.6.

Textured soy proteins produced from defatted soy flours or concentrates are the most important meat extenders available today—a boon

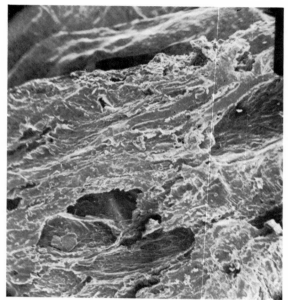

FIG. 9.6. MICROPHOTOGRAPH OF EXTRUSION-COOKED SOLVENT EXTRACTED
SOY FLOUR (MAGNIFICATION × 20)
Cellulose capsules around protein bodies have been ruptured by
extrusion cooking, all-owing protein bodies to run together in
rivulets. Proteins are denatured and made stretchable. Extrusion
forces twine the protein strands over one another to create a
chewy laminar structure similar to muscle tissue.

not only to household budgets in these days of high meat prices, but also
for their high protein content, and for making no known contribution to
serum cholesterol levels. Used widely in institutional feeding programs
(school lunch feeding programs, etc.), textured soy products are also
being incorporated into suitably labeled prepacked hamburger and
food-flavoring condiments sold in supermarkets. Textured plant proteins would also seem to have important potential markets in foods for
the military, for field workers, and in allergy diets. Usage of moisturized
textured soy as meat extenders includes the preparation of hamburger,
meatloaf, chili, soups, stews, salads, pizza, dry soup mixes, sausages,
potpies, tacos, gravies, curries, enchiladas, seasonings, tamales, pasta
casseroles, meat and spaghetti sauces, frozen dinners, canned foods, and
in vegetarian diets. They also are being used as one of the major ingredients in the third generation of textured protein products.

Density, chewiness, and rehydration characteristics of the textured
plant proteins may be controlled over a considerable range by selective
configuration of extruder components. Further textural modifications
can be made by careful adjustment of pH, before extrusion-cooking in

most cases. However, pH adjustments can also be made after extrusion-cooking.

DISADVANTAGES OF EXTRUSION-COOKING

(1) Extrusion-cookers process only floury or granular materials. Whole grains or oilseeds may be put through an extrusion-cooker, but in that event the extruder has to be designed in part as a grinder, with high shear forces, and thus loses cooking efficiency, capacity, and flexibility in textural versatility. It also loses some of the advantages found in biological performance of processed proteins.

(2) Mixtures containing milk proteins must be cooked in the lower third of the available range of extrusion temperatures—say from 100 to 135°C for optimum biological utilization of the protein (Smith 1969). A Maillard reaction can occur at higher temperatures, although this may be acceptable in certain foods for its contribution to flavor.

(3) It has not yet been possible consistently to bind or destroy the growth inhibitor, gossypol, present in cottonseed.

(4) Several of the *microencapsulated* vitamins can be premixed with cereals prior to HT/ST extrusion-cooking and show little loss in vitamin stability, probably due to the brevity of the period at high temperatures (12 to 20 sec) in an HT/ST system. However, certain vitamins, particularly vitamin C, show excessive loss in processing, and should be applied externally after extrusion-cooking and after drying.

CONTROL OF PROCESS VARIABLES TO EFFECT TEXTURAL PROPERTIES

The textures which can be achieved by extrusion-cooking are many. Experience has shown that there are 6 major means available to modify textures in extrusion-cooked foods:

(1) Control of product moisture levels and selection of the points of moisture application and selection of the form in which moisture is applied (as water, as steam, or as mixtures of both, or as syrup).

(2) Control of product temperatures at each point in the system.

(3) Selection of ingredients or mixtures of several ingredients for desired functional characteristics.

(4) Control of pH of ingredients or mixture (s).

(5) Selection of extruder components to provide the dwell time and the product temperatures desired in each section of the extruder. Interchangeable extruder components are designed to produce low, medium, or high temperatures of product within each section of the extruder. Extruder assemblies can be arranged to utilize only a short extruder (as needed for producing snacks) or a much extended extruder as needed for other products. Extruder heads are jacketed so that steam, cold water, or brine may be circulated as needed.

(6) Final dies are selected primarily to shape the extrudate as

needed, but die selection can also have an effect on the textural characteristics of the final product.

No capability of modern extrusion-cookers is more important than their ability to control product temperatures at each point within the system and to alter them quickly if the product temperature varies from the temperature preselected for any point. An automatic temperature-control system was developed for use where product uniformity is particularly important, such as a breakfast cereals or textured soy proteins. Manual control of product temperature is still in widespread use, particularly where slight irregularity in the product is acceptable.

TEXTURING OF EXTRUSION-COOKED PRODUCTS

It was indicated earlier that whenever any cereal and/or protein is extrusion-cooked, the extrudate is texturally and histologically restructured. Before this takes place, however, several steps occur during the cooking process, and these steps themselves often affect the texture of the final product:

(1)   The materials are uniformly moistened—sometimes with steam, sometimes only with water or sometimes with a combination of both.

(2)   The moistened (and sometimes heated) raw materials or mixtures are worked into a dough, followed by modification of the amorphous structure of an opaque, stretchable colloidal complex.

(3)   Proteins are denatured and rendered tractile, chewy, and capable of being stranded. Heat-labile growth inhibitors are destroyed during the extrusion process.

(4)   Gelatinization of starchy components occurs during this process, followed by a great uptake of moisture and substantial increases in dough viscosity.

(5)   During propulsion through the final coned section of the extruder the dough is elevated rapidly in temperature to a point at which its moisture content is well above the boiling point. However, since the area through which the dough is propelled (in the final coned section of the extruder) is being reduced, it is obvious that the moisture being converted to steam has no chance to expand. Hence the final coned section of the extruder itself becomes a small superheater. Since the dough has been rendered stretchable by being gelatinized or denatured, and since the moisture content is in superheated form at the instant of extrusion, the cell structure of the extrudate expands rapidly at the moment it is expelled from the extruder. The degree of expansion for any single ingredient or mixture will normally be directly proportional to the temperature of extrusion. Thus it is possible to control the degree of expansion within reasonable ranges by control of the extrusion temperature and moisture content.

(6)   Thermosetting follows normally within a few seconds of final extrusion. Most extrudates have a bread-like cell structure, and lose their plasticity rapidly after extrusion.

The texturing of extrusion-cooked foods is a process that can be used to provide certain characteristics of chewiness or tenderness, brittleness or plasticity, crunchiness or crumbliness. Much still has to be learned about this field: the use of additives, the functional selection of ingredients, and the effect of pH changes. Experience is being gained about the effects of and the selection of shortenings, emulsifiers, bleaching agents, humectants, glutens, and starches on the rheological properties of extrusion-cooked foods. Much more has been learned about the control and utilization of process variables and modifications in component configurations to achieve desired product forms, shapes, densities, and textures within the design limitations of the system.

FLATULENCE IN FABRICATED PLANT PROTEIN FOODS

Work has been done in a pilot plant over the past year in trying to deal economically with a problem which occurs occasionally when high levels of textured soy protein are ingested. This problem is flatulence. At normal levels of consumption of textured soy, flatulence seems not to exist. However, as the industry seeks methods of increasing the percentage of textured soy used in foods, it probably will be advisable to develop procedures which will cope with this problem.

The causes of flatulence are several, but most recent research seems to agree that fermentative degradation of carbohydrates of low molecular weight by the microflora in the ileum and colon are the primary causes (Steggerda et al. 1966; Calloway 1966). Of these, stachyose and raffinose appear to be the most likely culprits. Calloway (1966) showed that the human ileal and colonic microflora utilize stachyose to produce gas. Rackis et al. (1967) showed that raffinose and stachyose, hydrolyzed with yeast invertase and acid, produced large amounts of gas. Rackis et al. (1967) also showed that defatted cottonseed or peanut produced flatulent activity in dogs comparable to that of soy. Rackis et al. (1970) reported that oligosaccharides in defatted soybean meal are about 15%. Kawamura et al. (1963) showed that the oligosaccharides consisted of 6 to 8% sucrose, 4 to 5% stachyose, 1 to 2% raffinose, plus a trace of verbacose. Steggerda et al. (1966) reported the flatus volume of several soy protein products in man, and found there were considerable differences between individuals in this respect when each individual in the group was fed on a specific soy diet.

There are possible ways to deal with questions of flatulence in textured soy proteins. The first is to use a soy concentrate rather than a defatted soy flour as the raw material to be textured, since soy concentrates are generally prepared by an aqueous alcohol extraction of soy protein, in which process the sugars are largely removed. Isolated soy proteins are also relatively free of sugars. The soy concentrate or isolate has the advantage of working with a readily available raw material which has excellent properties for texturing. The disadvantage of such usage is a cost factor for concentrates or isolates that is much higher than that of defatted soy flour per unit of protein. The second method is to produce textured soy protein from defatted soy flour and to develop a method of washing it to leach out the sugars.

Defatted vegetable protein flours other than soy flours should also prove susceptible to such washing techniques. The washing alternative seems the most economical, and we have been examining it as one possible solution. The nitrogen in untoasted defatted soy flour is very soluble in water, and when one washes such a product in water, much of the protein is leached out in the wash water. However, one of the steps that occurs in extrusion-cooking of an untoasted or lightly toasted defatted soy flour is denaturation of the protein, the best evidence of which is a great reduction in protein solubility.

Lightly toasted defatted soy flour, such as is used in much production of textured soy protein, will have an NSI of 50 to 70% before extrusion-cooking, but an NSI of only about 5% after extrusion-cooking. Hence it seems practical to wash the textured soy protein after extrusion-cooking to remove the soluble sugars, safe in the knowledge that, while washing out most of the soluble sugars in water, the very low solubility of the extrusion-cooked protein would result in little if any leaching out of protein in the wash water.

The procedure then which seems most practical is the following:

(1)   To extrusion-cook defatted soy flour (with or without pH modification and with or without added vital wheat gluten), cut the extrudate into agglomerates of desired size at the die.

(2)   For greatest speed in leaching out the sugars, these agglomerates could be wet-milled immediately thereafter in an impact milling device (Urschel Comitrol or Fitz mill or the like) to a smaller particle size, such as pea-sized or smaller. This step may be avoided where large chunk size is desired, but is recommended where smaller particle size is required (such as the large granules of textured soy protein used in fortifying hamburger), since wet-milling will minimize the level of fines created, and will reduce the time required in the washing tank to leach out the sugars.

(3)   Textured soy proteins should be immersed in a continuous washing tank in warm water (180°F or thereabouts) for a period sufficiently

long to wash out the majority of the sugars. The length of period required in water will depend on the particle size of the textured soy protein and the temperature of the wash water. Cold water may be used if necessary, but will require a somewhat longer holding period in the washing tank.

It is believed that the washing tank should be designed to submerge the textured soy, to carry product continuously and uniformly beneath the surface of the water, and should be equipped with automatic temperature controls for the water. Fresh warm washing water should be run into the washing tank continuously; and a continuous and equal amount of water should be bled off to keep sugar concentration in the wash water at a low level.

(4)   A second washing tank may be used where it is desired to employ a coloring agent, or an acid or an alkaline salt as pH modifiers, or a bleaching or labeling agent in the wash water. Should a reagent be used in this second wash which later needed neutralizing, a third bath could be used as a neutralizing bath. Moisture content of the textured soy protein after soaking has been found to be 62 to 75%.

(5)   A continuous mechanical dewatering device might thereafter be used to remove as much moisture as possible by mechanical means, without drastically altering the desired structure of the textured soy protein. It is quite easy to squeeze moisture mechanically out of this chewy gel, which is sponge-like in nature. This mechanical dewatering device might be a fruit juice press (citrus, grape, cider, etc.), a roller mill, or some other suitable means of lowering the moisture content mechanically to the 40 to 50% range. Thereafter, the product should run through a suitable warm air dryer to bring final product moisture down to the desired 6 to 8% level. The protein content of the washed and dried product will jump to approximately 68 to 70% with loss of sugars. No drying of the washed product is needed if the washed textured soy is to be incorporated immediately into liquid-phase materials such as soup stock, chili, stews, etc., or foods that are to be canned or frozen.

Admittedly, the cost of this combined washing and drying is high because of added processing and some loss in weight of finished product due to washing out 12 to 15% of the weight as sugar. Since the flatulence problem is probably the major remaining obstacle to the maximum usage of textured soy, it seems logical that it should be dealt with by the industry. In addition to removing most of the stachyose, the protein content is increased from approximately 50% to about 70%, thus providing a salable explanation for the increased cost by an industry which seems unlikely to put together a discussion of flatulence in its public relations pronouncements.

EXPERIMENTAL DETERMINATION OF TEXTURAL REQUIREMENTS

The scope of this chapter does not permit the explanation of procedures and methods followed in extrusion-cooking to control product textures, rehydration characteristics, densities, uniformity, flavoring, mouthfeel, surface conditions, and sizing. Many years have been spent by Wenger in attempting to find answers to those problems. Today, it is possible to control most of these, but not yet as closely as desired. The answers to these questions have been the subject of systems analysis, and a wide range of interchangeable extruder components have been developed to permit production of the desired characteristics. "Cook factors" have been developed as a method of measuring the contribution to cooking made by interchangeable extruder components.

Uniformity of ingredients and processing conditions is necessary, of course, to maintain uniformity of extrusion-cooked product. The recognition of that need, plus the ability to maintain such uniformity, is one of the best available tools for production managers.

About 800 runs per year are made in the Wenger pilot plant, which is equipped with 7 different models of extrusion-cookers, two types of dryers/coolers, plus cooling and forming extruders, flavor conditioning feeder, external flavor applicator, hammermill, storage bins, batch mixer, pneumatic conveyors, large water-jacketed roller mill for flaking, a test dryer, dehulling system for soybeans, boiler, over 80 different configurations of extruder screws, and some 300 extruder dies. Interchangeable extruder heads, variable speed knives, a straightening and cutting conveyor, and a bevy of belt conveyors round out a pilot plant which is well equipped from every standpoint except that of a laboratory, which may be added soon.

The pilot plant has several important functions, in addition to the obvious ones of testing new machinery and new component configurations, new product development, and acting as a demonstration unit. Each time a product is extrusion-cooked, it is retextured. Its histology, chemistry, viscosity, tractility, mouthfeel, sheer strength, density, rehydration characteristics, and reactions to compression, heat, shear forces, and moisture are changed. When two or more ingredients are cooked simultaneously, or when mixtures are processed under differing conditions, the opportunity for management of textural properties jumps in quantum terms. In 11 years of pilot plant work, our major objective has been to learn how to control these changes and how to shape them to the rheological and functional requirements of the many industries served by extrusion-cooking. Data sheets are kept on all but the most routine of these pilot plant runs to record how well objectives were met, and what changes in processing conditions or extruder configuration are recommended for subsequent trials to achieve desired rheological properties.

Assignments to achieve a desired texture or mouthfeel are common in many industries served by extrusion-cooking. Hence, these thousands of trials have *all* taught some one thing or several things about how to achieve desired objectives. We have learned something about selection of ingredients, particle size, and pH; the points and nature of moisture application; certain effects of reducing sugars, enzymes, amylose, and amylopectins; the selection of lipids and emulsifiers; the management of Maillard reactions; the effects of product temperatures at various control points, and the effects of extrusion speeds. More important still in meeting textural assignments is the record of the changes made in textures by changes in configuration of extruder components. Many different configurations exist in primary screws, intermediate screws, coned screws, steamlock dies, final dies, and design of extruder heads. Also, extruder assemblies can be lengthened or shortened to meet a specific need.

Occasionally, extrusion-cooking cannot control all the rheological properties that are requested on some materials. Sometimes it is not possible to achieve the desired texture by using a given mixture. In some cases it has been possible to suggest an additive, a change in formulation, or a change in the properties of one or more of the ingredients to produce the desired texture.

Other than foods for human consumption, applications for extrusion-cooking in animal feeds include dry expanded dog foods and cat foods; semi-moist and intermediate-moisture pet foods; fish food, mink foods, starch-controlled urea (Starea) for ruminant feeds; and the use of extrusion-cooked full fat soy in broiler feeds and as partial replacements for milk proteins used in milk replacers and calf starters.

Many important new food products have been developed in the years since the first commercial delivery of the HT/ST extrusion-cooker. Many additional new products are in the development stage, or are close to test marketing. Many new food products will be extrusion-cooked in the future. For example, Wenger has designed a system to extrusion-cook a tube (round, square, oval or rectangular); to concomitantly fill that tube with a paste (meat, fruit, fish, vegetable, poultry, candy, cheese, cheese dips etc.); to keep that tube straight until it hardens and to shear it off into sticks of the desired length. Presently, this tube is made on a cereal flour base, but it should prove practical to use other sheathing materials. A new form of sausage or wiener can probably be made in such ready-to-eat or brown-and-serve forms.

Those of us who work every day with extrusion-cooking are bemused at the variety of applications which have been developed for extrusion-cooking, but are mindful that we cannot yet provide all the desired rheological properties. We do believe that the developing range of capabilities of extrusion-cookers will bring them into ever widening utilization by the food industry.

BIBLIOGRAPHY

ANSTAETT, F. R., SUNG, AN-CHEIN, PFOST, H. B. and DEYOE, C. W. 1969. Evaluating hydro-thermal process grains. Feedstuffs *41*(19), 19.

BERRY, S. 1972. Recycling, thermodynamics, and environmental thrift. Congressional Record, 92nd U. S. Congress, S. 2430 (February 23).

CALLOWAY, D. 1966. Respiratory hydrogen and methane as affected by consumption of gas-forming foods. Gastroenterology *51*, 383-389 (Sept. 3).

DANIELS, N., WOOD, P., RUSSELL-EGGITT, P., and COPPOCK, J. 1970. Studies on the lipids of flour. V. Effect of air on lipid binding. J. Sci. App. Agriculture (Brit.) *21*, 337-384.

DEMAEYER, E. 1965. Full-fat soy mixtures in the feeding of infants in Taiwan. P.A.G. Bulletin #5. United Nations, N. Y., pp. 50-59.

HAWTHORN, J. 1973. New protein processes. IUPAC/IUFOST Symposium, The Contribution of Chemistry to Food Supplies, Hamburg, Germany.

HOWE, E., JANSEN, G., and GILFILLAN, E. 1965. Amino acid supplementation of cereal grains as related to the world food supply. Am. J. Clinical Nutr. *16*, 315-320 (March).

JIMINEZ, A., PERRY, T., PICKETT, R., and BESSON, W. 1963. Raw and heat-treated soybeans for growing-finishing swine, and their effect on fat firmness. J. Animal Sci. *22* (2), 471-475.

KAWAMURA, S., TODA, M., and NARASAKI, T. 1965. Eiyo to Shokuryo. Japanese Society of Food and Nutrition. Journal *18*, 13.

MUSTAKAS, G., GRIFFIN, E., ALLEN, L., and SMITH, O. 1964. Production and nutritional evaluation of extrusion-cooked full-fat soybean flour. J. Am. Oil Chem. Soc. *41*, 607-614.

RACKIS, J., SESSA, D., and HONIG, D. 1967. Isolation and characterization of flavor and flatulence factors in soybean meal. *In* Soybean Protein Foods, ARS 71-35, U. S. Dept. of Agric., Peoria, Ill. p. 100-110 (May).

RACKIS, J., HONIG, D., SESSA, D., and STEGGERDA, F. 1970. Flavor and flatulence factors in soybean protein products. J. Agr. Food Chem. *18*(6) 977-982.

SLESSER, M. 1973. Energy analysis in policy making. New Science, p. 328 (November).

SMITH, O. 1969. History and status of specific protein-rich foods: extrusion-processed cereal foods. *In* Protein Enriched Cereal Foods for Human Needs. M. Milner (Editor). Am. Assn. Cereal Chem., St. Paul, Minn., pp. 140-153.

STEGGERDA, F., RICHARDS, E., and RACKIS, J. 1966. Effects of various soybean products on flatulence in the adult man. Proc. Soc. Exptl. Bio. Med. *121*(4) 1235-1239.

CHAPTER 10

Joel Sidel

Annette Woolsey

Herbert Stone

Sensory Analysis: Theory, Methodology, and Evaluation

Sensory evaluation is a relatively young, but still growing, branch of science that has recently experienced changes in emphasis and outlook, so much so that there is presently no generally accepted definition of sensory evaluation.

Sensory evaluation involves the evaluation of a product based on input from the five senses. Sensory information about a product originates not only from receptors in the nose and mouth, but also from visual, auditory and tactile systems. When signals from the sensory systems are received in the central nervous system, they may become integrated with expectations, past experience, and numerous conceptual factors before the response is measured. Judges in a sensory evaluation test should be viewed as measuring instruments that are not static, but rather are dynamic, processing many different stimuli simultaneously.

Primarily, sensory evaluation involves measurement. We are concerned with what a subject perceives in a product, and how to measure that perception. We measure responses to some combination of physical and conceptual stimuli and assume that the responses measured are related to either the subjects' perception of or attitude toward a test product, or both. We then generalize results from small test panels to larger populations and attempt to correlate the behavioral response measured to consumer acceptance. The main role of the sensory scientist is one of measuring and relating test panel data to consumer behavior.

A Model System

The sensory test serves as an experimental model for the consumer behavior we wish to predict. The value of any model is its ability to generate information regarding an end-object in the absence of that object (see Table 10.1). In terms of the sensory evaluation experiment, this refers to the relationship between test-panel judgments and consumer acceptance of the product. Sensory tests involve panelists, test products and a response, which is measured. Ideally, the test subjects should share some common functional characteristics with the target population so that data from them, in the absence of the target population, can have high predictive value.

TABLE 10.1

THE SENSORY EVALUATION TEST SERVES AS AN EXPERIMENTAL MODEL
FOR PREDICTING CONSUMER BEHAVIOR

Elements of Sensory Test	Consumer Counterpart
Panelists	Target population
Test product	Production product
Response measured	Acceptance

To be an effective model system, the sensory test must include test products that approximate the production product as nearly as possible. When a series of sensory tests are made with a product that is later changed in some way, as for example during scale-up from pilot plant to production, these changes could result in a very different product and consequently a different set of responses to it.

The third part of our model and, from our point of view, the most critical is response measurement. We must carefully and knowledgeably select both the response that we will measure and the most appropriate method for measuring that response. The primary information we are concerned with is consumer acceptance, and we may conduct a variety of tests, some appearing to be totally unrelated to acceptance, to satisfy that objective. The method of measurement selected will depend minimally on: (1) the product under investigation, (2) the type and number of judges desired, (3) the kind of information being sought, and (4) the availability of an appropriate method for measuring the desired response.

Product (Fabricated Foods)

For the moment, let us turn our attention to the product, fabricated foods. What is a fabricated food? As sensory specialists, it is important in designing the appropriate test, at the appropriate time, to understand something about the product—what it is, what it does, and for whom it is intended. We often encounter problems when we try to define those parameters. We find that some fabricated foods are created strictly to serve a nutrition or health need for people who desire to restrict their diet for health reasons. Other people may select fabricated foods because of cost; some fabricated foods are less expensive than the original. And still others may select fabricated foods because they offer added convenience, increased uniformity, and greater shelf stability.

Method (Fabricated Foods)

A review of the literature related to sensory testing of fabricated foods reveals very little in the way of specific methods developed or modified for use in evaluating these specialized foods. Frequently, only general acceptability or palatability of the product is reported. Statements made about products tend to be very broad, and a few details related to test methodology or immediate objectives are included. When dealing with general statements of acceptability, we note a lack of definition of "acceptance." It must be recognized that a particular set of circumstances may define the limits of acceptability. This may be particularly true of fabricated foods.

In the literature, the lack of details about sensory test procedures is a serious shortcoming that should not occur. The Institute of Food Technologists has published a set of guidelines for authors writing papers which include sensory evaluation data (Institute of Food Technologists 1971). These guidelines may also be helpful in the design of sensory experiments.

The Sensory Scientist

As the discipline of sensory evaluation developed, psychologists, psychophysicists, statisticians and others from branches of modern science contributed to the development of test procedures. Concomitantly, there evolved a group of specialists with titles such as sensory scientist, sensory specialist, or sensory technician, who were not experts with regard to products but were experts in the methods used to evaluate products.

Although the newly developed sensory techniques are objective, different responses to a product can be obtained, depending on the way the question is asked. For this reason, the sensory specialist should not be isolated from knowledge about the total overall objectives of a product. He must have an accurate overall definition of product objectives and information concerning the target consumer, as well as a definition of the specific problem under investigation, before he can adequately design tests that will give useful information. One way that this can be achieved is for the sensory scientist to be aware of all the "front-end" research that has occurred prior to product development.

Front-End Research

Front-end research refers to the kind of research usually conducted by marketing research groups responsible for development of ideas, or concepts, or product-positioning in the marketplace. Front-end research should have at least four results. The first is a measure of the concept's viability, that is, how the consumer responds to it. The measure of concept viability should include some measure of consumer intent to purchase, the frequency with which the consumer will purchase, the quantity that he will purchase, and the price he is willing to pay for the product. There are various ways of determining this; in fact, there are almost as many different ways as there are marketing research departments and market research companies. These measures are used to estimate the potential success of a specific product if the product were to be developed. If the consumer doesn't like the concept, there is a high risk that he would not like the product if it were made.

The second result of front-end research should be a list of consumer-defined attributes for the product. Behavioral researchers have long recognized the cultural role of semantics in meaningful communication between experimenter and human subjects. In sensory evaluation, the terms used to define product attributes, ideas, and opinions regarding the product are very critical, and must be adequately defined and communicated. If the subjects' use of descriptive or evaluative words is different from that of the sensory evaluation specialist or the developer, confusion may result.

Target population demographics, psychographics, etc., are a third result of front-end research. As discussed earlier, it is critical to define the consumer population as well as possible prior to initiating sensory tests. If such a definition is not accurate, the result could be introduction of the product to the wrong market, or worse, for the sensory scientist, the wrong population might be used to evalute the product. Subsequently, when the product did reach the marketplace, it could fail.

The final result of front-end research is some indication of what to use as an initial control sample in future sensory tests. Selection of control samples in fabricated foods can be extremely difficult and will be discussed in greater detail later in this chapter.

METHOD

Sensory evaluation groups should not operate in isolation from other evaluation groups, especially those who determine the concept and target population for new products. The sensory evaluation group not only must be aware of the research conducted previously, but it must design its own studies with knowledge about the character of the end-product and about the specific consumer population for whom it is intended.

Following concept development and the first attempts at product development, the sensory evaluation department becomes involved. Users and sensory scientists alike must recognize that there are limitations to the information that can be provided by the sensory evaluation laboratory. These limitations are based on (1) the kinds of tests and experimental designs available, (2) the kinds of questions and the manner in which they can be asked, and (3) the types and numbers of judges who can be used. All these must be added to the limitations posed by the types of products being investigated. Our task is to acquire certain information, which we obtain by asking questions. There are different structural ways of designing these questions, and the responses we observe, as well as the way we measure and analyze those responses, are dependent on the procedure used and the types of questions asked (Jones 1958).

Scales of Measurement

To measure behavioral responses to stimuli, there are 4 basic kinds of scales (or questions): nominal, ordinal, interval, and ratio. These have been clearly described by Stevens (1951) and will be discussed briefly below.

Table 10.2 is one example of a nominal scale in sensory testing. No assumptions are made regarding the relationship between categories except that all the responses in one category are equivalent and are different from the responses in another category. Numbers, letters, or words can serve as labels for each category.

Mathematical operations conducted on this kind of data are limited primarily to those dealing with frequency counts and percentages (e.g., mode).

A less desirable technique involves *post hoc* construction of nominal scales by categorizing responses to "open-end" type questions and then comparing the percentage of responses in each category. Because words as symbols may have multiple meaning to both respondents and experimenter, the primary criteria for nominal scales, "the members of one category are equal to each other and not equal to members of another

TABLE 10.2

AN EXAMPLE OF A NOMINAL SCALE

In which location(s) did you use this air freshener?	
Kitchen	☐
Bathroom	☐
Bedroom	☐
Living room	☐
Dining room	☐
Family room	☐
Closet	☐
Basement	☐
Garage	☐

category," may be violated in assigning responses to categories, thus rendering useless any data treatment and subsequent meaningful interpretation (Payne 1965). The open-end question can be of value in constructing scale questions for future tests.

Ordinal scales represent some improvements in sophistication and complexity over nominal scales. Ordinal scales are created when symbols (numbers, phrases, etc.) are assigned to samples according to some rank ordering that provides only that a number or a category is greater or less than another number or category. No assumption is made as to the degree or amount of difference between categories—only that there are "more or less," "higher or lower" differences between them. Because a group of categories may be ordered in a particular sequence, categories or numbers are *not* interchangeable. The 9 point quality scale ranging from 9-Excellent to 1-Extremely Poor is a good example of an ordinal scale (see Table 10.3).

Mathematical applications include those discussed for nominal scales with the addition of transformations that do not modify order (e.g., adding or subtracting a constant). Appropriate handling of data may also include a variety of nonparametric statistical tests that make no assumptions regarding the equality of intervals between points or categories on the scale (Siegel 1956).

To take full advantage of statistical techniques used for analysis of metric data, an interval scale is necessary. Interval scales are scales that have rank order, equal distance between intervals, and an arbitrary zero point.

Interval scales are the first truly quantitative scales and most metric statistics may apply to them. Means, standard deviations, and product mean correlations may be applied, whereas they are not applicable to data on ordinal or nominal scales.

Psychology aims to create quantitative scales and often treats ordinal

TABLE 10.3

THIS NINE POINT QUALITY SCALE IS AN EXAMPLE OF AN ORDINAL SCALE

Excellent
Very good
Good
Below good, above fair
Fair
Below fair, above poor
Poor
Very poor
Extremely poor

scales as though they were quantitative interval scales. The food-quality scale mentioned above often is inappropriately treated statistically as though it were an interval scale. Theoretically, this is not justified; however, our own empirical investigations suggest that the rules could be relaxed here.

One of the most popular sensory scales is the 9-point hedonic scale (Jones et al. 1955). The techniques selected for screening and ordering the descriptive categories, ranging from "like extremely" to "dislike extremely," may certainly justify analyzing this scale as though it were a quantitative interval scale. However, modifications of the scale seldom undergo similar rigorous prescreening of test categories, and consequently may best be treated as ordinal scales.

The fourth kind of scale is the ratio scale. It involves operations for determining equality, rank order, equality of intervals, and equality of ratios. Behavioral responses to physical stimuli empirically have been shown to fit ratio-scaling techniques. These techniques serve as the basis for the "new psychophysics" as presented by Stevens and his students (Cain and Marks 1971; Moskowitz 1974).

An example of a ratio scale may be seen in our perception of the physical stimulus of "weight." If a very light object is held in the hand, the amount of additional weight required before a perceptible change in weight is recognized is proportional to the original weight held. If we continue to add weights and record responses, we would have constructed a ratio scale, with the interval between points on this scale proportional to the original weight. Empirically, this has been performed, and the data indicate that, for the most part, the ratio or proportion is constant except near threshold and at the very high ranges.

This and similar information suggest that ratio scales are appropriate for measuring behavioral responses. For some investigators, the goodness of fit of behavioral responses to ratio scales has meaningful implications regarding receptor structure and function. These behavioral responses may serve as a model for the mechanisms of sensation.

The primary psychophysical techniques for developing ratio scales related to perception are: (1) Magnitude Estimation, (2) Magnitude Production, (3) Ratio Estimation, and (4) Ratio Production.

Magnitude estimation will be discussed because of its recent popularity with some investigators in sensory evaluation. In magnitude estimation, the judge may be given a sample identified with an arbitrary number (such as 100) or some scale attribute (e.g., sweetness). On succeeding sample presentations, judges are told to assign their own number to a test sample. They are instructed to assign a number twice as large, half as large, two-thirds as large, etc., depending on "how much more or less" the sample contains of the attribute being measured. One may say that if the first sample is 100 on a scale of sweetness and the second sample is half as sweet, then it should be scored a 50, and so on.

Ratio scales have the following advantages: (1) They seem to provide a better fit than other scales to much of the sensory data collected (Stevens and Galanter 1957). (2) They permit determination of the *"degree"* or proportion of perceptual intensity of a stimulus (e.g., a product may be twice as sweet as another). (3) They permit appropriate use of metric data analysis techniques. (4) They reduce the requirement for multiple verbal categories and subsequent interpretation.

Two major disadvantages are: (1) To use ratio scaling techniques, subjects are required to be knowledgeable in the method of "fractionation" or number generation. This limits their use to groups that receive adequate instructions and training on scale use. (2) There is a great deal of different use of numbers by subjects, (however, adjustment for use of the scale can be made by appropriate training, testing, and statistical techniques).

In sensory testing, measurement is necessary for effective determination of consumer response to products. According to Jones *et al*. (1955), "Most sensory scales are word or category scales which are ordered and numbered. This ordering and numbering is a convention, which allows for statistical treatment of data. The value of the scale will be reduced to the extent to which the words and phrases are ambiguous, or are not definitely in an order of meaning corresponding with the physical order of the scale intervals." The value of measurement will depend on developing scales that are unambiguous, valid, reliable, and appropriate to mathematical operations.

Types of Sensory Tests

Determining the kind of scale to use, the type of question to ask, and the terms to use are only part of the problem in designing an appropriate sensory test. There are 4 basic types of sensory tests: acceptance-preference, quality, discriminative, and descriptive. Each type is designed to provide very specific information (see Table 10.4). Acceptance-preference tests are used to determine whether the consumer will like a product well enough to purchase it. Consumer tests will be more meaningful if responses are correlated with purchasing behavior and if the test subject is a current or potential user of the commodity.

There are a number of test methods in which consumer panels are used to provide information that can be applied to a larger consumer

TABLE 10.4

TYPES OF SENSORY TESTS AND THE QUESTION EACH ANSWERS

Type of Test	Questions Asked
Acceptance-Preference	Does the consumer like our product? Will he/she buy it?
Quality	What product defects are present and to what degree?
Discriminative	Are selected products detectably different from each other or from a standard?
Descriptive	What are the perceptible sensory characteristics of a product and their intensities?

population. A consumer panel should be a group of consumers, selected on the basis of some criteria, whose response to a specific stimuli is measured. The reason for selecting the individuals forming the panel is to ensure that their responses will be indicative of responses from the large consumer population.

The test methods currently used fall into a number of categories. The subject may be simply asked what he likes or dislikes about a product. He then responds, using his own language, and describes why he feels as he does about a particular sample or set of samples. Such open-ended consumer tests are most effective in the early stages of concept or product testing when qualitative information is desired. Forced-choice methods may be used; these involve tests in which the consumer is presented with two or more samples and is asked to choose the one he prefers. Although useful, the forced-choice preference tests may lose much information by not measuring the degree of intensity of the preference. A similar criticism is true of ranking methods, in which the judge is given a number of samples and must rank these in order from "most preferred" to "least preferred." Rating scale methods, which include the hedonic or FACT (Schutz 1965) rating scales, require the subject to select one of many statements that best reflect his feelings about a product. The experimenter then assigns numerical values to the statements and does computations on the data. The selection of appropriate statistic operations for the data then becomes critical. Magnitude estimation methods, which require the judge to indicate how much he likes a sample, have been compared to rating scale techniques (Moscowitz and Sidel 1971) and suggest that greater use of ratio scaling in consumer acceptance studies is possible.

Consumer tests can be performed under several conditions. These include well-controlled laboratories, a central location (such as a large hall, hotel meeting room, or restaurant), and the home.

When selecting among laboratory, central location or home placement tests, we progress from the most controlled conditions, the laboratory (where lighting, ventilation, noise, etc., can be controlled), to a less controlled situation. One advantage of the central location test is that one generally uses a "true consuming population," whereas in the laboratory one is often restricted to using company employees. The home placement test most nearly represents actual use conditions. The consumer uses the test products in the way she normally would and there is an opportunity to obtain information about the performance of both the package and the product. Perceptual characteristics about the product and the attitudes formed, based on those perceptions, may be studied.

The second type of test is the quality test. Quality tests use trained judges to identify the product defects that are present, and to what degree. Quality tests often are misused and confused with acceptance-preference tests. Unless it has been empirically shown that quality and acceptance of a product are equivalent, quality tests should not be substituted for acceptance-preference tests. There are three basic requirements for a successful quality test. The first is a precise definition of product characteristics, indicating which are desirable and which are undesirable. The second is a standardized scoring system for judging the individual characteristics and their intensities. Third, judges must be trained to identify these characteristics in the product and to rate the product according to a standardized procedure that incorporates the above points and allows for an overall estimate of quality. The panel should consist of subjects who have been trained to use the same definition of terms for a product and to rate samples similarly. Trained panels can be expected to show little variability in quality judgments, and the homogeneity of their responses should be high.

The third type of test is the discrimination test. This is a test using an experienced judge. The object of the test is to determine if products are detectably different from one another. There are various classes of discrimination tests, for example, two-sample paired comparison tests, three-sample tests such as the duo-trio and triangle, and multi-sample tests that include dual standards. A variety of these methods are outlined in standard manuals and texts, such as the ASTM Manual on Sensory Testing Methods (1968) or the book entitled "Principles of Sensory Evaluation of Food" (Amerine *et al*. 1965). In discrimination tests, one may or may not choose to identify the specific sensory quality being investigated. Frequently there is a tendency to use the discrimination test too often as a solution for all sensory problems; yet in other cases it may not be used enough. The discrimination test is part of the total system of testing. The next section contains discussion as to how it can be used to save a company a great deal of time and expense. This test can be done rapidly, and data analysis is not difficult. The information gained may be useful in determining whether a product should be tested further.

The fourth type of test is the descriptive test. Included in this category are the familiar flavor and texture profiles and the newer quantitative descriptive analysis, a test technique developed at SRI (Stone *et al.* 1974). The primary objectives of a descriptive test are (1) to identify, by naming, the product characteristics or product attributes, such as sweet, sour, bitter, musty, etc.; (2) to indicate the order of perception of these characteristics by the judge; and (3) to determine subjective intensities for each individual characteristic. Obviously, it is critical to know not only whether the characteristic is there, but also to what degree it exists. Finally, an attempt is made to obtain an overall impression of the product in terms of liking, quality, or flavor blend.

The 4 test categories discussed above are used for different purposes during the development of a product for the consumer market. They are used in new-product development, during scale-up from pilot plant to production, and when cost reductions are being considered. When monitoring the uniformity of the product over time and describing the effects of package, process, or ingredient changes, appropriate use of these sensory evaluation techniques can be invaluable. Sensory testing of products during storage studies or when different plants should be producing identical products can highlight the characteristics that may be causing differences and indicate the degree of difference. Finally, these techniques may be used in competitive surveys when, perhaps annually, a company may wish to determine how its product compares with competitive products.

EVALUATIONS

The objectives of marketing and sensory testing during product development are to determine the relationship between a product concept, a control product (when available), and the experimental product for the purpose of aiding product development efforts to converge on these points. To accomplish this, and test in a logical sequence, requires much harmony between the marketing research, sensory, and product development departments. Let us consider an "ideal" system where interdepartmental teamwork can result in a testing sequence that will most benefit the developer of fabricated foods.

First, marketing research provides the concept, represented by a conceptual model, with proven consumer interest and clearly defined attributes. Consequently, what the product is, what it should do, how it should look, and some idea regarding its positioning in the marketplace should be established prior to commencing product development efforts. It is also the market researcher's responsibility to determine whether there is a product available in the market that can serve as a control for this project. In the case of fabricated foods development, the control could be a natural product or a synthetic analog, but it must have a close relationship to the conceptual model. Occasionally, the purpose of a project is to match a new product with an existing one. Then the control sample is identical with the conceptual model in both sensory properties and product objectives. At other times, because of differences in sensory properties or product objectives, the control is only somewhat similar to the conceptual model. In the third test situation, and this is often the case with fabricated foods, the objective is to manufacture an entirely new item, and therefore no control is available. Marketing provides the product concept, which may be represented by an artist's version of the item and a description of the product objectives.

Control Sample Available

Control Sample Identical with Conceptual Model.—Let us first consider the most straightforward test situation where a control identical with the conceptual model is available (Table 10.5). Market research has established that the concept is viable and there is a control available that is very similar to the conceptual model. Product development proceeds and, after a number of revisions and "bench-top" screening, the first-generation experimental product is supplied to the sensory evaluation group. It is decided that the first test conducted will be a discrimination test to determine whether there is a difference between the control and the experimental sample. For example, a paired-comparison, triangle or duo-trio test could be used. There are two possible outcomes. First, if no significant difference is found between the control sample and the experimental sample, the match must be verified by market testing; therefore the experimental product is returned to the market research department. However, if a significant difference is found, it must then be determined if this difference is going to affect the acceptability of the product; therefore the next test is an acceptance-preference test using a consumer-type laboratory panel. The reasons for choosing a smaller-scale laboratory acceptance-preference test, rather than going direct to the large-scale test, are that tests in a laboratory are generally more economical and can be done faster, and there is better control over the product and conditions of testing.

TABLE 10.5

A SEQUENCE FOR DEVELOPMENT AND TESTING OF A NEW PRODUCT
WHEN A CONTROL SAMPLE IS AVAILABLE

1. Market Research Testing	Establish that concept is viable and control sample is suitable
2. Product Development	Develop experimental sample
3. Sensory Evaluation Discrimination Testing	(1) When concept and control are identical, test experimental sample vs control (2) First-generation experimental sample vs second-generation experimental sample, etc.
Acceptance-Preference Testing (Laboratory-Type Consumer Panels)	Test control and experimental sample
Acceptance-Preference Testing (Large Scale Nonlaboratory Consumers Panels)	When necessary, use different scenarios with test samples
Descriptive Testing	Test control and experimental sample. When concept and control are not identical, develop "ideal models"
4. Further Market Research Testing	Using potential consumers, verify results from laboratory panels, as necessary
5. Further Product Development	Develop additional experimental samples as necessary

When determining acceptance-preference in a laboratory environment, the subjects are presented with unidentified samples and some measure of preference is obtained. It may be that although the control and first-generation experimental sample are discriminably different from each other, they are equally acceptable. If the laboratory consumer test indicates that the experimental sample is accepted (that is, statistical treatment of the data shows that either the experimental sample is significantly preferred, or that neither the experimental sample nor the control is significantly preferred), these results must be verified by large-scale market research consumer tests. However, if the experimental sample is rejected, one should proceed to large-scale acceptance-preference testing, or descriptive testing could be initiated. The decision of which test to choose at this point would depend on the degree of rejection by the laboratory consumer panel. Borderline rejection indicates that there may be value in obtaining acceptance-preference judgments from potential consumers, whereas when the sample is rejected outright, it is more appropriate to use descriptive techniques.

Acceptance-preference testing by a large-scale nonlaboratory consumer panel has the advantage that, as well as evaluating the unidentified samples, samples can be tested using qualifying statements, or "scenarios." For example, after asking which sample do you prefer, the subject could be told "Sample A costs 20 cents less than Sample B; now which one do you prefer?" A complete series of these scenarios may be used. If the experimental sample is only accepted under certain conditions (for example, at 20 cents less than the control), then a business decision must be made whether to market the product as qualified, or to further develop the product so that it can be marketed without qualifiers. When the experimental sample is rejected or if further development is desired, then descriptive techniques must be used.

The purpose of descriptive testing is to identify and measure the sensory components, in order of perception, for both experimental and control samples. The results should identify exactly which sensory attributes are causing the differences between the experimental sample and control, and indicate the magnitude of these differences. For this information to be of maximum usefulness to those fabricating a sample, it may also be necessary for the descriptive panel to identify physical correlates (e.g., ingredients) to the major sensory perception revealed in the descriptive test. These physical correlates would then act as references during further product development.

After further product development, when the research and development department supplies a second-generation experimental sample to the sensory group, it is desirable to determine that the revised sample is descriminably different from the first-generation sample. Often, time and money have been wasted evaluating samples in the laboratory, only to find later that the target population considered one or more of the test samples identical. Having established that the revised sample is different from its predecessor, the testing cycle may begin with laboratory or large-scale acceptance-preference or descriptive testing, depending on the development results.

Control Sample Not Identical with Conceptual Model.—The second possible test condition occurs when the control sample is somewhat similar, but not identical, with the conceptual model. Again, market research must establish that the concept is viable and that there is some degree of match between the control and the conceptual model. Product development conducts bench-top research and screening and produces the first generation experimental sample. Because the control sample is not identical with the conceptual model, the testing sequence will differ slightly from that in the first situation. Discrimination tests are unnecessary, since the objective is not to develop an experimental sample that is identical with the control.

The first test conducted by the sensory group in this case is an acceptance-preference test, using a laboratory-type consumer panel to determine whether the experimental sample is as acceptable as the control. If there is no difference in acceptance, the sample goes back to market research for verification of these results. However, if the experimental sample is rejected, either descriptive testing is conducted or the control and the experimental sample can be tested for acceptance by a larger group of potential consumers. When conducting nonlaboratory acceptance-preference tests, it is valuable to use scenarios. If the sample is accepted with qualifications, a business decision may be necessary to determine whether to market the sample as qualified or to develop the product further.

Descriptive testing is necessary when the first-generation sample is rejected. As well as identifying and measuring the sensory components of the control and the experimental sample, judges should next develop an "ideal model" for each sample (Green and Rao 1972). This is not necessary when the control and conceptual model are identical. An ideal model is constructed during descriptive testing in the following way. After evaluation of the samples, each subject is given a blank score sheet and asked to indicate where his "ideal" intensity for each sensory property of that sample is located. These results should indicate the perceptual distance between the actual sample and the ideal on each dimension. An ideal model of this type provides the development team with information about the deficiencies in the experimental sample, but it does have limitations. It is developed using a small laboratory panel; therefore the degree of agreement between subjects should be considered in evaluating the usefulness of their ideal model.

Further product development will provide a second-generation experimental sample that must be shown to be perceptually different from the initial sample. Then, retesting should be done with acceptance-preference or descriptive methods as needed.

No Control Sample Available.—The third possible test situation is when the proposed new product has no direct counterpart on the grocery shelf and marketing research has developed a viable concept, but can offer no control sample (Table 10.6). Now the task of the product development group is to develop what we call a protocept. The difference between a protocept and a prototype is that the protocept is not a potentially manufacturable product, whereas a prototype is. A protocept is made in an experimental kitchen from the best of ingredients.

TABLE 10.6

A SEQUENCE FOR DEVELOPMENT AND TESTING OF A NEW PRODUCT
WHEN NO CONTROL SAMPLE IS AVAILABLE

1. Market Research Testing	Establish that concept is viable and there is no control available.
2. Product Development	Develop a protocept
3. Market Research Testing	Test viability of protocept
4. Product Development	Develop experimental sample
5. Sensory Evaluation Discrimination Testing	Test experimental sample vs protocept
Acceptance-Preference Testing (Laboratory-Type Consumer Panels)	Test experimental sample
Acceptance-Preference Testing (Large Scale Nonlaboratory Consumer Panels)	When necessary, use different Scenarios with test samples
Descriptive Testing	Test experimental sample. Not necessary to develop "ideal"
6. Further Product Development	Develop additional experimental samples as necessary.

It is not intended as a production model, but embodies all the product attributes identified in previous concept delineation.

The protocept must then be tested by marketing to determine if it is as viable as the concept. It if is not viable, even with qualifying statements, then another protocept must be developed, or consideration must be given to abandoning the project for the time being. Remember, the marketplace is dynamic and the protocept may become viable at some later date. If market research testing establishes that the protocept is as viable as the concept, we return to product development and develop the first-generation experimental sample.

During the early stages of sensory evaluation, the protocept may serve as a control, but care should be taken not to use it for too long. Initially, a discrimination test between the protocept and first generation experimental sample may be conducted. The testing sequence would then be similar to the situation where a control was available, that is, acceptance-preference testing in the laboratory, then tests using a consumer panel, and on to descriptive testing. During descriptive testing it may not be necessary to develop an ideal model for the protocept because the viability of the protocept was established earlier by market research. If the first generation experimental sample is rejected, further development is required. When the product development group supplies the sensory scientist with the second-generation sample, we would recommend that the first and second generation samples be tested to determine whether they are significantly different from one another. If they are not different, this information should be reported back to product development. However, if the samples are different from each other, the recommended test sequence is acceptance-preference testing of both the first and second-generation samples. By including the first-generation sample in these tests, we can determine whether the second sample is indeed an improvement over the first. If the result of the nonlaboratory acceptance-preference test is favorable, then market research testing is necessary to determine that the current sample is as viable as the concept.

If market research establishes that the sample is viable, then the sample becomes a potential product and the project to date is a success. However, if market testing indicates that the experimental sample is not viable, the sensory group must initiate descriptive testing in preparation for further product development and the resumption of this test cycle.

Throughout the ideal sequence of tests outlined above, there is a continuous interplay between tests conducted by marketing research and tests conducted by the sensory evaluation group. Therefore, close communication between these two groups is necessary. At certain stages (for example, before the acceptance-preference testing outside the laboratory), the test-design, questionnaire, etc., should be reviewed by personnel from both groups to ensure continuity in product testing. When products are tested according to one set of objectives by sensory personnel and according to completely different objectives by the marketing research group, different conclusions regarding product acceptance may be reached. This must be avoided at all costs.

SUMMARY

The problems facing the developer and merchandiser of fabricated foods—especially those to be sold retail as a finished product—are more than technical in nature. The sensory scientist, using the available tools of his profession and developing new tools when needed, can make a significant contribution to the solution of these problems and should be a participating member of the market product development team. If successful products are to be developed and tested in an efficient and economical manner, adequate communication and a skilled team effort are essential.

BIBLIOGRAPHY

ASTM, 1968. Manual on Sensory Testing Methods. Special Technical Publication 434.
AMERINE, M. H., PANGBORN, R. M., and ROESSLER, E. B. 1965. Principles of Sensory Evaluation of Food. Academic Press, New York.

CAIN, W. S., and MARKS, L. E. (Editors). 1971. Stimulus and Sensation, Readings in Sensory Psychology. Little, Brown & Co., Boston.

GREEN, P. E., and RAO, V. R. 1972. Applied Multidimensional Scaling, A Comparison of Approaches and Algorithms. Holt, Rinehart, and Winston, Inc., New York.

INSTITUTE OF FOOD TECHNOLOGISTS COMMITTEE OF SENSORY EVALUATION. 1971. Author guidelines for IFT research papers reporting sensory evaluation data. Food Technol. 21, 254.

JONES, F. N. 1958. Prerequisites for test environment. In Flavor Research and Food Acceptance, A.D. Little, Inc. (Editor). Reinhold, New York.

JONES, L. V., PERYAM, D. R., and THURSTONE, L. M. 1955. Development of a scale for measuring soldiers' food preferences. Food Res. 20, 512-520.

MOSKOWITZ, H. R. 1974. Sensory evaluation by magnitude estimation. Food Technol. 28, 16, 18, 20, 21.

MOSKOWITZ, H. R., and SIDEL, J. L. 1971. Magnitude and hedonic scales of food acceptability. J. Food Sci. 36, 677-680.

PAYNE, S. L. 1965. Are open-ended questions worth the effort? J. Market Res. 2, 417-419.

SCHUTZ, H. G. 1965. A good action rating scale for measuring food acceptance. J. Food Sci. 30, 361-375.

SIEGEL, S. 1956. Nonparametric Statistics for the Behavioral Sciences. McGraw-Hill Book. Co., New York.

STEVENS, S. S. 1951. Mathematics, measurement and psychophysics. In Handbook of Experimental Psychology, S. S. Stevens (Editor). John Wiley & Sons, New York.

STEVENS, S. S., and GALANTER, E. 1957. Ratio scales and category scales for a dozen perceptual continua. J. Exptl. Psychol. 54, 377-411.

STONE, H., SIDEL, J. L., OLIVER, S., WOOLSEY, A., and SINGLETON, R. C. 1974. Sensory evaluation by quantitative descriptive analysis. Food Technol. 28, 24, 26, 28, 29, 32, 34.

CHAPTER 11

Malcolm C. Bourne

Texture Properties and Evaluations of Fabricated Foods

Definition

Although the word "texture" has meaning as a quality attribute to most people who work with foods, it comes as a surprise to many to find that there is really no completely satisfactory definition of the word "texture" for food technologists. The dictionary definition of texture is of little help. Under the term "texture" Webster's Dictionary refers to textiles and weaving in general and then continues, "it is the manner of structure, interrelation of parts, structural quality", it gives for examples textiles, fabrics, artistic compositions, music, poetry, petrography, bones and plants, but makes no mention at all of foods.

Even among food technologists there is no accepted definition of texture. Some consider that texture describes properties such as hardness and chewiness, while others, such as those in the meat industry, consider texture to be the microscopic appearance in terms of smoothness or fineness of grain. This approach is shared by the dairy industry and baking industry who consider "texture" to mean the smoothness and uniformity of ice-cream and bread. Kramer (1973) provides a good discussion of the problem of defining food texture and relating it to other quality attributes.

Rather than go through a long description of the various definitions of texture, I would like to introduce the term "textural properties". For too long, many people have considered texture to be a one-point measurement (for example, like pH), which it is not. "Textural properties" points out that there are a number of parameters associated with texture and that texture cannot be measured completely by a single-point measurement.

A useful breakdown of "texture" into its component parts is shown in Table 11.1. This table should be sufficient to dispel any idea that texture is a simple one-parameter property of food. In the Texture Profile Technique (which will be explained in more detail later) a panel will usually identify and quantify 10 to 30 different textural properties within a single food. There is, therefore, merit in abandoning the word "texture", with its implied association of a single parameter, and turning to some more descriptive term, such as "textural properties," with its implied association of a number of parameters.

One definition of textural properties is as follows: "The textural

TABLE 11.1

RELATIONS BETWEEN TEXTURAL PARAMETERS AND POPULAR NOMENCLATURE

Mechanical Characteristics		
Primary parameters	Secondary parameters	Popular terms
Hardness		Soft→Firm→Hard
Cohesiveness	Brittleness	Crumbly→Crunchy→Brittle
	Chewiness	Tender→Chewy→Tough
	Gumminess	Short→Mealy→Pasty→
		Gummy
Viscosity		Thin→Viscous
Elasticity		Plastic→Elastic
Adhesiveness		Sticky→Tacky→Gooey
Geometrical Characteristics		
Class		Examples
Particle size and shape		Gritty, Grainy, Coarse, etc.
Particle shape and orientation		Fibrous, Cellular, Crystalline, etc.
Other Characteristics		
Primary parameters	Secondary parameters	Popular terms
Moisture content		Dry → Moist → Wet → Watery
Fat content	Oiliness	Oily
	Greasiness	Greasy

Szczesniak 1963

properties of a food are that group of physical characteristics that are sensed by the feeling of touch, are related to the deformation, disintegration and flow of the food under the application of a force, and are measured objectively by functions of force, time, and distance". This definition excludes those physical characteristics such as optical and electrical properties that have nothing to do with texture and restricts the meaning to those properties that are felt in the mouth or in the hand. The sensation of temperature is also excluded.

Other Definitions

The word "mouthfeel" is generally meant to include those non-chemical stimuli that are sensed in the mouth during mastication. Interactions between the food and the saliva constitute an important part of the total mouthfeel sensations.

"Viscosity" refers to the resistance of a fluid to flow. There is a tendency among food technologists to restrict the word viscosity to Newtonian fluids or fluids that exhibit near-Newtonian behavior and use the word "consistency" for those fluids that deviate substantially from Newtonian behavior. The word consistency includes those foods that exhibit plastic flow.

"Rheology" is the study of the deformation and flow of matter. "Food rheology" is "the study of the deformation and flow of the raw materials, the intermediate products, and the final products of the food industry" (White 1970).

"Mastication" refers to the entire complex of processes that occur as the food is chewed in the mouth and brought into a condition ready to be swallowed. This is an extremely complex set of processes that is generally not understood or appreciated. Its complexity has been well described by Yurkstas (1965) as follows, "We sometimes fail to appreciate the complexity of the chewing apparatus. It is truly remarkable that most people perform this function daily with little or no forethought. Mastication involves the use of forces that sometimes exceed 100 lb and pressures that are probably over 10,000 lb per sq. in. One hundred blows per min are often delivered for periods of 0.5 to 1 hr at a time. These blows are automatically controlled and are precise to within a few hundredths of an inch; a mistimed blow or a misguided stroke can cause intense pain or result in considerable damage."

IMPORTANCE OF TEXTURAL PROPERTIES

The majority of people select their food primarily for the enjoyment they drive from eating, and only secondarily for its nutritional value. The fact that the consumption of foods is a pleasurable experience is evidenced by the great pains that food suppliers take to ensure that the food they provide comes up to the quality expected by the consumer. They know from long, and often bitter, experience that unless the food provides the eating quality demanded by the customer they will be out of business, no matter how nutritious their product line.

The range of textural characteristics found in foods is enormous. There is the chewiness of meat, the softness of the marshmallow, the crispness of celery, the juiciness of fresh fruits, the smoothness of ice-cream, the soft toughness of bread, the flakiness of fish, the viscosity of thick soup, and the crumbliness of cake. The great range and types of texture arise from the human demand for variety in the nature of their food.

A classic example of this desire for variety is found in the Old Testament. When the children of Israel were traveling through the desert from Egypt to Palestine, God supplied them with manna to eat. Manna was "bread from Heaven", and by all accounts a very enjoyable food. Despite the high quality and excellent organoleptic characteristics of manna, the people tired of eating it every day and demanded a change. The record says, "and the children of Israel wept again and said 'Who shall give us flesh to eat?' We remember the fish, which we did eat in Egypt freely; the cucumbers, and the melons, and the leeks and the onions and the garlic. But now our soul is dried away. There is nothing at all, besides this manna before our eyes" (Numbers, Chapter 11). Twentieth century humans are just as insistent in demanding a variety of textures and flavors in their food as were the children of Israel many centuries ago.

Dr. Schiffman (1973) indirectly pointed out the importance of texture by feeding 29 different foods to people who were blindfolded and asking them to identify the foods. The samples had been puréed by blending and straining in order to eliminate textural clues. Table 11.2 lists some representative figures from Schiffman's data. It is remarkable to discover how poorly many foods are identified when their texture and color are concealed. Young adults of normal weight were able to identify correctly only 40.7% of the 29 foods used in the study.

Szczesniak and Kleyn (1963) gave a word association test to 100 people to determine their degree of texture-consciousness and the terms used to describe texture. Seventy-eight different descriptive words were used by the participants. The authors concluded that texture is a discernible characteristic, but is more evident in some foods than in others. Foods that elicited the highest number of texture responses were either bland in flavor or possessed the characteristics of crunchiness or crispness.

In a later study (Szczesniak 1971), a word association test was given to 150 respondents with results similar to the first study. This test again showed that texture is a discernible characteristic of foods and that awareness of it generally is equivalent to that of flavor. It was also found

TABLE 11.2

% CORRECT IDENTIFICATION OF PURÉED FOODS

Food	Normal Weight Young	Obese Young	Normal Weight Aged
Apple	81	87	55
Strawberry	78	62	33
Fish	78	81	59
Lemon	52	25	24
Carrot	51	44	7
Banana	41	69	24
Beef	41	50	27
Rice	22	12	15
Potato	19	69	38
Green pepper	19	25	11
Pork	15	6	7
Cucumber	8	0	0
Lamb	4	6	—
Cabbage	4	0	7
Mean for 29 foods	40.7	50.0	30.4

From Schiffman 1973.

that women, and people in the higher economic brackets, showed an increased awareness of the textural properties of foods.

Yoshikawa *et al.* (1970) conducted a similar test in Japan, using 140 female college students and 97 food words and collected 406 different words that describe characteristics of food. These studies show the importance of textural properties as a factor in food quality and the great variety of textures found in food. The ten most frequently used words in these two studies are listed in Table 11.3. It is interesting to notice that seven of the ten words are common to both lists although Japanese culture and food habits are substantially different from those of Americans, and that the Japanese used 406 descriptive words as compared to 78 words in the U.S.

Szczesniak and Kahn (1971) conducted in-depth interviews with homemakers and found that texture awareness is often apparent at a subconscious level and that it is taken more or less for granted; however, when the textural aspects did not come up to expectations, there was a sharp increase in awareness of texture and criticism of its deficiencies. The authors state, "If the texture of a food is the way people have learned to expect it to be, and if it is psychologically and physiologically acceptable, then it will scarcely be noticed. If, however, the texture is not as it is expected to be, ... it becomes a focal point for criticism and rejection of the food. Care must be taken not to underestimate the importance of texture just because it is taken for granted when all is as it should be."

In yet another report Szczesniak (1972) studied the attitudes of children and teenagers to food texture and found that it is an important aspect of their liking or disliking specific foods. The young child prefers simple soft textures that he can manage within the limited development

TABLE 11.3

MOST FREQUENTLY USED TEXTURE WORDS

United States[1]	Descending Order of Frequency	Japan[2]
crisp		
dry		hard
juicy		soft
soft		juicy
creamy		chewy
crunchy		greasy
chewy		viscous
smooth		slippery
stringy		creamy
hard		crisp
78 words		crunchy
		406 words

[1]Szczesniak and Kleyn 1963.
[2]Yoshikawa, Nishimaru and Tashiro 1970.

of the structures of the mouth, and he extends his range of relished textures as his teeth, jaws, and powers of coordination develop. Teenagers have a high degree of texture awareness that sometimes surpasses that of adults, suggesting that the next generation of adult consumers may be more sophisticated and demanding in terms of textural qualities of the foods they purchase.

MEASUREMENT OF TEXTURE

Objective Methods

A great number of objective tests have been developed over the years to measure many different textural properties of foods. Table 11.4 lists and classifies the various methods used for measuring food texture. This classification system has been discussed in some detail by Bourne (1966). Many of these methods are unsuitable for fabricated foods, and many of them have used laboratory-built equipment that is not commercially available. This discussion will restrict itself to a description of those instruments that are commercially available and that appear to have promise for measuring the textural properties of three types of fabricated foods. Appendix I gives the names and addresses of the manufacturers of the equipment discussed in this paper. An extensive list of commercial equipment has been given by Szczesniak (1973). The instruments that are discussed are listed below according to the textural type of commodity for which they are suited.

Crisp or Crunchy Foods.—Crunchy foods fracture on the first bite, giving sharp force peaks and steep force-distance curves. A satisfactory method of measuring the textural properties almost always requires a strip chart recorder as an integral part of the testing machine in order to follow the step-by-step breakdown of the food. Single-point measuring devices in which one number is read from a scale are generally unsatisfactory. The instruments that would be useful on this kind of test are the Instron (Bourne *et al.* 1966), G-F Texturometer (Friedman *et al.* 1963), and the Ottawa Texture System (Voisey 1971). Since rapid changes in forces are involved in testing these foods, it is necessary to use a high-speed pen response type recorder.

The Instron machine consists essentially of two parts, (1) a driving mechanism that moves a horizontal crosshead in a vertical direction by means of twin lead screws at selected speeds in the range 0.5 to 50 cm a min; and (2) a load-sensing and recording system that consists of electric bonded-wire strain gauges whose output is fed to a strip chart recorder. Forces from less than 1 newton to 5,000 newtons (100 gm to 500 kg, approximately) can be measured in the bench model machines, and

TABLE 11.4

OBJECTIVE METHODS FOR MEASURING FOOD TEXTURE

Method	Measured Variable	Dimensional Units	Examples
1. Force	Force (F)	mlt^{-2}	
a. Puncture	"	"	Magness Taylor
b. Extrusion	"	"	Shear Press, Tenderometer
c. Shear	"	"	Warner-Bratzler Shear
d. Crushing	"	"	—
e. Tensile	"	"	—
f. Torque	"	"	Rotary Viscometers
2. Distance			
	a. length	1	Penetrometers
	b. area	1^2	Grawemeyer Consistometer
	c. volume	1^3	Bread Volume
3. Time	Time (T)	t	Ostwald Viscometer
4. Energy	Work (F x D)	ml^2t^{-2}	—
5. Ratio	F or D or T measured twice	dimensionless	Specific gravity
6. Multiple	F and D and T	mlt^{-2}, 1, t	Instron, Ottawa System, GF Texturometer Durometer
7. Multiple Variable	anything	unclear	
8. Chemical Analysis	concentration	dimensionless (%)	Alcohol Insoluble Solids
9. Miscellaneous	anything	anything	Optical Density, Crushing Sounds

Adapted from Bourne 1966.

forces from less than 20 millinewtons to 100 kilonewtons (approximately 2 gm to 10,000 kg) can be measured in larger models (see Fig. 11.1).

A wide variety of test cells can be attached to the moving crosshead, in effect making this machine universal because it can perform almost any kind of test that utilizes rectilinear motion, including puncture, extrusion, shear, crushing, tensile, and snapping tests (see Fig. 11.l). The chart records the complete history of the changes in force during the course of the test. Since both the crosshead and chart are driven by synchronous motors, the time axis on the chart becomes a true measure of distance or some simple ratio of distance traveled by the moving crosshead. Consequently it is possible to measure forces, distances, times and areas (work). In addition, the crosshead can be set to recipro-

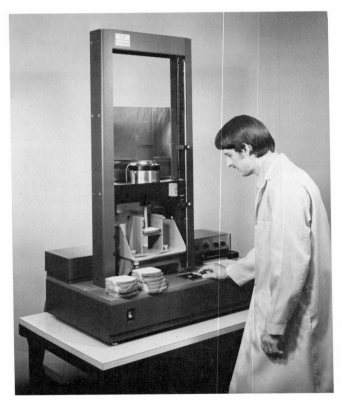

Courtesy of Instron Corporation

FIG. 11.1. THE BENCH MODEL INSTRON MACHINE ADAPTED FOR FOOD USE

cate in a vertical direction similar to the action of the jaws, giving repeated compression tests on a single sample of food which enables a texture profile to be measured (Bourne 1968).

For crunchy foods, the most common type of test is to place an article of food between two horizontal extensive surfaces, crush the material, examine the chart and attempt to pick out from the chart those features that correlate with the textural properties that are desirable. A second "bite" is sometimes useful here.

The General Foods Texturometer (Friedman *et al*. 1963) is designed to imitate the chewing action of the mouth. It consists of a moving arm that reciprocates in the arc of a circle compressing bite-size pieces of food 2 times. A force-time recorder records the history of the changes in force during the 2 strokes (see Fig. 11.2). The group at General foods have analyzed these curves and identified 6 textural properties that can be obtained from them, namely, hardness, cohesiveness, elasticity, adhesiveness, fracturability, chewiness, and gumminess. The Texturometer has 2 chewing rates, 12 and 24 chews per min. The force available at the tooth ranges from less than 1 newton to approximately 600 newtons (approximately 100 gm to 60 kg). Total stroke length is approximately 1½ in. This machine lends itself readily to the testing of bite-size pieces of food.

The Ottawa Texture-Measuring System (Voisey 1971) is somewhat similar to the Instron in design and operation, using a load cell that is connected to a strip chart recorder and a number of different attachments. The moving parts are driven by means of a single screw (see Fig. 11.3). This instrument would probably be effective in testing many crunchy foods.

A number of "laboratory-made" testing instruments have been used on crunchy foods. Perhaps the best known of these is the Bailey Shortometer (Bailey 1934). This consists of two vertical beams across which the material such as a cookie is placed. A descending beam coming between the two rigid beams snaps the article in half and the maximum force required for snapping is measured. Bruns and Bourne (1974) studied this type of test using the Instron and found that the snapping force on cookies and chocolate agrees with engineering theory in that the snapping force is directly proportional to the width, directly proportional to the square of the thickness, and inversely proportional to the length of the test specimen.

Chewy Foods.—The best-known instrument for measuring the tenderness of meat is the Warner-Bratzler Shear (Bratzler 1932). This instrument shears across the fibers of a cylinder of meat, usually ½ or 1 in. in diam, by means of a stainless steel blade 0.050 in. thick, and the

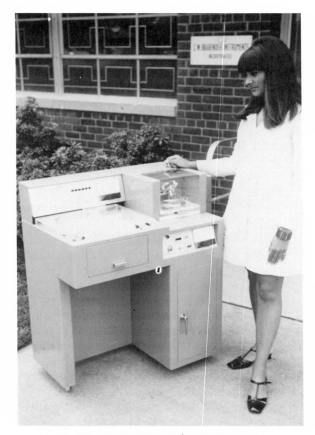

FIG. 11.2.   THE GENERAL FOODS TEXTUROMETER

maximum force encountered during shearing is measured (see Fig. 11.4). The test sample is cut so that the fibers lie longitudinally in the test specimen.

The Shear Press (Kramer 1961) has also been used for fibrous foods. This is a hydraulically driven instrument that may use a maximum force-measuring gauge or a strip chart recorder. The latest model consists of a rectangular aluminum box with internal dimensions 2⅝ × 2¾ × 2½ in. high and ⅛ in. wide slits in the bottom. A set of aluminum

Courtesy of Mr. Peter Voisey

FIG. 11.3.   THE OTTAWA TEXTURE MEASURING SYSTEM (OTMS)

bars ⅛ in. wide passes down through the box, meshing through the slits in the bottom (Fig. 11.5). In this test the food is first compressed and then extruded or sheared. The Shear Press and Warner-Bratzler Shear usually give statistically significant correlations with panel evaluations of meat tenderness, but the numerical values of the correlation coefficients are not high enough to be completely satisfactory. However, no commercial instrument has yet been developed that is consistently

FIG. 11.4.   THE WARNER-BRATZLER SHEAR FOR MEASURING TENDERNESS OF
MEAT

The meat sample is represented by a cylinder of wood.

better than the two named above. Methods for measuring meat texture
have been extensively reviewed by Szczesniak and Torgeson (1965).
Corey (1970) has discussed some of the problems involved in measuring
textural properties of fibrous foods, including meat analogs.

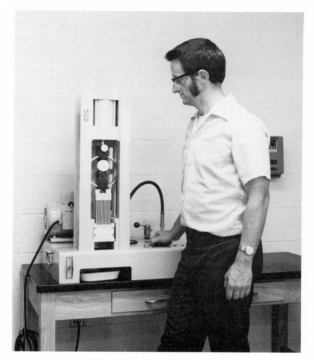

FIG. 11.5.   THE SHEAR PRESS

A new instrument in the field of measuring texture of chewy foods is the Armour Tenderometer (Hansen 1971, 1972). In this instrument the maximum force required to push a set of 10 large pins into a piece of uncooked beef is measured. It is claimed that this force reading is a reliable index of the tenderness of the meat after cooking, although some workers dispute this (Parrish *et al.* 1973; Carpenter *et al.* 1972; Dikeman *et al.* 1972). Nevertheless the Armour Tenderometer received the Institute of Food Technologists' Industrial Achievement Award in 1973. It is possible that this type of instrument may be of use in measuring the texture of chewy foods.

The working parts of the Warner-Bratzler Shear, the Shear Press and Armour Tenderometer have been mounted and used in the Instron and the Ottawa Texture-Measuring System.

Soft and Smooth Foods.—Foods such as yogurt, starch puddings, and whipped toppings require an instrument that can measure small forces. A common way of measuring these products is by use of a Penetrometer (see Fig. 11.6). The Penetrometer consists of a cone and shaft assembly that is allowed to sink into the soft food by the force of gravity. The distance that it sinks into the food is measured after a fixed time, usually 5 sec. The softer the product the farther the cone sinks into it. Several weights of cone and angles of cone are available from commercial suppliers.

FIG. 11.6.   THE PENETROMETER

Several cones and needles are shown in the foreground.

Another type of instrument that is similar in principle to the Pentrometer is that of the falling plummet. A good example of this is the Hilker-Guthrie sour cream body tester (Hilker 1947; Guthrie 1963). It consists of a hollow aluminum rod 4½ in. long, ½ in. in diameter, with a tapered end that is allowed to fall freely from a height of 20 in. into the food (see Fig. 11.7). The depth of penetration, which is read immediately after the falling rod comes to rest, gives an index of the firmness of the commodity.

Another principle used for measuring the firmness of certain soft foods is that of puncture, in which the force required to push a probe into

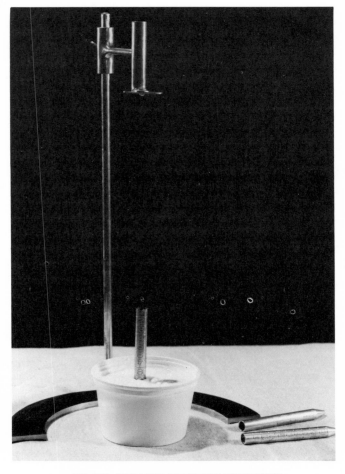

FIG. 11.7.   THE HILKER-GUTHRIE FALLING PLUMMET

the foods is measured. The best-known of these is the Bloom Jelly Tester (Bloom 1925), which is used for measuring the firmness of gelatin gels and similar products. Another instrument in this class is the Marine Colloids Gel Tester, used for measuring the strength of gels made from marine colloids (see Fig. 11.8). The Instron has also been used for performing puncture tests on soft products (Bourne 1966).

The General Foods Texturometer can be used for measuring the textural properties of soft foods. In this case rather than crushing the food, a large-diameter disk is pushed into a small container filled with the food and withdrawn, 2 times (Friedman *et al.* 1963).

Viscometers are sometimes used for measuring the textural properties of soft foods. Generally speaking these are of the rotating type. The Couette type (for example, the MacMichael Viscometer), consists of a cylindrical cup containing the food. A cylindrical bob is suspended in the

Courtesy of Marine Colloids

FIG. 11.8. THE MARINE COLLOIDS GEL TESTER

cup, the food occupying the space between the cup and the bob. The geometry is highly standardized and the gap between the cup and bob is small. The cup is rotated at constant speed and the drag of the soft food on the bob is measured by means of a torsion wire or force transducer.

Other viscometers in which the geometry is not so well defined are also used, for example, the Brabender Viscocorder and the Brookfield Viscometer. In the latter two it is difficult to obtain exact viscosity measurements since the geometry is not well-defined, but they are frequently used and are often effective in obtaining comparative empirical data that are useful.

Subjective Methods

A number of processes occur while a food is being masticated. These include deformation, flow, comminution, mixing and hydration with saliva, and sometimes changes in temperature and surface roughness. The entire complex of effects that occurs and are sensed in the oral cavity cannot be measured completely by instrumental methods. Furthermore, no matter how sophisticated and elegant the instrumental methods of measurement are, it must never be forgotten that the ultimate calibration of any instrument must be against the human palate; for if the palate says a food has undesirable textural properties then the texture is undesirable regardless of the readings given by instruments.

Sensory methods of measuring food quality are difficult. They are time-consuming and expensive, and they lack the precision that is desirable in scientific research because of the variability from person to person and variability from hour to hour and day to day in the likes and dislikes of each person. Nevertheless, despite these serious obstacles, sensory measurement of texture is a very important aspect that cannot be ignored. Sensory evaluation is the best method for evaluating texture of new types of fabricated foods in the early stages of development, and for providing a basis on which instrumental methods might later be designed for use as a quality measure and production control tool.

The most complete system of sensory texture measurement is the General Foods Sensory Texture Profiling Technique (Brandt *et al*. 1963; Szczesniak *et al*. 1963; Civille *et al*. 1973). This technique is based on the order of appearance of the textural characteristics of a food during mastication. This can be divided into three phases: (1) the first bite, which is the initial sensation; (2) the masticatory phase, which consists of those sensations perceived during chewing; and (3) residual sensation, those sensations experienced just before, during, and after swallowing. In effect, this technique trains the human mouth to behave as an analytical instrument with precision and reproducibility and the power of measuring every textural property that can be sensed during mastication.

The textural characteristics are divided into three classes:

Mechanical Characteristics.—These are both qualitative and quantitative. The mechanical characteristics are made quantitative by means of standard rating scales, analogous to Mohs scale of hardness used by minerologists. In this case there is a standard hardness scale that consists of 9 food products ranging from very low hardness (Philadelphia cream cheese) to high hardness (rock candy) (see Table 11.5 and Table 11.1).

Other standard scales are brittleness (7 points), chewiness (7 points), gumminess (5 points), adhesiveness (5 points) and viscosity (8 points). The items selected to be used for the standard rating scales are chosen on the basis of having that particular textural property as a dominant characteristic and fairly uniform intervals between points in the desired characteristic. A panel of 5 to 8 people with adequate training can rate the mechanical properties of a sample on each of the 6 standard scales to within about 1/5 of a point with a high degree of reproducibility.

Geometrical Characteristics.—Geometrical characteristics are qualitative and partly quantitative in nature. They consist of characteristics of foods that relate to particle size, shape, and orientation, and include such terms as powdery, chalky, grainy, gritty, coarse, lumpy, beady, flaky, fibrous, pulpy, cellular, aerated, puffy, and crystalline.

TABLE 11.5

STANDARD HARDNESS SCALE FOR GF TEXTURE PROFILE

Panel Rating	Product	Brand or Type	Manufacturer
1	Cream cheese	Philadelphia	Kraft Foods
2	Egg white	hard-cooked 5 min	—
3	Frankfurters	large, uncooked, skinless	Mogen David Kosher Meat Products Corp.
4	Cheese	yellow, American, pasteurized process	Kraft Foods
5	Olives	exquisite giant size, stuffed	Cresca Co.
6	Peanuts	cocktail type in vacuum tin	Planters Peanuts
7	Carrots	uncooked, fresh	—
8	Peanut brittle	candy part	Kraft Foods
9	Rock candy	—	Dryden & Palmer

From Szczesniak *et al.* 1963.

Reference foods are used as examples of each of the geometrical properties (Brandt *et al.* 1963).

Other Characteristics.—Sometimes called chemical characteristics, these include the factors of moistness, dryness and oiliness. The term, "moistness" in this sense does not mean the actual moisture content as can be determined by chemical analysis, but the sensation of moistness that is experienced in the mouth. For example, it is possible to have 2 cuts of beef that have been shown to have equal moisture contents by chemical analysis, and yet one cut will be termed juicy because of the sensation of moistness in the mouth while the other cut might be termed dry because the sensation of moistness is lacking.

Once a panel has been trained, it operates by chewing a sample of food for which the texture profile is desired and scoring all these parameters on a standard score sheet. In this way differences in texture that result from changes due to formulation, processing, and storage can be pinpointed. Table 11.6 shows the basic texture profile score sheet.

Where it is necessary to quantify small differences in textural properties of similar materials caused by differences in formulation and pro-

TABLE 11.6

TEXTURE PROFILE BALLOT

Product: _____ Name: _____ Date: _____

Initial (perceived on first bite)
  (a) Mechanical
        Hardness (1-9 scale)
        Fracturability (1-7 scale)
        Viscosity (1-8)
  (b) Geometrical
  (c) Other
Masticatory (perceived during chewing)
  (a) Mechanical
        Gumminess (1-5 scale)
        Chewiness (1-7 scale)
        Adhesiveness (1-5 scale)
  (b) Geometrical
  (c) Other
Residual (change made during mastication)
  Rate of breakdown
  Type of breakdown
  Moisture absorption
  Mouth coating

Courtesy of Dr. Szczesniak, General Foods Corporation.

cessing, a comparative texture profile ballot is derived from the standard score sheet shown in Table 11.6. In the comparative texture profile one material that is the "target" material, whose textural properties it is desirable to reproduce, is set up as a control and has a score of zero. The textural properties that have been identified during mastication are then listed in order of appearance and experimental samples are graded equal to, less than, or greater than the control sample in that particular quality factor. The grading is made semi-quantitative by grading from 1 to 5 plus and from 1 to 5 minus. One plus means slightly greater than the control and 5 plus, much greater than the control in that particular textural property. The minus score is used to indicate slightly less than to much less than the control sample. A comparative texture profile ballot is shown in Table 11.7.

By means of the comparative texture profile ballot it is possible to identify those formulations and processing variables that bring the experimental samples closer to the target. In my opinion, this is definitely the best technique for obtaining the desirable textural properties in fabricated foods that seek to imitate natural foods. I predict that the Texture Profiling Technique will be used more extensively in the future as the manufacturers of fabricated foods realize the importance of building desirable textures into their products.

The texture profiling technique can be used under a wide range of conditions. For example, Bourne *et al.* (1974) trained a texture profile panel in Colombia which identified 28 different textural characteristics in arepa (a widely used Colombian food made from corn). The work of this panel has been of great value in developing a protein-fortified food of acceptable textural quality for the Colombian population. The texture profile ballot used by this panel is shown in Table 11.7.

DESIRABLE TEXTURES IN THREE TYPES OF FOODS

In developing fabricated foods it is important that desirable textural properties be engineered into the food from the early stages in development; it is, therefore, necessary to attempt to spell out exactly what textural characteristics are desirable. This is a difficult problem and there is very little literature in this area at the present time. Szczesniak and Kahn (1971) found in consumer interviews that crispness, tenderness, juiciness, and firmness are generally considered to be desirable textural attributes while crumbliness, sogginess, mealiness, and hardness generally have a negative connotation. Corey (1970) suggests that only a restricted portion of the spectra of physical properties of foods are texture-inducing and proposes the word, "texturogens" to identify them.

In the absence of definitive studies on this point, an attempt is made

TABLE 11.7

COMPARATIVE TEXTURE PROFILE BALLOT FOR AREPA

	–	Control 0	+
I. Initial Sensation			
(a) Measure force to: bite off with incisors / pull out with hand			
(b) Hardness			
(c) Sideways sliding of center			
(d) Toughness of skin			
(e) Doughiness of center			
(f) Dryness of skin			
(g) Moistness of center			
II. Mastication			
(a) Chewiness (number of chews)			
(b) Adhesiveness			
(c) Pastiness of center			
(d) Graininess of center			
(e) Toughness of skin			
(f) Roughness of skin pieces			
(g) Dryness of skin pieces			
(h) Moistness of center			
III. Final Sensations			
(a) Rate of breakdown of skin			
(b) Rate of breakdown of center			
(c) Moistness of paste			
(d) Graininess of paste			
(e) Dryness of skin particles			
(f) Roughness of skin particles			
(g) Presence of coarse particles other than skin			
(h) Absorption of moisture by mass			
(i) Absorption of moisture by pieces of skin			
(j) Mouthcoating of mass			
(k) Presence of skin particles around mouth			
(l) Scratchiness of residual skin particles			

INSTRUCTIONS: Put an X in "0" column if sample is equal to control
Put 1X to 5X in (+) column if sample is more than control
and in (−) column if less than control
X = Slightly different
XXXXX = Strongly different

From Bourne *et al.* 1974.

below to classify and identify the desirable textural characteristics in 3 types of fabricated food using a general knowledge of texture and a limited amount of experimental data as the foundation on which to build this classification. Since there are many different textural types of foods, this discussion will be restricted to 3 types that are of great current interest to food fabricators (see Table 11.8).

One important aspect that is required in all foods is that the food hydrate and mix with the saliva to form a non-abrasive paste, slurry, or emulsion in readiness for swallowing. There should be no sensation of a "foreign body" in the mouth, because anything that causes discomfort in the mouth tends to make people gag and choke, and such unpleasant sensations inhibit consumption of that food. All foods should be free

TABLE 11.8

DESIRABLE TEXTURAL CHARACTERISTICS OF SOME FABRICATED FOODS

1. All Fabricated Foods
   Rapid hydration and mixing with saliva to form a non-abrasive paste or slurry; no sensation of "foreign body" in mouth; no sharp particles; not excessively sticky; not shear-thickening.
2. Crisp or Crunchy
   Rigid, non-deformable structure that collapses suddenly with brittle fracture and rapid decay of force after fracture; very low shear strength.
   Breaks up under simple compression between teeth with little or no grinding or tearing.
   Rapid breakdown into small pieces; small number of chews per piece; not chewy.
   Low work content required for mastication.
   Sound effects associated with brittle fracture often desirable.
   Structure usually comprised of cellular aggregates:
   (a) Dry types (e.g., potato chips): rapid softening and mixing with salvia; sharp edges from brittle fracture quickly become non-abrasive; moisture content usually below 5%.
   (b) Moist types (e.g., celery, raw apple): high turgor, juicy, moist spherical cells with no sharp edges; moisture content usually above 85%.
3. Chewy (e.g., meat and simulated meat)
   Highly deformable under a low force; measurable shear strength (toughness); no brittle fracture.
   Intermediate work content required for mastication (high work content renders product too tough).
   Requires grinding and/or tearing in addition to compression for proper mastication.
   Usually fibrous or laminated structure; sensation of moistness or juiciness.
4. Soft and Smooth (e.g., pudding)
   Smooth homogeneous texture; soft, not brittle, not tough, not chewy, not rigid.
   Exhibits plastic flow with a low slope and yield point above 1G.
   Manipulate with tongue rather than masticate with teeth.
   Need shear-thinning or melting effect in mouth.
5. Multicomponent Systems (e.g., cherry pie, caviar)
   Firm discrete particles in a soft continuous matrix or firm layers alternating with soft layers.

from sharp, hard particles that can cause injury to soft tissues. Excessive stickiness should be avoided, and in most foods it should be practically absent. Products that are difficult to manipulate in the mouth (e.g. a rheopectic gel) should also be avoided. This property of easy mixing with saliva and the feeling of "at-home" in the mouth applies to every type of food described below.

Crisp or Crunchy Foods

These foods are characterized by having a rigid, non-deformable, stiff structure that suddenly collapses with a brittle fracture and rapid decay of the force after fracture. Multiple fractures are usually evident in a single bite. These foods have a very low shear strength. In mastication they break up under simple compression with little or no lateral motion of the jaw, and are rapidly reduced to small pieces; the number of chews per piece is usually small.

These characteristics are shown in Figs. 11.8 and 11.9 which are traces from the chart of an Instron machine in which pieces of crunchy foods 10 mm high were compressed to 2 mm between 2 extensive parallel surfaces (first bite) then released and compressed to 2 mm again (second bite) in a reciprocating motion resembling the chewing action of the jaw. This is called the Texture Profile Test and is adapted from the G.F. Texturometer test (Friedman *et al.* 1963; Bourne 1968).

Fig. 11.9 shows that breadsticks and pretzel sticks (both crunchy foods) have very similar chewing patterns. The steep initial slope of the force-compression curve indicates the rigidity and resistance to deformation. The rapid decrease in force after the first break indicates brittle fracture of the whole piece. The series of smaller peaks that follow indicate successive brittle fractures of smaller pieces as the food is further compressed. A pretzel stick is much harder than a bread stick, having an initial fracture force of about 400 newtons compared with about 110 newtons for the breadstick, but the common property of

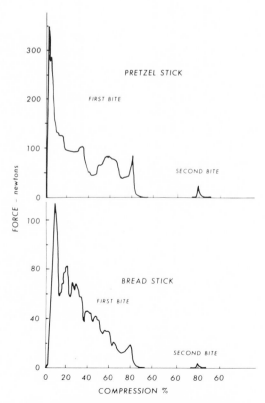

FIG. 11.9.   TEXTURE PROFILE OF TWO CRUNCHY FOODS

crunchiness is shown in the similarities in the curves for the two commodities. The second bit is very small compared with the first bite in respect to peak force and area under the curve, indicating that most of the work of breaking the structure is done on the first bite.

Fig. 11.10 shows another type of crunchy food (corn curls), that has a foamed or aerated structure as distinct from the more solid structure of the pretzel and breadsticks. In this case there is still the initial steep slope (indicating rigidity) and the sudden drop in force (indicating brittle fracture); however, as compression proceeds there are repeated brittle fractures at approximately constant force. In this product part of the rigid aerated structure collapses with brittle fracture, while the other part remains intact, only to collapse with brittle fracture in a succession of steps as the compression increases. The second bite has much smaller peak force and area, but not as small as in the pretzel sticks or breadsticks. The second bite (like Fig. 11.8), shows no brittle fracture force peaks.

Another desirable effect with many crunchy foods is the sound that accompanies the brittle fracture. The sounds that are produced by chewing foodstuffs have been analyzed by Drake (1963, 1965), who tape-recorded the chewing sounds obtained as people masticated crunchy foods. The sound on the tapes was then analyzed for the amplitude, frequency and duration of sound. Drake found significant correlations between sensory scores for tenderness and amplitude of sound of a standard frequency for crisp or crunchy foods. He obtained correlation coefficients of 0.74 to 0.97 for crisp Swedish bread, biscuits and wafers, rusks and carrot. However, on samples of meat (a non-crunchy food) the correlation coefficient fell to -0.26 and -0.28.

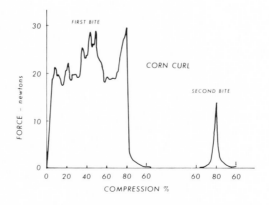

FIG. 11.10   TEXTURE PROFILE OF CORN CURLS

The structure of crunchy foods is usually a cellular aggregate with very little fibrous or laminar tissues present. Crisp or crunchy foods may be divided into two general types—dry and wet. Potato chips, rusks, pretzels, and most snack foods are examples of the dry type. Their moisture content is usually below 10% and often less than 5%. Their texture is characterized by very rapid softening and mixing with the saliva. The brittle fracture gives rise to sharp edges and corners that have an abrasive effect in the mouth. It is important that these sharp edges become softened quickly by saliva and lose their abrasive characteristics.

The second type are the moist foods, for example, celery and apples, which are characterized by having high turgor, juiciness, and no sharp edges after fracture. Their crunchiness or crispness arises from the high turgor that is found only in living tissue . A small amount of dehydration results in loss of turgor and a limp, noncrunchy structure. The moisture content of these products is usually above 85%.

It is interesting to notice that crisp or crunchy foods have either a low moisture content (below about 5%) or a high moisture content (above 85%). It is difficult to conceive of any crunchy food that has an intermediate moisture content.

Chewy Foods

Good examples of this group are meat and simulated meat products. These are characterized by being deformable, not rigid, and without brittle fracture. They have a measurable shear strength or toughness, and the work required for mastication is significant. Too high a work content, however, is undesirable because the product becomes tough.

Chewy foods require grinding and/or tearing in addition to compression for proper mastication; this is achieved by lateral or sideways motion of the jaw in addition to simple up and down compression strokes.

Fig. 11.11 shows the force-distance curve of cylinders of two kinds of cooked meat and one kind of soymeat analog that have been compressed from an initial height of 10 mm to 2 mm in the Instron machine two times. Note the considerable compression that occurs at low force. The initial low slope and absence of multiple-fracture force peaks is in marked contrast to the curves obtained on crunchy foods. The second bite has an area and force peak height about two-thirds that of the first bite, indicating that the food does not "chew down" rapidly as in crunchy foods.

The peak height for the chuck is about twice that of the tenderloin. This difference is worth $2.20/lb in the market place (chuck cost $2.29/lb and tenderloin $4.49/lb in a New York supermarket in February 1974). The soymeat analog gives a curve that is similar in shape to the cooked beef and with a peak force intermediate between that of chuck and tenderloin. There are two important differences between the curve for soymeat analog and beef: (1) The soymeat analog more nearly returns to its orginal height after the first bite. Notice the long tail to the left of the second bite curve for soymeat compared to the short tail for chuck and tenderloin. This tail (defined as "elasticity" in the G. F. Texture Profile)

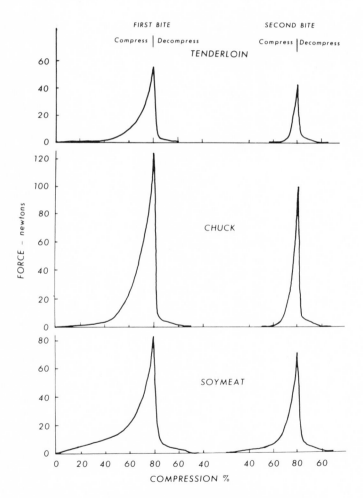

FIG. 11.11.   TEXTURE PROFILE OF COOKED BEEF AND SOYMEAT

is 0.25 of the original sample height of the tenderloin, 0.30 for chuck and 0.60 for soymeat analog. (2) The initial slope of the curve on the first bite is much steeper for soymeat than for beef. Fig. 11.12 shows traces from the chart for the gentle compression of equal size pieces of meats in the Instron. In effect, this is a magnified look at the initial slope of the first bite in Fig. 11.11; the chuck has a steeper slope than the tenderloin, and the soymeat has a much steeper slope than the chuck.

Another difference between soymeat analog and beef that is not easy to measure objectively is quickly sensed in the mouth. This is the sense of moistness or juiciness. Chuck and tenderloin give a sensation of moistness in the mouth while the soymeat analog feels dry. A frequent comment made by persons eating soymeat analog is that it feels like chewing cotton, that is, the fibers do not give the sensation of moistness and ease of hydration that is found in meat.

Stanley *et al.* (1971, 1972) performed tensile tests on meats and soy protein fibers and presented data for work of rupture, breaking strength, break elongation, elasticity, and stress relaxation. Cumming *et al.* (1972) performed similar tensile tests on soy protein that was texturized by thermoplastic extrusion.

There is another class of chewy foods that is not fibrous, exemplified by caramel candy. In this case the chewiness seems to arise from the combination of extensive plastic deformation without shear thinning, moderate hardness, and rather slow solution in saliva.

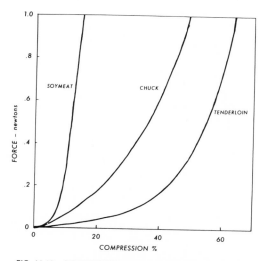

FIG. 11.12.   DEFORMATION OF COOKED BEEF AND SOYMEAT

Soft and Smooth Foods

This group is exemplified by milk pudding, yogurt, and whipped toppings. These products are soft, not brittle, not tough, not chewy, not rigid and have low shear strength and a smooth homogeneous texture with no cellular, fibrous or laminated structure. Many of these products are emulsions. They might be classed in general as Bingham or plastic solids because they do not flow under force of gravity, but a force slightly greater than gravity is sufficient to initiate flow. These products are characterized by having a yield point (see Fig. 11.13), in contrast to a Newtonian liquid which has no yield point. The yield point should be higher than gravity (1G) so that no flow occurs when the food rests on a plate unrestrained, but in most of these products the yield point should be only slightly higher than 1G so that they will flow readily upon the application of a small force. The other characteristic required of these homegenous foods is that the slope of the curve should be low so that, once flow begins, a small increase in applied force gives considerable increase in the rate of flow.

In Fig. 11.13, product A would be considered to have a desirable mouthfeel providing it has a suitable yield point. Product B would be considered undesirable because it would not move in the mouth as desired. Product C (a viscous Newtonian fluid, exemplified by corn syrup or pancake syrup) has no yield point and a steep slope, and cannot be classed as a soft smooth food. It should be noted that curve A is

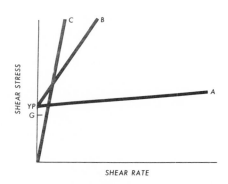

FIG. 11.13.   SOME VISCOSITY RELATIONSHIPS IN FOODS

A has a desirable texture for a soft and smooth food and B has an undesirable texture. C is a viscous Newtonian fluid and is not a soft solid. G represents the shear stress that would be developed by the force of gravity. The yield point (YP) represents that shear stress at which flow begins.

idealized. In practice, it is found with many products that these curves are not straight lines but have various bumps in them because of low-strength structures that have to be broken down. These foods are so soft that in general they are not masticated with the teeth to any great extent but tend to be manipulated with the tongue against the roof of the mouth and mixed with the saliva.

In some cases (for example gelatin gels), there is a melting effect in the mouth; as the product reaches mouth temperature it actually melts and blends easily with the saliva. This is one of the principal differences between a gelatin gel and an agar gel. Although they may have the same firmness when tested at refrigerator temperature, they have completely different sensations in the mouth because the gelatin gel will melt at body temperature and the agar gel will not.

Another desirable textural characteristic for most of these foods is the property of shear-thinning, i.e., a decrease in viscosity as the shear rate increases. Szczesniak and Farkas (1962) found that gums that are Newtonian or nearly Newtonian in aqueous solution have a slimy mouthfeel which was considered undesirable. The more the food deviated from Newtonian behavior by showing shear-thinning, the better the panel liked the product. These results were confirmed by Stone and Oliver (1966).

Multi-Component Foods

In many cases a fabricated food consists of more than one component. Examples are: caviar, where firm fish eggs are embedded in a jelly, and cherry pie, where whole cherries are embedded in a soft starchy matrix and the whole is surrounded by the pastry crust. In these cases it is necessary to separate the different components, evaluate their texture independently and then evaluate the interactions of the various components put together in the whole product. In general, multi-component systems consist of firm, discrete particles in a continuous matrix that is considerably softer than the particles. The matrix is usually a smooth-textured product, while the free particles may be chewy, crunchy, or tough. In some instances, multi-component systems consist of firm layers alternating with soft layers, for example, a cream-filled chocolate. It is likely that there will be an increasing interest in fabricating multi-component foods in the near future. Some Russian workers have already obtained a patent for synthetic caviar (Nesmeyanov et al. 1971).

CONCLUSION

The information that has been presented in this volume leaves no doubt that a new wave of advances in the fabrication of textured foods is well under way. We are quite accustomed to the fabricated foods made from cereal grains (bread, cake, cookies), milk (cheeses, butter), and sugar (candies), because they have been with us for many generations. These foods were developed by empirical "cut and try" methods and probably took centuries to evolve to the forms that are familiar to the present generation.

Unlike our forebears, the food industry of today cannot afford to spend a hundred years or so developing new types of fabricated foods—it wants these new structured foods within a few years. Fortunately, it has well-trained scientists and technologists, well-equipped laboratories and pilot plants, and a good communications system to accelerate the development lrocess.

The new technologies that are now being developed will place heavy demands on our understanding of what texture is, how it can be precisely defined and specified, and how it can be measured quickly and accurately. However, the field of food texture is presently in a highly empirical state; there is no solid foundation of general theoretical concepts on which to proceed intelligently with measuring and specifying texture. Part of the present effort in fabricated foods should be employed to develop food texture as a field of study in its own right in order to provide an organized and rational foundation for our understanding of the problems involved and a means of finding satisfactory solutions to these problems more quickly. Without this foundation, there is a likely possiblity that texture problems will become the limiting factor in the development of fabricated foods, and that time-consuming "cut and try" methods will be the only tool available to break these bottlenecks.

BIBLIOGRAPHY

BAILEY, C. H. 1934. An automatic shortometer. Cereal Chem. *11*, 160-163.

BLOOM, O. T. 1925. Machine for testing jelly strength of glues, gelatins and the like. U.S. Patent 1,540,979.

BOURNE, M. C. 1966. A classification of objective methods for measuring texture and consistency of foods. J. Food Sci. *31*, 1011-1015.

BOURNE, M. C. 1968. Texture profile of ripening pears. J. Food Sci. *33*, 223-226.

BOURNE, M. C., SANDOVAL, A. M. R., VILLALOBOS, M., and BUCKLE, T. S. 1974. Training a sensory texture profile panel and development of standard rating scales in Colombia. J. Texture Studies (in press).

BOURNE, M. C., MOYER, J. C., and HAND, D. B. 1966. Measurement of food texture by a universal testing machine. Food Technol. *20*, 522-526.

BRANDT, M. A., SKINNER, E. Z., and COLEMAN, J. A. 1963. Texture profile method. J. Food Sci. *28*, 404-409.

BRATZLER, L. J. 1932. Measuring the tenderness of meat by means of a mechanical shear. M. S. Thesis, Kansas State College.

BRUNS, A. J., AND BOURNE, M. C. 1974. Use of a mathematical model in designing the triple beam snap test and its application to baked goods and agricultural products. Manuscript in preparation.

CARPENTER, Z. L., SMITH, G. C., and BUTLER, O. D. 1972. Assessment of beef tenderness with the Armour Tenderometer. J. Food Sci. 37, 126-129.

CIVILLE, G. V., and SZCZESNIAK, A. S. 1973. Guidelines to training a texture profile panel. J. Texture Studies 4, 204-223.

COREY, H. 1970. Texture in foodstuffs. CRC Critical Reviews in Food Technology, May 1970, 161-198.

CUMMING, D. B., STANLEY, D. W., and DEMAN, J. M. 1972. Texture-structure relationships in texturized soy protein. II. Textural properties and ultrastructure of an extruded soybean product. J. Can. Inst. Food Sci. Technol. 5, 124-128.

DIKEMAN, M. E., TUMA, J. H., GLIMP, H. A., GREGORY, K. E., and ALLEN, D. M. 1972. Evaluation of the Tenderometer for predicting bovine muscle tenderness. J. Animal Sci. 34, 960.

DRAKE, B. K. 1963. Food crushing sounds: An introductory study. J. Food Sci. 28, 233-241.

DRAKE, B. K. 1965. Food crushing sounds: Comparison of objective and subjective data. J. Food Sci. 30, 556-559.

FRIEDMAN, H. H., WHITNEY, J. E., and SZCZESNIAK, A. S. 1963. The Texturometer—a new instrument for objective texture measurement. J. Food Sci. 28, 390-396.

GUTHRIE, E. S. 1963. Further studies of the body of cultured cream. Cornell Agr. Expt. Sta. Bull. 986.

HANSEN, L. J. 1971. Meat tenderness testing. U.S. Pat. 3,602,038.

HANSEN, L. J. 1972. Development of the Armour Tenderometer for tenderness evaluation of beef carcasses. J. Texture Studies 3, 146-164.

HILKER, L. D. 1947. A method for measuring the body of cultured cream. J. Dairy Sci. 30, 161-164.

KRAMER, A. 1961. The Shear Press, a basic tool for the food technologist. Food Scientist 5(1), 7-11.

KRAMER, A. 1973. Food texture—definition, measurement, and relation to other food quality attributes. In Texture Measurements of Foods, A. Kramer and A. S. Szczesniak (Editors). Reidel Publishing Co., Dordrecht, Holland.

NESMEYANOV, A. N., ROGOZHIN, S. V., SLONIMSKY, G. L., TOLSTOGVZOV, V. B., and ERSHOVA, V. A. 1971. Synthetic caviar and a method of preparing it. U.S. Pat. 3,589,910.

PARRISH, JR., F. C., OLSON, D. G., MINER, B. E., YOUNG, R. B., and SNELL, R. L. 1973. Relationship of tenderness measurements made by the Armour Tenderometer to certain objective, subjective and organoleptic properties of bovine muscle. J. Food Sci. 38, 1214-1219.

SCHIFFMAN, S. S. 1973. The dietary rehabilitation clinic: a multi-aspect, dietary, and behavioral approach to the treatment of obesity. b. Taste and smell of foods. Presented at Assoc. Adv. Behavior Therapy, Miami Beach, Florida, December 7, 1973.

STANLEY, D. W., PEARSON, G. P., and COXWORTH, V. E. 1971. Evaluation of certain physical properties of meat using a universal testing machine. J. Food Sci. 36, 256-260.

STANLEY, D. W., CUMMING, D. B., and DE MAN, J. M. 1972. Texture-structure relationships in texturized soy protein. I. Textural properties and ultrastructure of rehydrated spun soy fibers. Can. Inst. Food Sci. Technol. J. 5, 118-123.

STONE, H., and OLIVER, S. 1966. Effective of viscosity on the detection of relative sweetness intensity of sucrose solutions. J. Food Sci. 31, 129-134.

SZCZESNIAK, A. S., and FARKAS, E. 1962. Objective characterization of the mouthfeel of gum solutions. J. Food Sci. 27, 381-385.

SZCZESNIAK, A. S. 1963. Classification of textural characteristics. J. Food Sci. 28, 385-389.

SZCZESNIAK, A. S., and KLEYN, D. H. 1963. Consumer awareness of texture and other foods attributes. Food Technol. 17, 74-77.

SZCZESNIAK, A. S., BRANDT, M. A., and FRIEDMAN, H. H. 1963. Development of standard rating scales for mechanical parameters of texture and correlation between the objective and sensory methods of texture evaluation. J. Food Sci. *28*, 397-403.

SZCZESNIAK, A. S., and TORGESON, K. 1965. Methods of meat texture measurement viewed from the background of factors affecting tenderness. Adv. Food Res. *14*, 33-165.

SZCZESNIAK, A. S. 1971. Consumer awareness of texture and of other food attributes. J. Texture Studies *2*, 196-206.

SZCZESNIAK, A. S., and KAHN, E. L. 1971. Consumer awareness of and attitudes to food texture. I. Adults. J. Texture Studies *2*, 280-295.

SZCZESNIAK, A. S. 1972. Consumer awareness of and attitudes to food texture. II. Children and teenagers. J. Texture Studies *3*, 206-217.

SZCZESNIAK, A. S. 1973. Instrumental methods of texture measurement. *In* Texture Measurements of Foods, A. Kramer, and A. S. Szczesniak (Editors). Riedel Publishing Co., Dordrecht, Holland.

VOISEY, P. W. 1971. The Ottawa texture measuring system. J. Can. Inst. Food Technol. J. *4*, 91-103.

WHITE, G. W. 1970. Rheology in food research. J. Food Technol. *5*, 1-32.

YOSHIKAWA, S., NISHIMARU, S., TASHIRO, T., and YOSHIDA, M. 1970. Collection and classification of words for description of food texture. I. Collection of words. J. Texture Studies *1*, 437-442.

YURKSTAS, A. A. 1965. The masticatory act. A review. J. Prosthetic Dent. *15*, 248-260.

APPENDIX I
Source of Instruments Discussed in this Chapter

Instron Universal Testing Machine. Instron Corporation, 2500 Washington Street, Canton, Mass. 02021.

General Foods Texturometer. Elnik Instruments Inc., 410 Garibaldi Ave., Lodi, N.J. 07844.

Ottawa Texture Measuring System. Canners Machinery Ltd., Simcoe, Ontario, Canada.

Warner-Bratzler Shear. G-R Electric Mfg. Co., Route #2, Manhattan, Kansas 66502.

Shear Press. Food Technology Corp., 11425 Isaac Newton Square South, Reston, Va. 22070

Penetrometers
   (a)   Precision Scientific Co., 3739 W. Cortland Street, Chicago, Ill. 60647.
   (b)   Lab-Line Instruments, Inc., Labline Plaza, Melrose Park, Ill. 60160.

Hilker-Guthrie Sour Cream Body Tester. Whitman Laboratories, 7 Wedgewood Road, New Hartford, N.Y. 13413.

Bloom Gelometer. Precision Scientific Co., 3739 W. Cortland St., Chicago, Ill. 60647.

Marine Colloids Gel Tester. Marine Colloids Inc., Gel Tester Division, 2 Edison Place, Springfield, N. J. 07081.

MacMichael Viscometer. Fisher Scientific Co., 711 Forbes Avenue, Pittsburgh, Pa. 15219.

Viscocorder. C. W. Brabender Instruments, Inc., 50 E. Wesley Street, South Hackensack, N. J. 07606.

Brookfield Viscometer. Brookfield Engineering Labs., 240 Cushing Street, Stoughton, Mass. 02072.

CHAPTER 12

S. Kuramoto
I. Katz

Flavoring Fabricated Foods

A bacon-like product called Baco's was offered in the supermarkets with resounding success during the last decade. It was one of the first attempts by a major food corporation to introduce a meat analog into the American diet. While it may not have displaced bacon, it did find a position on supermarket shelves as a convenient condiment for use in salads, soups, sandwiches, and the like. In 1971, the U.S. School Lunch Program authorized the use of up to 30% rehydrated textured soy flour in combination with meat, fish, or poultry. The principle use was in hamburger, and some 25 million school children began consuming vegetable protein in patties, chilies, meat loaves, and spaghetti sauce.

In 1973, when meat prices were beginning to arouse the ire of consumers, the Red Owl Stores in Minneapolis pioneered the 25% extended raw hamburger, which presented the housewife with the meat-extender concept. Today beef patty mixes and "juicy burgers" appear to have become a permanent product in the meat case. While such practices were being followed in portion-control meats for the HRI industry, where users were totally unaware of these blends, acceptance of meat extenders at the consumer level was a breakthrough indeed. Perhaps this kind of crisis was required to launch these products, since only a few years ago the consumer's negativity to soy or anything fabricated was a tremendous hurdle to overcome.

Markets for meat flavors closely parallel the development of these fabricated meat analogs. While there exists an attractive opportunity for meat flavors in soups, gravies, and casserole mixes, the potential for flavors, for example in the 4 billion lb hamburger market, are significant. As the technology and need arise, markets for total replacement of such items as chicken, ham, luncheon meat, and sausages are realistic in the near term. Flavors for these items must be developed and a huge effort is under way by many companies to take advantage of the potential that exists today and in the future.

Flavors other than the savory types have been highly developed, principally because of need. We have the capability of making totally synthetic fruit flavors with nuances like the freshness of orange juice or the tinniness of canned pineapple. With the advent of gas chromatography, flavorists are able to "sniff" chemicals as they are eluted, and identifications can be made by extrapolating retention curves or by comparison with reference compounds when they are available. The new methodologies have made possible the identification of hundreds of chemicals occurring in natural products that were previously unavailable for observation in pure form. The use of these data resulted in a tremendous upsurge in the flavor industry in the late 50's which is still continuing. Better fruit flavors have resulted in the diminution of natural fruit flavors. In some instances, products were developed which could not be marketed without the use of imitations because supply of the natural materials could not supply the need. Synthetics were not always equivalent in quality to naturals but quality was judged adequate while contributing considerable cost savings.

More recently, the invention of molecular separators like the Watson-Biemann and Becker-Ryage type resulted in rapid interfacing of mass spectrometers and all types of GC columns. The application of this new analytical technique to flavor chemistry increased the quantity and the rate at which unknowns could be identified by several orders of magnitude. Components heretofore undetected were not only detected but identified. Thus, a large number of unknown nitrogen and sulfur chemicals began to emerge and flavor chemists were presented with new chemicals which had previously eluded their creative efforts. It is ironic that some heterocyclic nitrogen compounds were reported to be important in heated foods back in 1926 by Reichstein and Standinger, but their use in flavor compounds did not materialize until recently.

Pyrazines, for example, may have been rejected for their importance in flavors because the people evaluating them may not have had experience in their use nor the idea of their interaction with other chemicals. Perhaps, they could not be properly evaluated because many other important chemicals were not yet synthesized or had not yet been discovered. Researchers have rediscovered pyrazines, and recent publications have indicated their presence in every type of heated or roasted product. Similar statements can also be made about other heterocyclic sulfur compounds like the thiophenes, furyl mercaptans and sulfides, thiazoles, etc. Interest in these alicyclic and heterocyclic compounds was not simply a result of their rediscovery via revolutionary techniques. Much of this information would be academic were it not for the fact that new markets for fabricated foods were created which forced the demand for flavor chemicals which had been previously unattainable.

Application of computer technology to analytical procedures will have immediate and far-reaching effects. The development of high resolution GC and GC—Mass Spectrometer techniques buried analytical flavor chemists under mountains of spectra; one of the bottlenecks now is the time required to interpret the spectra. For example, to count and normalize the spectra of interest obtained in a 200-peak chromatogram which is commonly obtained from 500 to 1000 ft open tubular columns could easily consume 30 hr, to say nothing of the time needed for interpretation. Computer systems are now available or are being developed that will allow automatic searching of libraries of standard spectra with printout of the most probable structure.

Computers also enable us to do things not possible heretofore by using well-known mathematical treatments. Techniques introduced by Milutinovic *et al.* (1970) and Biggers *et al.* (1969) allow the flavor chemist to compare 2 samples of coffee, for example, analyzed in the same manner, and obtain a digital representation of the area of one peak as a function of the other. These ratios can then be matched with comparable ratios from the other chromotogram to determine which peaks are more closely correlated with differences in flavor. Also, changes determined organoleptically in the flavor of a substance can be correlated with digital changes and then weighing factors can be assigned. In this manner, one may be able to reduce the vast number of probablity factors affecting critical differences in flavor to a relatively small number. For example, a chromatogram containing 50 peaks will produce 1200 terms when expanded from a 49 X 49 matrix, but this reduces to a small number of items where discriminate analysis is applied. This is just another way to answer the question of which components and combinations are responsible for flavor differences noted organoleptically.

Previously, the flavor chemist used a combination of the sniff test and experience to glean the important constituents from a 100 to 300-component system. Where proper flavor reference standards are available, discriminate analysis with the help of the computer and the proper sensory evaluations can be used to select the important components for flavor much more efficiently and methodically with less chance of omission or error. Using only subjective analysis, the obvious is picked up quickly and some of the unobvious is determined properly from experience. For the most part, this amounts to only "skimming the cream", and much of the information is lost because we are unable to properly discriminate a 100 to 300-component system. The computer may offer the best possible means for determining those components and concentrations that relate to flavor.

These new technologies have undoubtedly expedited the development of fruit flavors, and while there is a need for continued improvement, perhaps a greater need exists now for better, more authentic meat flavors.

The first meat flavors sold by the flavor industry were skillful spice blends. In many cases, these compositions are still being used in the meat industry; in the meat-soy blends where soy is used at the 25% level, spice blends are partially satisfactory to blend out the mixture.

Once the utility of MSG and ribotides became known, these were combined to give a level of brothy, mouth fullness character to these compositions. The development of high-quality HVPs and yeast autolyzates made further contributions; and, in today's markets, compositions with MSG, ribotides, and spices make up the bulk of what are considered to be meat flavors. As a matter of fact, HVP blends have almost eliminated beef extract as an ingredient in soups, bouillons, and gravies. This occurred, not so much because of the superior flavor qualities of HVP, but by economic conditions resulting in higher prices for beef extract along with inconsistent quality. Gradual changes and concomitant consumer acceptance have created a new flavor standard to the extent that beef extract would have a difficult time replacing HVP if it were to become more economical and available.

As good as HVP, autolyzates, MSG, ribotides, and spice blends are in flavoring soups, bouillons, and gravies, they are a long way from the type and quality needed for fabricated meat analogs. For example, in the meat extenders mentioned earlier, when extension goes beyond 25% to 40 to 50%, meat dilution is so great that enhancers and HVP just do not perform. There is a need also for flavor systems that can be processed as a precursor, so that flavor development occurs when heating ensues. In the spun Bontrae types, a beef slice or chunk requires meaty, bloody notes which are unattainable today with HVP's, ribotide, and MSG.

Meat flavor research embraces two principal areas, notably studies directed at physiology and nutrition as they affect flavor, and biochemical constituents and their relationship to flavor.

Hornstein et al. (1960) and Wasserman and Spinelli (1972) were responsible for delineating which parts of meat are responsible for flavor. Experiments showed that meatiness is derived principally from muscle tissue, and the species characteristic of beef, pork, chicken and the like originate in the fat. More recent reports by Pepper and Pearson (1971) and Wasserman and Talley (1968) indicate that it is the water-soluble components of adipose tissue that are responsible for species character rather than the fat itself.

It was found that chicken fat had little effect on the flavor of chicken broth and meat but did have an effect on the aroma (Peterson 1957). It was reported also that 2,4- decadienal, an important carbonyl compound in chicken extracts, arose from tissue fatty acids (Lineweaver and Pippen 1961). Patton et al. (1959) reported that 2, 4-decadienal resulted from the heating of linoleate to high temperature in the presence of water, and it is generally concluded that an important component of chicken flavor, namely 2,4-decadienal, results from the oxidative breakdown of esterified or free linoleic acid during cooking.

A myriad of other saturated and unsaturated aldehydes have been identified in chicken volatiles, the major precursor of which must be unsaturated lipid material (Wilson and Katz 1972). These chemicals are nearly always found at very low levels, but while their threshold values are very low, they contribute to mouthfeel and aroma without imparting a characterizing flavor of their own.

The work of Batzer *et al.* (1960, 1962) indicated the importance of reducing sugars in the formation of flavor during heating. The role of reducing sugars in cooked meat flavor has been extended by work of Mabrouk *et al.* (1969A; 1969B) in which ribose, deoxyribose, glucose, mannose, and galactose or sorbose were identified in diffusate fractions from semimembranous beef tissue. Further, the fraction containing these sugars and methionine and cysteine produced meaty aromas when heated. Tonsbeek *et al.* (1968) isolated 4-hydroxy-5-methyl-3-(2H)-furanone, an important component of beef broth, and determined that its precursors were ribose 5-phosphate and pyrrolidone carboxylic acid. The latter compound was formed readily on heating of glutamine. The ribose phosphate is available by virtue of its production directly from autolytic breakdown of IMP and the "shunt" pathway of anaerobic glycolysis. Other known volatile compounds that originate from carbohydrates include acetaldehyde, acetoin, acetone, benzaldehyde, and diacetyl. (Pippen *et al.* 1958; Hornstein 1960, 1967; Hornstein and Crowe 1960, 1964; Pippen and Nonaka 1960; Pippen and Nonaka 1963; Bender 1961; Burks *et al.* 1959; Jacobson and Koehler 1963; Kramlich and Pearson 1960; Merritt *et al.* 1959; Yueh and Strong 1960; Hodge *et al.* 1972; Hodge 1967). Perhaps the most important volatile components resulted from the reaction of H_2S which is produced in part from cysteine. Sulfur-containing compounds can then arise from the reactions of H_2S with NH_3, with amino acids, sugars, and fats. Thus, the production of volatile chemicals during heating of muscle tissue appears to be very complex; it involves the reactions of reducing the sugars and sugar phosphates and their Maillard reaction products with amino acids and the Strecker degradation products of amino acids.

In an attempt to capitalize upon this basic information, a large number of patents have been granted that are essentially flavors by process. One of the earliest was that issued to Morton *et al.* (1960), who described the preparation of a meat flavor by refluxing cysteine with glyceraldehyde or a reducing sugar. Giacino of I.F.F. (1968) described the reaction of carbohydrate-free HVP, cysteine, and thiamine hydrochloride followed by spray drying (see also Giacino *et al.* 1968).

Giacino (1970) also described the production of a poultry type flavor by substituting taurine for amino acids and including an appropriate vegetable fat. Perret (1968) of Pfizer prepared a meatless beef-flavored bouillon by reacting α-ketobutyric acid, disodium inosinate, MSG, and HVP. Hack and Konigsdorf (1969) produced a meat flavor by reacting essentially cysteine-free amino acid mixture with lactic acid, phosphate salts, 5'-nucleotide, and water. The 1970 Lever patent issued to Soeters (1970) is interesting in that a meat flavor is prepared by dry-reacting a mixture of HVP, cysteine, glucose, and fat at 140°C. The Canadian Unilever patent (Tonsbeek 1971) claims the production of a meat flavor by reacting a mixture of casein hydrolyzate, lactic acid, and 5'-nucleotides. It is noteworthy that in many of these patents, thiol groups or thiol-forming moieties are important in the eventual formation of meaty flavors. (Ohara et al. 1970)

While some of the patents described have enjoyed commercial success, they are certainly not the final answer. These flavors that result from reaction processes are expedients until another generation of meat flavors becomes available. In order to achieve this, the flavor chemist must have available the chemicals responsible for the flavor of raw and cooked meat. When analytical identification and organic synthesis of the essential chemicals are developed, the flavor chemist can resourcefully compound flavors that will solve the apparent problems. Thus, we find today in both the technical and patent literature a rapid movement towards the identification and utilization of individual chemicals with meat-like characteristics. These are structurally different, as can be expected from most of the chemicals used by the flavor chemist today. An entirely new synthetic and creative learning must evolve in order to commercialize this new generation of meat flavors. Some of these which are considered important are shown in Table 12.1

While the previously mentioned chemicals were reported in the analysis of cooked meat, there are many others common to cooked meat that are found also in other heated foods like coffee, nuts, and chocolate. These include aliphatic sulfides, alcohols, enols, and dienals. Many of these contribute organoleptic effects to meat flavor.

Of increasing importance in the compounding of meat flavors are chemicals that have yet to be detected in natural products. An awareness of these materials can only be obtained by careful reading of the patent literature. A few of the more interesting patents and applications are discussed below.

In 1968 Tonsbeek et al. (1968) at Unilever reported the identification of two furanones (4-hydroxy-5-methyl-3-(2H)-furanone and 4-hydroxy-2,5-dimethyl-3-(2H)-furanone). Both of these are interesting

TABLE 12.1

CHEMICALS ISOLATED FROM COOKED BEEF

Compound	References
2,4,5-Trimethyl= 3-oxazoline	Chang et al. 1968 Hirai et al. 1973
2,4,6-Trimethyl-S= trithiane	Wilson et al. 1973
2,2,4,4,6,6-Hexamethyl= S-trithiane	Wilson et al. 1973
5,6-Dihydro-2,4,6= trimethyl-1,3,5	Brinkman et al. 1972 Wilson et al. 1973
3,5-Dimethyl-1,2,4= trithiolane	Brinkman et al. 1972 Chang et al. 1968 Hirai et al. 1973 Persson and von Sydow 1973
1-Methyl thioethanethiol	Wilson et al. 1973 Brinkman et al. 1972
3-Methyl-2-butanethiol	Wilson et al. 1973
2-Methyl-1-butanethiol	Wilson et al. 1973
2-Acetyl-2-thiazoline	Tonsbeck et al. 1971

flavor chemicals; the dimethyl compound was reported by Rodin *et al.* (1965) to occur in pineapple. In 1970 and 1971, Unilever (Van der Ouweland 1970) and I.F.F. (Katz *et al.* 1971) were assigned patents that describe the reaction of dimethyl furanone with H_2S to form meat flavors. Unilever has reported that the furans and thiophenes form as a result of the reaction; although these chemicals have not been identified in meat or other heated natural products, their presence can be predicted *a priori* and their discovery in nature remains a challenge to the analytical chemist.

Another interesting chemical that is the subject of an I.F.F. patent application (Katz and Mussinan 1973) is dimethyl dihydroxydithiane.

It is described as having a roasted chicken character. This chemical is interesting because it forms from mercaptoacetones at ambient temperature. The mercaptoacetone and other alpha-keto mercaptans have intense meat-like aroma and are the subject of other I.F.F. patents.

It is apparent that we have only scratched the surface of information pertinent to creating meat flavors, let alone those of poultry, fish, and seafood. The very resourceful work of a very few individuals has led to the commercialization of a few meat flavors which, at best, serve as a stopgap until better, more authentic materials are discovered and synthesized. We must pursue intensive research into raw meat analyses and the pyrolytic effects of blood and skeletal tissue. Perhaps insights into the cellular chemistry of lipid-protein interaction may be necessary to discover what is responsible for the succulence of meat. It appears that the most difficult tasks lie ahead, and most likely flavor and fabrication must be treated as a whole to arrive at organoleptic effects that more effectively mimic what we have become accustomed to eating.

The discussion to this point has been exlusively flavors for fabricated meat analogs but let me briefly delineate some other interesting possibilities.

The starchy part of our diet—notably the potatoes of our meat-and-potatoes diet—appears to be undergoing innovation. The very fact that potatoes are perishable necessitates either storage or preservation, the latter being the preferred procedure in view of the fact that potatoes continue to respire during storage. Dried potatoes (granules or flakes) are an accepted form for instant-mashed potatoes, but what looks particularly interesting is the activity by a potato processor in producing what amounts to a fabricated french fry. A particular necessity was to develop a flavor that would make these fabricated products more closely resemble the product made from fresh potatoes. Such flavors are reported to have been developed.

Two years ago markets for tomato flavor were nonexistent. Today, an opportunity has been created for fabricated tomato solids because of the tremendous success of the one-step, heat-in-skillet casserole mixes. We have the capability of extending tomato powder with skillful blends of starches, acids, color, and flavors.

Cheese has traditionally been one of the more expensive food flavorings used in convenience foods and snacks. The inflationary cost of dairy products has given incentive to many food and flavor companies to produce functional products that perform like processed cheddar or parmesan/romano. Flavor is, of course, a vital key and some excellent products are emerging that duplicate the proteolytic and lipolytic transformation that is indeed cheese.

As in the case of many economics forced fabricated products, chocolate compound coatings are perhaps a classic example of cost-induced innovation. Unfortunately, these "chocolate" coatings, composed principally of vegetable fat, cocoa, sugar, and vanillin, are poor replicas of real chocolate. The duplication of chocolate liquor has indeed been one of the more difficult flavor tasks, but as in the case of cheese, some innovative inventions that have departed from the usual, and have utilized some new and "never-before" flavor systems have resulted in break-throughs in what was once a vanillin-dominated flavor system.

Other fabricated foods, notably margarine, coffee lighteners, and whipped toppings, are well developed both technically and flavorwise and there appears little need for flavor improvement of a gross nature. The greatest advances will no doubt be in the areas mentioned and there is every indication that changes are forthcoming which will make the contributions necessary for sophisticated product development.

BIBLIOGRAPHY

BATZER, O. F., SANTORO, A. T., TAN, M. C., LANDMANN, W. A., and SCHWEIGERT, B. S. 1960. Precursors of beef flavor. J. Agr. Food Chem. 8, 498-501.

BATZER, O. F., SANTORO, A. T., and LANDMANN, W. A. 1962. Identification of some beef flavor precursors. J. Agr. Food Chem. 10, 94-96.

BENDER, A. D. 1961. A preliminary examination of some of the compounds responsible for meat flavour. Chem. Inc. (London) 52, 2114-2115.

BIGGERS, R. E., HILTON, J. J., and GIANTURCO, M. A. 1969. Differentiation between coffea arabica and coffea robusta by computer evaluation of gas chromatographic profiles—comparison of numerically derived quality predictions with organoleptic evaluations. J. Chromatogr. 7, 453-472.

BRINKMAN, H. W., COPIER, H., de LEUW, J. J. M., and TJAN, S. B. 1972. Components contributing to beef flavor. Analysis of the headspace volatiles of beef broth. J. Agr. Food Chem. 20, 177-181.

BURKS, R. E., BAKER, E. B., CLARK, P. ESSLINGER, J., and LACEY, J. S. 1959. Detection of amines produced on irradiation of beef. J. Agr. Food Chem. 7, 778-782.

CHANG, S. S., HIRAI, C., REDDY, B. R., HERZ, K. O., KATO, A., and SIPMA, G. 1968. Isolation and identification of 2,4,5-trimethyl-3-oxazoline and 3,5-dimethyl-1,2,4-trithiolane in the volatiles flavor compounds in boiled beef. Chem. and Ind. 1639-1641.

GIACINO, C., BIDMEAD, D. S., GROSSMAN, J. D., and KRATZ, P. D. 1968. Roasted meat flavor and process for preparing same. U.S. Patent 3,394,016. July 23.

GIACINO, C. 1968. Product and process of reacting a proteinaceous substance with a sulfur containing compound to provide a meat like flavor. U.S. Patent 3,394,015. July 23.

GIACINO, C. 1970. Meat flavor composition. U.S. Patent 3,519,437. July 7.

HACK, A. W., and KONGISDORF, W. 1969. Production of seasonings with a flavor similar to meat extract. U.S. Patent 3,480,447. Nov. 25.

HIRAI, C., HERZ, K. O., POKORNY, J., and CHANG, S. S. 1973. Isolation and identification of volatile flavor compounds in boiled beef. J. Food Sci. 38, 393-397.

HODGE, J. E. 1967. Origin of flavor in foods nonenzymatic browning reactions. In Chemistry and Physiology of Flavors, H. W. Schultz, E. A. Day, and L. M. Libbey (Editor). Avi Publishing, Co., Inc. Westport, Conn.

HODGE, J. E., MILLS, F. D., and FISHER, B. E. 1972. Compounds of browned flavor derived from sugar-amine reactions. Cereal Sci. Today 17, 34-38, 40.

HORNSTEIN, I. 1960. The isolation and identification of precursors and compounds responsible for development of flavor in beef and pork. *In* PhD. Dissertation, Georgetown Univ., Washington, D.C.

HORNSTEIN, I. 1967. Flavor of red meats. *In* Chemistry and Physiology of Flavors. H. W. Schultz, E. A. Day, L. M. Libbey (Editors) Avi Publishing Co., Inc, Westport, Conn.

HORNSTEIN, I., and CROWE, P. F. 1960. Flavor studies on beef and pork. J. Agr. Food Chem. *8*, 494-498.

HORNSTEIN, I., and CROWE, P. F. 1964. Meat flavor—a review. J. Gas Chromatogr. *2*, 128-131.

JACOBSON, M., and KOEHLER, H. H. 1963. Components of the flavor of lamb. J. Agr. Food Chem. *11*, 336-339.

KATZ, I., and MUSSINAN, C. J. 1973. I. F. F. Patents applied for.

KATZ, I., PITTET, A. O., WILSON, R. A., and EVERS, W. J. 1971. Procedure for and composition of the flavoring agents. French Patent 2, 675,449. Jan. 12.

KRAMLICH, W. F., and PEARSON, A. M. 1960. Separation and identification of cooked beef flavor components. J. Food Sci. *25*, 712-719.

LINEWEAVER, H., and PIPPEN, E. L. 1961. *In* Proc. of Flavor Chem. Symp., Campbell Soup Co., Camden. N.J.

MABROUK, A. F., JARBOE, J. K., and O'CONNER, E. M. 1969A. Water soluble flavor precursors of beef. Extraction and fractionation. J. Agr. Food Chem. *17*, 5-9.

MABROUK, A. F., JARBOE, J. K., and O'CONNER, E. M. 1969B. Nonaqueous beef flavor components composition of petroleum ether-extractable intra muscular polar lipids. J. Agr. Food Chem. *17*, 10-14.

MERRITT, C., BRESNICK, S. R., BAZINET, M. L., WALSH, J. T., and ANGELINI, P. 1959. Determination of volatile components of foodstuffs. Techniques and their application to studies of irradiated beef. J. Agr. Food Chem. 7, 784-787.

MORTON, I. D., AKROYD, P., and MAY, C. G. 1960. Flavoring substances and their preparation. U.S. Patent 2,934,437. April 26.

MILUTINOVIC, L., BARGMANN, R. E., CHANG, KUN-YU, CHASTAIN, M., and POWDERS, J. J. 1970. Comparison of flavor and volatiles of tomato products and of peanuts. J. Food Sci. *35*, 224-228.

OHARA, M., OTA, S., ENCI, H., EGUCHI, S., and OKUMURA, S. 1970. Seasoning compositions and related products and methods. U.S. Patent 3,524,747. Aug. 18.

PATTON, S., BARNES, I. J., and EVANS., L. E. 1959. n-Deca-2,4-dienal. Its origin from linoleate and flavor significance in fats. J. Am. Oil Chem. Soc. *36*, 280-283.

PEPPER, F. A., and PEARSON, A. M. 1971. Possible role of adipose tissue in meat flavor. The nondialyzable aqueous extract. J. Agr. Food Chem. *19*, 964-968.

PERRET, M. A. 1968. Beef type flavoring composition, soup and gravy. U.S. Patent 3,365,306. Jan. 23.

PERSSON, R., and VON SYDOW, E. 1973. Aroma of canned beef: gas chromatographic and mass spectrometric analysis of the volatiles. J. Food Sci. *38*, 377-385.

PETERSON, D. W. 1957. The source of chicken flavor. Chemistry of natural food flavors. A symposium sponsored by the Nat. Acad. of Sci., Nat'l Res. Council for the Quatermaster Food and Container Institute for the Armed Forces, Washington, D.C.

PIPPEN, E. L., NONAKA, J., JONES, F. T., and STITT, F. 1958. Volatile carbonyl compounds of cooked chicken. I. Compounds obtained by air entrainment. J. Food Sci. *23*, 103-113.

PIPPEN, E. L., and NONAKA, M. 1960. Volatile carbonyl compounds of cooked chicken.II. Compounds volatilized with steam during cooking. J. Food Sci. *25*, 764-769.

PIPPEN, E. L., and NONAKA, M. 1963. Gas chromatography of chicken and turkey volatiles: the effect of temperature, oxygen and type of tissue on composition of the volatile fraction. J. Food Sci. *28*, 334-341.

REICHSTEIN, T., and STAUDINGER, H. 1926. Producing artificial coffee oil, a new or improved method. British Patents 260, 960 and 246, 454.

RODIN, J. O., HIMEL, C. M., SILVERSTEIN, M., LEEPER, R. W., and GORTNER, W. A.

1965. Volatile flavor and aroma components of pineapple. I. Isolation and tentative identification of 2,5-dimethyl-4-hydroxy-3(2H)-furanone. J. Food Sci. *30*, 280-285.

SOETERS, C. J. 1970. Process for preparing a savory meat flavoring. U.S. Patent 3,493,393. Feb. 3.

TONSBEEK, C. H. T. 1971. Flavor composition. Canadian Patent 862,685. Feb. 2.

TONSBEEK, C. H. T., COPIER, H., and PLANCKEN, A. J. 1971. Components contributing to beef flavor. Isolation of 2-acetyl-2-thiazoline from beef broth. J. Agr. Food Chem. *19*, 1014-1016.

TONSBEEK, C. H. T., PLANCKEN, A. J., and VAN DER WEERDHOT, T. 1968. Components contributing to beef flavor. Isolation of 4-hydroxy-5-methyl-3(2H)-furanone and its 2,5-dimethyl homolog from beef broth. J. Agr. Food Chem. *16*, 1016-1021.

VAN DER OUWELAND, G. A. M., and PEER, H. G. 1970. Furans and thiophenes—meat like flavor components. West Germany Patent 1,932,800. Jan. 8.

WASSERMAN, A. E., and TALLEY, F. 1968. Organoleptic identification of roasted beef, veal, lamb, and pork as affected by fat. J. Food Sci. *33*, 219-223.

WASSERMAN, A. E., and SPINELLI, A. M. 1972. Effect of water-soluble components on aroma of heated adipose tissue. J. Agr. Food Chem. *20*, 171-174.

WILSON, R. A., and KATZ, I. 1972. Review of literature on chicken flavor and report of isolation of several new chicken flavor components from aqueous cooked chicken broth. J. Agr. Food Chem. *20*, 741-747.

WILSON, R. A., MUSSINAN, C. J., KATZ, I., and SANDERSON, A. 1973. Isolation and identification of some sulfur chemicals present in pressure-cooked beef. J. Agr. Food Chem. *21*, 873-876.

YUEH, M. H., and STRONG, F. J. 1960. Some volatile constituents of cooked beef. J. Agr. Food Chem. *8*, 491-494.

CHAPTER 13

George M. Briggs | # Nutritional Aspects of Fabricated Foods

If a particular fabricated food product is attractive, good-tasting, economical, safe, and has good texture, mouthfeel, and good shelf-life, is this enough?

Nutritional scientists, generally, do not believe these factors alone are always sufficient in designing a new food today—especially when the food resembles or imitates a traditional nutritious food and is going to be used in significant amounts. It is important, for reasons to be discussed here, that the new fabricated food also be equal, or superior to, the imitated food in nutritional value.

Actually, many types of fabricated foods have been provided by the food industry for many years, in the sense that they are "fabricated" from a variety of rather purified or highly milled ingredients. Among the traditional ones not generally considered to be nutritious are many candies, soft drinks, cookies, gelatin desserts, pastries, and various other kinds of snacks.

On the other hand, examples of fabricated foods similar in nutritional value to the food they imitate are margarine, filled milks, and ice-creams (in which a vegetable fat is substituted for the butter fat), and special infant formulas which replace human milk.

Bread, one of the oldest foods known to man, can be considered a fabricated food, made somewhat more nutritious by enrichment with iron, thiamine, riboflavin, and niacin, or by the use of whole grain or similar additions. Sausages and processed meats are fabricated. Some modern breakfast foods, often enriched with many nutrients, are fabricated in every sense, and may have superior nutritional values (though the latter statement cannot be made for all modern breakfast cereals, which are often very high in sucrose). Also, those special foods used as various therapeutic diets, for infant feeding, and in parenteral feeding are fabricated foods in every sense of the word.

Primarily this chapter will consider the nutritional aspects of those newer types of foods of current interest made in part or entirely from various vegetable sources (primarily soybean) which can replace similar-appearing traditional animal foods and which are usually less expensive than the original.

WHY THE INCREASED INTEREST IN NUTRITION?

Heightened interest in nutrition by the food industry and consumers is a fact of life today for a number of reasons, chiefly high food prices and resource and energy shortages. Also, interest has been stimulated by the presence of much more information in the communication media on world hunger and starvation, as well as on the malnutrition problems which are being found in the U.S. The increasing amount of information (not generally very sound) in popular books and in the press on weight-reducing diets has stimulated public interest in nutrition. Nutrition advertising by the food industry on radio and T.V. and in magazines and newspapers is a multi hundred-million dollar industry. Expanded nutrition education programs of all types are being sponsored by local, state, and federal agencies, as well as by schools, by non-profit foundations and by some segments of the food industry. Nutrition societies and groups of specific nutrition interests are proliferating at a rapid rate, such as the National Nutrition Consortium, a new Nutrition Division of the Institute of Food Technology, the "Nutrition Today Society," the Community Nutrition Institute, the Society of Nutrition Education, and many other "nutrition action" groups at the national level and in most states. The renewed interest in ecology and the environment, especially among the younger generation has resulted in much publicity for poorly defined "natural" and "organic" foods. Nutrition, also, has become a political issue, with much interest being shown today by many government agencies, members of the U.S. Congress, and local governments.

The New U.S. RDA'S

Of particular importance in stimulating an interest in nutrition today are the new Federal Food and Drug Administration's regulations on nutritional labeling of foods. These regulations will be of special importance to the development, acceptance, and growth of the fabricated-food industry. Because of this, the new "U.S. RDA's" (Recommended Daily Allowance), which form the basis for the new regulations, are given in Table 13.1 These values are the Food and Drug Administration's standards, effective July 1, 1975 (with exceptions), for statements about the nutritive value of foods appearing voluntarily on food labels.

Incidentally, the new U.S. RDA's (Table 13.1) should not be confused with the Recommended Dietary Allowances of the Food and Nutrition Board of the National Academy of Sciences (NAS-RDA's)—though the U.S. RDA's are based on these. The NAS-RDA's are given in much more detail. They were recently revised (National Academy of Sciences—1974), although the U.S. RDA legal standards for food cannot be revised so easily. Significant changes were made in 1974 in the NAS recommendations for protein, vitamin C, vitamin B-12, and vitamin E among others, though these changes are not reflected in the current U.S. RDA's as yet.

TABLE 13.1

U.S. RDA'S' USED IN NUTRITION LABELING

Nutrients which Must Be Declared on Label (If foods are labeled)	Adults & Children 4 or More Years of Age (Used in labeling conventional foods; also for "special dietary foods")	Infants & Children Under 4 Years of Age	Pregnant or Lactating Women
		(Used only with "special dietary foods")	
Protein[2]	"High quality protein": 45 gm	20 gm	—
	"Proteins in general": 65 gm	28 gm	—
Vitamin A	5,000 I.U.	2,500 I.U.	8,000 I.U.
Vitamin C (ascorbic acid)	60 mg	40 mg	60 mg
Thiamine (vit. B-1)	1.5 mg	0.7 mg	1.7 mg
Riboflavin (vit. B-2)	1.7 mg	0.8 mg	2.0 mg
Niacin	20 mg	9 mg	20 mg
Calcium	1.0 gm	0.8 gm	1.3 gm
Iron	18 mg	10 mg	18 mg
Nutrients Which May Be Declared On The Label:			
Vitamin D	400 I.U.	400 I.U.	400 I.U.
Vitamin E	30 I.U.	10 I.U.	30 I.U.
Vitamin B-6	2.0 mg	0.7 mg	2.5 mg
Folic acid (folacin)	0.4 mg	0.2 mg	0.8 mg
Vitamin B-12	6 ug	3 ug	8 ug
Phosphorus	1.0 gm	0.8 gm	1.3 gm
Iodine	150 ug	70 ug	150 ug
Magnesium	400 mg	200 mg	450 mg
Zinc	15 mg	8 mg	15 mg
Copper[3]	2 mg	1 mg	2 mg
Biotin[3]	0.3 mg	0.15 mg	0.3 mg
Pantothenic acid[3]	10 mg	5 mg	10 mg

Notes:
  1. The U.S. RDA is not the same as the RDAs of the National Research Council but is a term adopted by FDA to replace the term "Minimum Daily Requirement" (MDR). The U.S. RDA's are derived from the 1968 NRC-RDA's for the adult male.
  2. "High quality protein" is defined as having a protein efficiency ratio (PER) equal to or greater than that of casein. "Proteins in general" are those with a PER less than that of casein. Total protein with a PER less than 20% of that of casein are considered "not a significant source of protein" and would not be expressed on the label in terms of the U.S. RDA.
  3. There are no NRC-RDA's for copper, biotin, or pantothenic acid.

Adapted from Federal Register, March 14, 1973, pp. 6950-6964.

INDICATORS OF NUTRITION PROBLEMS IN THE UNITED STATES

Nutritional surveys, including biochemical and clinical studies, made in the U. S. in the past few years show many pockets of borderline nutritional deficiencies and other forms of malnutrition (Abraham *et al.* 1974, Davis *et al.* 1969, Kelsay 1969, USDA 1969, U.S.DHEW (Ten State Survey) 1972). These studies, in summary, show that the nutrition situation in the U.S. is no better—and possibly worse—than 10 or 20 years ago, with evidences of malnutrition existing today in the form of inadequate intake of nutritious foods and of specific nutrients (especially iron, calcium, vitamin A, vitamin C, and riboflavin). Malnutrition in this country is demonstrated directly by the high incidence of anemia and obesity, and indirectly by diseases closely associated with under- or over-nutrition, such as diseases of the circulatory system (heart disease, hypertension, stroke, etc.), diabetes, severe incidences of dental and peridontal diseases, and problems associated with excessive alcohol intake. At least 25 to 30% of the population is affected by significant nutritional problems, not including dental decay, according to my own estimates. Especially vulnerable to malnutrition are infants, young children, adolescents, young pregnant women, families of the poor, handicapped persons, and people over 65 years of age. It needs to be noted, especially in the context of fabricated foods, that specific *protein* deficiencies are actually very uncommon in the U.S.

A second indicator of nutrition problems in the U.S. is a comparison of the nutrients available per day for civilian consumption on a per capita basis (Table 13.2) with the U.S. Recommended Daily Allowances (Table 13.1). Table 13.2 gives the estimates of nutrient availability from food availability figures with *no deduction for loss on processing or waste of*

TABLE 13.2

NUTRIENTS AVAILABLE FOR CIVILIAN CONSUMPTION,
PER CAPITA PER DAY, SELECTED PERIODS[1]

Nutrient	Unit	Aver-age 1957-59	1967	1971	1972	1973 prelim-inary	1973 as a percentage of 1957-59	1967	1972
Food energy	cal	3,140	3,210	3,320	3,320	3,390	105	102	99
Protein	gm	95	98	101	101	100	105	102	99
Fat	gm	143	150	158	158	156	109	104	99
Carbohydrate	gm	374	373	380	381	382	109	102	100
Calcium	gm	.98	.94	.94	.94	.95	.97	101	101
Phosphorus	gm	1.51	1.52	1.53	1.53	1.53	101	101	100
Iron	mg	16.1	17.2	17.9	18.0	17.7	110	103	98
Magnesium	mg	348	343	343	344	343	99	100	100
Vitamin A value	I.U.	8,000	7,900	8,200	8,100	8,100	101	103	100
Thiamine	mg	1.84	1.91	1.97	1.93	1.90	103	99	98
Riboflavin	mg	2.28	2.33	2.37	2.35	2.35	103	101	100
Niacin	mg	20.6	22.4	23.3	23.3	23.0	112	103	99
Vitamin B_6	mg	2.01	2.18	2.28	2.29	2.25	112	103	98
Vitamin B_{12}	mcg	8.9	9.5	9.9	9.9	9.7	109	102	98
Ascorbic acid	mg	105	108	115	115	117	111	108	102

[1]Quantities of nutrients computed by Agricultural Research Service, Consumer and Food Economics Institute, on the basis of estimates of per capita food consumption (retail weight), including estimates of produce of home gardens, prepared by the Economic Research Service. No deduction made in nutrient estimates for loss or waste of food in the home, use for pet food, or for destruction or loss of nutrients during the preparation of food. Civilian consumption data include iron, thiamine, ribo-flavin, and niacin added to flour and cereal products; vitamin A value added primarily to margarine, milk of all types, and milk extenders; ascorbic acid added primarily to fruit juices and drinks, flavored beverages and dessert powders, milk extenders, and cereals. Quantities for 1960-66 were estimated in part by Consumer and Food Economics Institute. (From the National Food Situation, Economic Research Service, U.S.D.A., Washington, D.C., November 1973 (NFS-146), p. 24).

food in the home, or use for pet food. Allowing for a deduction for waste and loss of nutrients in processing (probably amounting to at least 20% of the figures in Table 13.2), it can be seen that the amount of certain nutrients available on a daily per capita figure is very close to, or even less than, the U.S. RDA (Table 13.1) for a number of nutrients (especially magnesium, calcium, iron, thiamine and vitamin B-6). Magnesium availability is actually less than the U.S. Recommended Allowance.

This admittedly theoretical approach becomes especially important when one puts individual eating habits into the usual bell-shaped curve. Roughly as many people would be eating below these averages as above the averages. Though there is room for flexibility in these standards (since minimum requirements are actually less than allowance figures), and though it is true that a person will not necessarily be deficient in an nutrient if he or she eats less than the RDA, the Food and Nutrition Board report (National Academy of Sciences 1974, pp. 12-13) states that "since the requirements of individuals are not known, it must be assumed that the farther the habitual intake falls below the RDA standard for a particular nutrient and the longer the low intake continues, the greater is the risk of deficiency." The Food and Nutrition Board report also states (on p. 14), to strengthen my argument, that "Results of the recent Ten-State Nutrition Survey (USDHEW 1972) bear out the fallacy of depending on averages; for, even in a country as well supplied with nutrients as the U.S., a portion of the population obviously has a less-than-adequate diet."

Persons eating diets low in calories, such as many aged persons and many young persons interested in dieting, are especially vulnerable in this connection. For example, for sake of argument, a person eating a diet of "average foods" of around only 1550 calories would be consuming only half of the values of the nutrients in Table 13.2 which, when allowances are made for waste and losses on heating, would bring his nutrient intake considerably below the recommended allowances. Such values would be considered by many nutritionists, including myself, to be nutritionally unsafe.

Another barometer, or theoretical indicator, of possible nutritional problems in the U.S. is seen in important information prepared by the USDA showing the contribution of major food groups to supplies of nutrients available for civilian consumption. These values are given in Table 13.3 (data from the USDA National Food Situation, 1973—see reference in footnote to Table 13.3). This table probably means many things to different people, but to me it means that we as a nation are in a very delicate nutritional balance because of our choices of foods—often with little thought about nutritional value. Inspection of the values in

TABLE 13.3

CONTRIBUTION OF MAJOR FOOD GROUPS TO NUTRIENT SUPPLIES AVAILABLE FOR CIVILIAN CONSUMPTION,[1] 1973[1]

Food groups	Food energy %	Protein %	Fat %	Carbohydrate %	Calcium %	Phosphorus %	Iron %	Magnesium %	Vitamin A value %	Thiamine %	Riboflavin %	Niacin %	Vitamin B6 %	Vitamin B12 %	Ascorbic acid %
1973 (preliminary)															
Meat (including pork fat cuts), poultry and fish	19.9	41.2	34.2	0.1	3.5	25.9	29.3	13.6	22.2	27.7	24.2	45.7	45.6	68.9	1.1
Eggs	2.0	5.3	3.0	0.1	2.3	5.5	5.4	1.3	6.1	2.3	5.2	0.1	2.0	8.5	0
Dairy products, excluding butter	11.6	23.1	12.9	6.9	76.5	37.0	2.4	22.4	13.2	9.5	41.7	1.6	10.6	21.0	4.1
Fats and oils, including butter	17.9	0.1	42.7	[2]	0.4	0.2	0	0.4	8.1	0	0	0	0	0	0
Citrus fruits	0.9	0.5	0.1	1.9	0.9	0.7	0.8	2.2	1.5	2.8	0.5	0.9	1.2	0	25.9
Other fruits	2.2	0.6	0.3	4.8	1.2	1.1	3.4	4.0	5.9	1.8	1.5	1.7	5.7	0	12.1
Potatoes and sweet potatoes	2.7	2.3	0.1	5.3	0.9	3.8	4.4	7.0	4.8	6.1	1.6	7.0	11.1	0	17.9
Dark green and deep yellow vegetables	0.3	0.4	[2]	0.5	1.5	0.6	1.6	2.1	20.7	0.9	1.1	0.7	1.7	0	8.3
Other vegetables, including tomatoes	2.5	3.2	0.4	4.6	4.7	4.9	9.0	10.2	15.0	6.8	4.4	5.9	9.0	0	27.3
Dry beans and peas, nuts, soya flour	2.9	5.0	3.7	2.0	2.6	5.7	6.0	10.9	[2]	5.2	1.8	7.0	4.0	0	[2]
Flour and cereal products	19.3	17.8	1.3	35.0	3.3	12.4	28.9	17.8	0.4	36.8	17.2	24.3	8.9	1.5	0
Sugars and other sweeteners	17.1	[2]	0	38.1	1.2	0.3	6.2	0.2	0	[2]	[2]	[2]	0	0	[2]
Miscellaneous[3]	0.7	0.4	1.3	0.6	1.0	1.8	2.5	7.9	2.3	0.1	0.7	5.0	0.1	0	3.6
Total[4]	100.0	100.0	100.0	100.0	100.0	100.0	100.0	100.0	100.0	100.0	100.0	100.0	100.0	100.0	100.0

[1]Percentages for food groups are based on nutrient data included in totals in Table 13.2.
[2]Less than 0.05 percent.
[3]Coffee and chocolate liquor equivalent of cocoa beans and fortification of products not assigned to a specific food group.
[4]Components may not add to total due to rounding
(From the National Food Situation, Economic Research Service, USDA, Washington, D. C., November, 1973, (NFS-146), p. 27).

Table 13.3, for example, will show that sugar and other sweeteners contribute as much as 17.1% of our caloric intake, which along with the 17.9% of our calories from isolated fats and oils (including butter), gives a total of 35% of our caloric intake from sugar and isolated fats. Though these are basic foodstuffs, they supply no protein, no minerals, and no vitamin C or B vitamins whatsoever. Another major contributor to our caloric intake (about 15 to 17%) is white flour which contributes, proportionately, very small amounts of fat-soluble vitamins, calcium, or trace elements to the national diet at its present high-extraction rate. These three food items, along with alcohol, supply about half of the nation's caloric intake, but a much smaller proportion of protein and almost all vitamins and minerals (with a few partial exceptions—see Table 13.3). Any individual's diet based mainly on these 3 food items would obviously be nutritionally unbalanced. It is important to point out that these 3 food items add 5% *more* of our total caloric intake to our diet today than they did in the 1957-59 period, even though our average caloric intake is less. This trend, too, is of concern to me because of our bell-shaped curve of eating habits and because this "dilution effect" with sugar, fat, and white flour is more than we can afford, nutritionally speaking.

Another indicator of malnutrition problems is our high health care costs, now over the 80 billion dollar mark annually—or nearly $380 per capita (compare with our total annual food bill of 140 billion dollars). These costs include, among other things, doctor's bills, hospitalization (and hospital insurance), dental care, and drugs. It surprises many people to know that we are not the healthiest nation in the world; indeed, we are quite far down on the list (the Scandinavian countries being at the top). There is no doubt that malnutrition and poor food habits contribute greatly to these health care costs, though just how much is a debatable point. According to my admittedly rough calculations, the costs due to malnutrition and food misuse are as much as 30 billion dollars a year in the U.S.—over $140 per capita (also see Wier, 1971). This estimate is made in consideration of the relationship of nutrition and food to such costly diseases as atherosclerosis and other forms of heart disease, hypertension, bone disorders, diabetes, kidney diseases, obesity, digestive diseases, alcohol misuse and liver cirrhosis, dental decay, certain mental health problems, certain infectious diseases, absenteeism due to nutritional related illness, shortened life span (when related to nutritional disorders), and to other nutrition-related problems in general in infancy, childhood, pregnancy, and old age.

It is important, therefore, in summarizing this section, that any new fabricated foods we may develop for widespread use in this country be equal or superior in nutritional value to the foods they replace in our diets. To do otherwise would result only in further deterioration of the nation's nutritional problems.

REASONS FOR MALNUTRITION PROBLEMS IN THE UNITED STATES

Persons directly concerned with manufactured foods in this country need to be more aware of the nutritional problems outlined above, since these persons are closely connected with some of the causes of these problems. That the problem exists in a modern, enlightened country such as the U.S. is a fact which many people still care to ignore today, or refuse to believe. No longer can we always blame an individual for his malnutrition or food-misuse problems—the problem is greater than just his or her poor food habits, as outlined in the next paragraph.

The reasons for malnutrition and food misuse in this country are many and varied, but include:

(1) Economic causes, including lack of adequate food, poor food distribution programs (especially for children in schools, for the incarcerated, and for the aged), and because of population pressures.

(2) Social, cultural, and religious differences in food habits, changes in living habits (such as urbanization, decline of home gardens, different snacking habits), and growth of food quackery.

(3) Widespread ease of availability and use of highly processed and highly advertised foods with low nutritional value (including alcoholic beverages). There has been a notable lack of interest, or emphasis in advertising, in the subject of nutrition by many segments of the food industry on the mistaken notion, or excuse, that "nutrition doesn't sell."

(4) Decreases in caloric requirements due to labor-saving devices, and inadequate exercise and activity.

(5) Lack of adequate nutrition education in schools, in the home, and in the communications media.

(6) Poor or misdirected motivation of individuals to eat properly; also complacency, and overuse of fat, sugar, and alcohol.

(7) Inadequate training of physicians, food communicators, food technologists, advertisers, and health professionals about nutrition.

(8) Inadequate recognition by local, state, and national public officials, and industry leaders of the importance of good nutrition. (Attempts are being made by many to have the U.S. government adopt a much-needed national nutrition policy—see National Nutrition Consortium Inc. 1974.)

WHAT ARE THE BASIC NUTRIENTS?

I commend food chemists and technologists for their recently renewed interest in, and concern about, nutrition. However, from what I recently have seen in food advertisements, on food packages, and in the food technology literature, I question if the homework about nutrition of those who must translate food science to the kitchen has been of sufficient depth. Human nutrition is a very complicated science, concerned not only with food chemistry and food composition but also with biochemistry, physiology, and the clinical and sociological sciences. When I read that "eight basic nutrients" have been added to a certain breakfast cereal, or are contained in an imitation egg product, for example, I become troubled. The ones added are not necessarily the ones most limiting in a daily diet. There are not just 8 basic nutrients—there are at least 43 basic nutrients, all required in the diet of man for life. We cannot survive on 8, or 15, or 25, or even 40 of them alone, no matter how popular a few of them might be. (Generally, the popular ones turn out to be the ones easiest to measure in a laboratory!)

It is important here to review some basic nutrition facts for those who are concerned with fabricated foods. The human organism cannot exist without obtaining a relatively few simple organic and inorganic compounds (the 43 basic nutrients) from the environment (primarily this means compounds in his food supply). From these few compounds the human body manufactures thousands of chemicals essential for life, including proteins, enzymes (actually thousands of different ones), hormones, fats, phospholipids, coenzymes and cofactors, nucleic acids, carbohydrates, intermediates, and many, many others.

The basic nutrients (numbered in parentheses) we need from the environment in order to live are:

GENERAL
    Oxygen   (1)
    Water   (2)
    Sources of Energy
        Carbohydrates   (3)
        Fats   (4)
        Protein in excess   (5)
            (also serves as an essential nitrogen
            source)

SPECIFIC ESSENTIAL SUBSTANCES
    Fat Constituents
        Linoleic acid   (6)
        (a fatty acid essential in the diet)

Protein Constituents
  Amino Acids
    Histidine (7)
    Isoleucine (8)
    Leucine (9)
    Lysine (10)
    Methionine (supplies essential sulfur) (11)
    Phenylalanine (12)
    Threonine (13)
    Tryptophan (14)
    Valine (15)
  Additional Nitrogen (see #5)
Vitamins
    (organic substances needed in small amounts
    in the diet—other than fatty acids, carbo-
    hydrates, and amino acids)
  Fat-soluble:
    Vitamin A (16)
      (including plant precursors)
    Vitamin D (17)
    Vitamin E (18)
    Vitamin K* (19)
  Water-soluble:
    Thiamine (vitamin B-1) (20)
    Riboflavin (21)
    Pantothenic Acid (22)
    Biotin (23)
    Niacin (24)
    Vitamin B-6 (25)
    Folacin (26)
    Vitamin B-12 (27)
    Choline
      (a deficiency has not been
      demonstrated as yet in man, though it
      is a vitamin for many animals)
    Vitamin C (ascorbic acid) (28)
Inorganic Elements (the "Minerals")
    (other than oxygen, sulfur, and nitrogen sources
    already listed)
  Macrominerals
    Calcium (29)
    Phosphorus (30)

Sodium*	(31)
Potassium*	(32)
Chlorine*	(33)
Magnesium	(34)
Trace Elements	
Iodine	(35)
Iron	(36)
Copper	(37)
Manganese*	(38)
Zinc	(39)
Fluorine*	(40)
Cobalt	
(only needed as a component of vitamin B-12)	
Molybdenum*	(41)
Selenium*	(42)
Chromium*	(43)

Nickel ⎫
Tin ⎬ Essentiality shown only in experimental
Vanadium ⎪ animals; it is probable that they are
Silicon ⎭ needed by man, though this remains to be proved.

*Essential nutrients *not* listed in the U.S. RDA standards (see following discussion).

The substances with an asterisk (*), primarily among the minerals, are those substances not on the U.S. RDA list of nutrients used as the standard for nutritional labeling. This is important to understand, since this shows why the value of any fabricated food must be measured on the basis of everything within it that contributes to health, not just a relatively few so-called "basic" nutrients.

There are undoubtedly other organic and inorganic substances present in our food supply which contributes to health, though they remain either to be proved or to be identified. Fiber is one of these of current popular and scientific interest because of its apparent beneficial effect on the intestine, though proof of the essentiality of fiber is still lacking. We are working on an unidentified growth factor for the guinea pig in our laboratory, and other unidentified beneficial substances in food have been reported.

Though synthetic mixtures of the above nutrients have served to support the life of humans under certain experimental conditions, it is still a practical and economic necessity to supply these essential nutrients in our diets by eating, primarily, a wide variety of the traditional natural-type foods' sufficiently processed when necessary to make them palatable, safe, and capable of being stored from one growing season to another.

MAKING FABRICATED FOODS NUTRITIOUS

The whole point of the long background I have given is to make it clearly evident that from a nutritional viewpoint fabricated foods can be very important in the American diet, but only if they:

(1)   Provide an equal amount, or more, of all essential nutrients than the food(s) which they replace, and

(2)   Provide an economic and/or an ecological benefit, either by giving equal nutritional value at less cost, or by conserving or stretching what would be a limited supply of foods of animal origin in the coming period of energy and land shortages.

It is true that there is no food which is an absolute necessity in our diet, though some are more important nutritionally than others. Foods are not essential—only nutrients—all 43 of them. Soybeans and other similar legume seeds and most grains are excellent foodstuffs and contain a wide spectrum of amino acids, vitamins, and minerals. Therefore, "dilution" of a meat or other animal or plant food (such as bread) with soybeans or soybean flour makes good nutritional sense, as long as the minor differences in nutrient composition are either added back through fortification or are consumed by eating other foods. In the case of soybean versus meat, among the nutrients that are lower in soybeans are iron and several other trace elements, sulfur amino acids, and some of the B-vitamins.

One could go "all the way" with soybeans in a totally meatless diet (as many people prefer to do in this country) as long as the nutritional differences are otherwise made up and as long as it is justifiable by taste, economics, or the personal desires of the consumer. Soybeans have some arguable advantages over meat: they contain no cholesterol, have less saturated fat, and contain plant fiber, as well as being more economical. The proven successful and healthy dietary practices of the Seventh-Day Adventists in this country, who by and large do very well without any meat in their diet, is proof that soybeans and other vegetable foods (along with milk and eggs in this case) provide a fully adequate and nutritious diet.

As another piece of evidence for the nutritive value of the soybean, I refer you to the tremendous use of soybean meal, properly heated to destroy various naturally occurring growth inhibitors, in the animal nutrition industry. Soybean meal, supplemented with certain vitamins and minerals, has now replaced practically all animal feedstuffs. Animal foods (meat, poultry, and eggs) would be scarce items and at least 2 to 4 times their current price if we had to depend on animal by-products for feeding farm animals today to the extent that they were used in the 1930's and early 1940's.

Though soybeans have been emphasized here, the same principle would apply to other vegetable foods such as defatted peanuts, cotton-seed, wheat germ, corn germ, and to some extent whole corn, oats, and other grains. These are excellent foodstuffs—part of the traditional "four food" groups. Isolated proteins, however, are not traditional foods in themselves and are not part of any food group plan. (See next section.)

Use of Isolated Texturized Proteins Not Nutritionally Sound

Now, what about using isolated texturized proteins, concentrates of protein 80% or higher, in making fabricated foods (the preceding discussion was about the benefits of using soybean flour or other vegetable foods not far removed from their natural state). To me, to use isolated proteins in fabricated foods is an entirely different sort of problem, and nutritionally unsound.

In the first place, nutritionally speaking, protein deficiencies as such are very uncommon in the U.S. Deficiencies of protein do not appear in nutritional surveys, for example. In fact, the average intake of protein in the U.S. is about 100 gm a day (see Table 13.2), roughly twice the recommended allowance and about 3 times the basic requirement. Very seldom is there need for protein supplementation of a diet—though there are some limited uses for protein in certain speciality foods and therapeutic diets.

In the second place, isolated proteins are expensive—more so than the original crude proteins existing in the natural food source of the protein. To use or promote expensive isolated proteins as a nutritional saving is wrong in my mind, and is an injustice to the American consumer, with very few exceptions. I agree that they may have a place in speciality items for functional purposes or to increase the aesthetic value of certain foods where cost is not a factor.

In the third place it is *a nutritional step backward* to dilute the American diet still further with foodstuffs lacking a broad spectrum of vitamins and minerals, as pointed out earlier. Every time our overall diets are "diluted out" in appreciable amounts (even if with products fortified with the "basic RDA nutrients"), our intake of potassium, folic acid, pantothenic acid, and many other essential nutrients not considered "basic" is decreased accordingly. It would be impractical and uneconomical to try to fortify a product made with isolated protein with all these missing nutrients. We are still a long way, knowledge-wise, from being able to balance the diets of the American public to any large extent from enrichment with the entire spectrum of nutrients because of such widespread differences in food habits. We still need to depend on eating a variety of "crude" foodstuffs to ensure an adequate intake of nutrients along with any enrichment that still might be necessary.

NEED FOR BIOLOGICAL TESTING OF FABRICATED FOODS

Because it is probable that we will be consuming an increasingly greater amount of fabricated foods in future years, many made with isolated proteins in spite of what I have stated here, it is essential that a routine biological test with animals be made on these new products. Some type of standard "biological score" will need to be given to their overall nutritional value compared with the product they imitate. This is now done routinely in testing the comparative value of protein used in foods (PER test as an example); but to test for protein quality only, in measuring fabricated foods, is entirely inadequate. No food manufacturer should market a new type of meat extender or any type of food which imitates another without having tests run on its biological value; the test results should be available to others. Rigid federal standards need to be established. Especially necessary is the development of biological tests to be used to evaluate substitutes for foods of the traditional "four food groups", such as substitutes for citrus juices, other fruit juices, hamburger, eggs, milk, cream, cheese, processed meats, and whole grain.

I fully recognize that we normally eat a total diet composed of a wide variety of foods, and that in most diets there is a margin of safety for most nutrients. Nevertheless, with the wide availability of fabricated foods, what are the chances that many persons may be eating diets consisting mainly of such foods? To use a hypothetical example, it is entirely possible that a school-age child might have a breakfast of an imitation citrus drink high in vitamin C (only), a sugar-rich breakfast cereal with limited milk intake, a lunch of isolated protein-diluted meat with a white flour bun, an afternoon candy bar, and an evening meal of imitation potato chips, a soft drink and some overcooked meat, fish, or poultry. This is not an adequate diet—it is low in important nutrients.

Biological testing of fabricated foods is also essential because of the possible presence of toxic artifacts or loss of amino acids developed in the manufacturing practice—something always possible when proteins are highly processed.

FOOD HABITS AND FABRICATED FOODS

How fast will fabricated foods replace traditional foods? Not very fast, I feel, based on the fact that people's food habits are difficult to change.

However, they do change or we would not have a multi-billion dollar food-advertising industry. There is no doubt, for instance, that fear of toxic substances and the amount of money in the pocketbook are two important factors which motivate food changes quite rapidly. The taste, texture, and appearance of foods are other factors. Nutritional value will be an increasingly greater factor as knowledge about good nutrition and its importance to health reaches more and more consumers. In connection with our food habits, if I were to ask how many of you would go to a restaurant tonight and order from a hypothetical menu a fabricated prime rib instead of a regular prime rib, I would expect very few to respond positively. Food habits are much ingrained in us.

SUMMARY

Fabricated foods, from a nutritional viewpoint, will play an increasingly important role in the American diet provided that they are made from ingredients which provide an equal amount of, or more than, all the essential nutrients in the food which they replace and, in addition, provide an economic benefit. However, if the resulting food product is nutritionally inferior to the food it replaces in the diet, as measured by adequate biological tests, they serve little or no nutritional function. This is because the American diet is already "diluted out", as much as is nutritionally sound by wide use of foods lacking, or low in, the essential vitamins and minerals.

I consider a fabricated food made with defatted seeds, such as soybean flour, cottonseed meal, peanut meal, or one based on whole corn, wheat, or oats, for example, to be a nutritious food (and a part of the traditional four food groups), and to be nutritionally far superior to a fabricated food based on isolated proteins, for reasons explained.

Malnutrition and food misuse in America are very costly to our society, as evidenced by results of nutritional status surveys, a high incidence of nutritional related diseases, a record of poor food habits and borderline intake of nutrients, and high health-care costs. The reasons for malnutrition in this country are reviewed. Fabricated foods can play an increasingly important role in overcoming these problems, but only with careful scientific planning.

BIBLIOGRAPHY

ABRAHAM, S., LOWENSTEIN, F. W., and JOHNSON, C. L. 1974. Preliminary findings of the first health and nutrition examination survey, United States, 1971-1972: Dietary intake and biochemical findings. U.S. Department of Health, Education, and Welfare Publication No. (HRA)) 74-1219-1, Washington, D. C.
BOGERT, L. J., BRIGGS, G. M., and CALLOWAY, D. H. 1973. Nutrition and Physical Fitness, 9th Edition, W. B. Saunders Co., Philadelphia.

DAVIS, T. R. A., GERSHOFF, S. N., and GAMBLE, D. F. 1969. Review of studies of vitamin and mineral nutrition in the United States (1950-1968). J. Nutr. Educ. *1* (Supplement to No.2), 41-57.

FDA. 1973. Food labeling. Federal Register *38,* No. 49, pp. 6950-6964, Washington, D. C., March 14.

FRIEND, B. 1973. Nutritional review. National Food Situation, NFS-146, Economic Research Service, ERS, USDA, Washington, D. C.

KELSAY, J. L. 1969. A compendium of nutritional status studies and dietary evaluation studies conducted in the United States, 1957-1967. J. Nutr. *99* (Supplement 1), 123.

NATIONAL ACADEMY OF SCIENCES. 1974. Recommended Dietary Allowances (of the Food and Nutrition Board), 8th Edition. National Academy of Sciences, Washington, D.C.

NATIONAL NUTRITION CONSORTIUM, INC. 1974. Guidelines for a national nutritional policy. Nutrition Rev. *32,* 153-157.

USDA. 1969. Food intake and nutritive value of diets of men, women, and children in the United States, Spring 1965: A preliminary report. ARS 62-18. USDA, Beltsville, Maryland 1-69.

USDHEW. 1972. Ten-state nutrition survey, 1968-70. Publication No. (HSM) 72-8130-8134, Washington, D. C.

WIER, C. E. 1971. Benefits from Human Nutrition Research. Human Nutrition Research Division, Agric. Res. Service, USDA, Washington, D. C.

CHAPTER 14

Constance Kies | # Nutritional Evaluation of Fabricated Foods

As fabricated foods gain an increasingly prominent place in the diets of humans, the greater will be the need for them to be carriers of nutrients of appropriate kinds and amounts. The need of and stress on the nutritive value of these products will be proportionally increased.

In a true sense, a food product has no nutritional value in itself: its nutritional value is merely a reflection of the physiological needs and wants of the individual consuming it. Thus, the nutritional value of a food product in reality is a very variable, changeable quality depending upon the specific consumer under specific circumstances. Practicality demands a somewhat more definable method of approach.

Approaches to Measurement of Nutritive Quality

Definition of nutritive quality in theory should take into consideration all the nutrients known to be or suspected to be required by the human, plus all the interrelations existing between these nutrients known to influence the requirements of any of them. This also is an almost impossible task.

While fabricated foods must act as carriers of many vitamins, minerals and energy, much of the stress has been on protein quality. Even limiting nutritive evaluation to protein value offers complications.

Various interacting factors are involved in determining the value of food products as sources of protein. Some of the defined direct determinants are as follows:

(1) Amino acid proportionality patterns. Lysine and sulfur-containing amino acid content has received much stress but other interrelationships may well be involved.
(2) Total protein content.
(3) Protein digestibility and amino acid availability.
(4) Total nutritional environment.

Indirect determinants of value of food products as sources of protein may involve the following:

(1) Palatability and acceptability. Regardless of the nutritional merits of a product if people won't eat it or if dietary habits limit its inclusion in the diet to very small amounts, its value is nil.
(2) Availability.
(3) Cost.
(4) Other constituents of the product. These may enhance or detract from value as protein resources.

(5)   Other constituents of the food pattern.

Obviously, no single assay procedure could possibly take all these factors into account. An idealized approach to evaluating the value of a supplementary protein would involve a sequential progression from chemical evaluations, to biological evaluations with animals, to biological evaluation with humans, to controlled field and uncontrolled field trials. For routine evaluation of large numbers of test materials such a procedure is prohibitive in terms of time, money and limitations of test materials.

The Department of Food and Nutrition, University of Nebraska, for many years has specialized in one of these steps—that of human bioassay of protein nutritive value. Human bioassay approaches are expensive in terms of time, money and effort. They present special legal and ethical problems. Human bioassay procedures certainly should not be used as for everyday screening, but they offer invaluable information as a final check. The remainder of this paper will discuss experiences using humans in the bioassay of one type of fabricated food ingredient, namely, vegetable protein products processed to resemble ground beef.

Several years ago the Department of Food and Nutrition, University of Nebraska, was approached by the Archer Daniels Midland Company to evaluate the protein value of one of their products (a defatted, extruded soymeal product processed to resemble ground beef) using human bioassay techniques. Following an initial study which was financially sponsored by the ADM company, a series of studies investigating various aspects of the protein value of this material was undertaken using other sources of financial support. In order to give continuity to this project, the same product, referred to here as TVP (textured vegetable protein), was used throughout. There are several other somewhat similar products marketed by other companies which originate from different raw materials or which are produced by quite different processing techniques. Although this chapter will deal chiefly with the results of studies using the ADM product, this should not be interpreted to indicate that the Department of Food and Nutrition, University of Nebraska, feels that the ADM product is superior or inferior to that of any other company.

The PER method, in spite of its many limitations, is the most popular small animal bioassay method of evaluation of protein quality of food products. When humans are used as the bioassay experimental models, the most popular method of evaluation is the nitrogen balance technique.

Nitrogen balance equals nitrogen content of the diet consumed minus the nitrogen content of the excreta (urine and feces) over a stated period of time. An improvement in nitrogen balance, that is, a less negative or more positive balance in comparison to a control is an index of the protein quality of a test product.

Some variations in application of the nitrogen balance technique to human subjects exist from laboratory to laboratory. Therefore, the routine procedures used at the University of Nebraska which apply to all studies to be discussed in this chapter are explained.

For each study, approximately 10 volunteers from the student body of the University of Nebraska, inmate population of the Nebraska Penal and Correctional Complex for Men, or (in the case of the adolescent boy studies) from the student body of a local junior high school are selected as subjects.

All subjects receive all experimental variables. The test product is incorporated into the test diet shown in Table 14.1 Each product is fed for a period of 4 to 10 days before the next product or product variation is substituted. All dietary items are weighed. Subjects are required to eat everything served and nothing else.

TABLE 14.1

BASAL DIET

	Amount
Breakfast	
Applesauce	100 gm
Starch bread	⅓ recipe
Jelly	Varied
Butter oil	Varied
Tea or coffee	Varied
Lunch	
Casserole	
Green beans	50 gm
Stewed tomatoes	50 gm
Test product	Varied
Peaches	100 gm
Starch bread	⅓ recipe
Jelly	Varied
Soft drinks	Varied
Butter oil	Varied
Vitamin supplement	
Mineral supplement	
Supper	
Casserole	
Green beans	50 gm
Stewed tomatoes	50 gm
Test product	Varied
Pears	100 gm
Starch bread	⅓ recipe
Jelly	Varied
Hard candy	Varied
Butter oil	Varied

During the feeding phase of each study, subjects make complete collections of urine and feces. Nitrogen content of urine, feces, and food used in calculation of nitrogen balance are analyzed and are reported in terms of mean values for 24 hr.

Comparison of Protein Value of Ground Beef, TVP and Methionine-Enriched TVP at Two Levels of Intake

The objective of the first study in the series (Kies and Fox 1971) was to compare the protein value of TVP, a 1% D,L-methionine-enriched TVP and ground beef at two levels of nitrogen intake in respect to its ability to meet the protein needs of adult men.

The experimental plan is given on Table 14.2. The 62-day study consisted of two 31-day parts in which total dietary nitrogen was maintained at either 4.8 gm N/day or 8.8 gm N/day. During part A, beef, TVP, or the methionine-enriched TVP was fed to provide 4.0 gm N/day in randomized periods of 7 days each. During part B, the test materials were fed at an 8.0 gm N/day level. Diets were maintained adequate in vitamins, minerals and calories.

At the 4.0-gm N intake level, mean nitrogen balances of the 10 adult human subjects were: -0.30, -0.70, and -0.45 gm N/day, respectively, for beef, TVP and methionine-enriched TVP. This suggested a lower protein nutritive value for TVP, which can be overcome at least in part by methionine supplementation. It also indicates methionine as being the first limiting amino acid in the product.

TABLE 14.2

EXPERIMENTAL PLAN

Period[1]	No. of Days	Source of Dietary Nitrogen	Amount (gm N/day)	Total Dietary Nitrogen[2] (gm N/day)
Part A				
Adj. A	10	50% beef/50% TVP	4.0	4.8
Exp. 1	7	Beef	4.0	4.8
Exp. 2	7	TVP	4.0	4.8
Exp. 3	7	TVP + 1% methionine	4.0	4.8
Part B				
Adj. B	10	50% beef/50% TVP	8.0	8.8
Exp. 4	7	Beef	8.0	8.8
Exp. 5	7	TVP	8.0	8.8
Exp. 6	7	TVP + 1% methionine	8.0	8.8
	62			

[1]Periods of Part A and Part B randomly arranged for the 10 adult male subjects.
[2]Includes 0.8 gm N/day from basal diet.

At the 8.0-gm N intake level, feeding of the 3 products resulted in almost identical nitrogen retentions. This should not be interpreted as meaning that the products were equal in protein value, but rather that if sufficent quantities are fed, the TVP can meet the protein nutritional needs of humans. It does suggest, however, that discussion of protein quality in relationship to TVP and beef is really more academic than practical.

Part A of this study was repeated in a second project designed to compare the protein nutritional value of beef, TVP, and 1% D,L-methionine-enriched TVP for adolescent boys (Korslund et al. 1973). Adolescent boys aged 12 to 16 years believed to be in the rapid growth stage are used in this laboratory for comparison studies on protein needs for growth (Table 14.3).

Mean nitrogen balances of 9 subjects while receiving TVP, methionine-enriched TVP and beef at the 4.0-gm N intake level were: -0.08, +0.48, and +0.32 gm N/day, respectively. Again, results indicated a poorer protein quality for the TVP product in comparison to beef, which could be overcome with methionine supplementation. The degree of improvement resulting from methionine supplementation was much greater in the case of the boys than in the case of the adult men.

Somewhat similar results were found earlier by Bressani et al. 1967. In that study, there was no evidence of difference in protein quality between skimmilk and a test soybean textured food when fed to children at a protein intake level of 2.0 gm/kg./day. However, an intake of 138 mg N/kg/day from the soy food in comparison to only 97 mg N from skimmilk was necessary for achievement of N equilibrium. Turk et al. 1973, also reported on the adequacy of spun-soy protein containing egg albumin for human nutrition. In this study, the product was fed to provide various levels of dietary protein in either descending or ascending order. Results indicated that good protein nutriture could be achieved if sufficient amounts were fed.

TABLE 14.3

COMPARATIVE PROTEIN VALUE OF BEEF, TVP, AND TVP + METHIONINE
FOR ADOLESCENT BOYS

Period	No. of Days	N Intake Source	Amount	Nitrogen Balance
			gm N/day	gm N/day
Adjustment	5	Varied	4.0	—
Expt. 1*	6	Beef	4.0	0.32
Expt. 2*	6	TVP	4.0	0.08
Expt. 2*	6	TVP + methionine	4.0	0.48

*Randomly arranged.

Effect of Varying the Ratio of Beef and TVP Nitrogen on Protein Value

Although results of these two earlier studies indicated that beef and TVP are not equal in protein nutritive value, it has been suggested that a food composed of 30% soy analog and 70% beef gave a PER value equal to that of 100% beef.

There are several possible explanations for the apparent disagreement in these results. It is possible that the PER methodology was not sufficiently sensitive to detect differences in protein value. Failure to detect a difference does not necessarily mean that no difference exists. Since it is unknown how the protein contents of the rations were calculated, it might be that different nitrogen conversion factors were used for the soy analog material and the beef. To feed at equal protein intakes is not necessarily the same as feeding at equal intakes of nitrogen. A third possibility might be that the mixture of soy analog and beef resulted in a total amino acid pattern of improved protein value, thus promoting better growth or better nitrogen retention than predicted on the basis of the performance of the two products individually. Methionine (or a total S-containing amino acids) is assumed to be the first limiting amino acid in soybeans and in beef. Mutual supplementation would be not likely to take place by mixing these two materials. However, protein quality is not merely a matter of supply of the first limiting amino acid but is also related to interplays among all amino acid constituents.

Therefore, a third project was undertaken to further investigate these relationships (Kies and Fox 1973A,B.) The specific objective was to determine the effect of changing the beef to TVP nitrogen ratio on nitrogen balances of adult humans.

The 32-day study consisted of a 2-day nitrogen depletion period, a 5-day nitrogen adjustment period, and 5 experimental periods of 5 days each. The experimental plan is shown on Table 14.4. Order of the experimental periods was randomly arranged for each subject.

During the 5-experimental periods beef provided 4.0, 3.0, 2.0, 1.0, or 0.0 gm N while in concurrent periods, TVP provided 0.0, 1.0, 2.0, 3.0, or 4.0, gm N. Thus, N intake from the test sources was maintained constant at 4.0 gm N per day but the beef N to TVP N ratio was altered from 4/0 to 3/1 to 2/2 to 1/3 to 0/4. The other items in the basal diet provided 0.8 gm N per day.

Mean nitrogen balances of the 8 subjects while receiving the beef to TVP N in the ratios of 4/0, 3/1, 2/2, 1/3, and 0/4 were: -0.44, -0.56, -0.75, -0.90 and -1.11 gm N per day, respectively. Mean nitrogen balance figures were significantly different from one another at the 5% level with each change in ratio.

Seemingly a straight-line relationship exists as a result of changing the beef/TVP nitrogen ratio. This is what would be expected if the difference in nitrogen retention as a result of feeding 4.0 gm nitrogen from either source were the result of either a lower total protein content or lower methionine content in the case of the TVP. The improvement in nitrogen retention in moving from a 0/4 to 4/0 beef/TVP nitrogen ratio is a simple mathematic relationship predictable from the rules of ratio relationships, since intermediate points where mixtures were made fall on the straight line. If mixing the two resources resulted in diminishing weaknesses of both, as in the case of the mutual supplementation effect, the intermediate points should fall above the straight line, resulting in a positively curved line. The opposite, a negatively curved line, would be the result of mixing the two sources resulting in an intensifying of unfavorable tendencies. This was clearly not the case.

No significant differences were found in the following fasting blood analysis as a result of changing the beef/TVP nitrogen ratio: calcium, inorganic phosphorus, glucose, urea nitrogen, albumin, cholesterol globulin, total protein, albumin/globulin ratio, uric acid, phosphatase, lactic dehydrogenase, SGPT, hematocrit, and hemoglobin. This was also true in earlier studies.

Comparison of Protein Quality of Several Commecially Available Plant Protein Products Processed to Resemble Ground Beef

No information is currently available in the literature on comparative protein value for humans of presently available meat-like vegetable protein products produced by different techniques. Therefore, another study was done which sought knowledge in this area (Doraiswamy 1972).

TABLE 14.4

EXPERIMENTAL PLAN

Period[1]	No. of Days	N Intake Beef	(gm N/day) TVP[2]	Total[3]	Beef N/Day TVP N Ratio
Depl.	2	0	0	0.8	—
Adj.	5	4.0	0	4.8	4/0
Expt. 1	5	4.0	0	4.8	4/0
Expt. 2	5	3.0	1.0	4.8	3/1
Expt. 3	5	2.0	2.0	4.8	2/2
Expt. 4	5	1.0	3.0	4.8	1/3
Expt. 5	5	0	4.0	4.8	0/4

[1]Experimental periods randomly arranged for each of the 8 subjects.
[2]TVP (soy textured vegetable protein), an extruded soy product processed to resemble beef.
[3]Includes 0.8 gm N provided by basal diet.

The objective of the study was to determine the protein nutritional value of several vegetable protein products processed to resemble ground beef. The tests were run on soybean protein products made by different industrial processing methods, using either extruded defatted soy flour or spun concentrated soy protein and a wheat protein product. Ground beef and dried whole egg were used as comparative control proteins. Complete description of the products used is as follows:

(1)   Extruded defatted soybean product.
          Ingredients: defatted soy flour, salt, monosodium gluta-mate, spices, whey solids, flavorings, hydrolyzed vegetable protein, caramel and U.S. certified colors, disodium inosi-nate and disodium guanylate (12.85 gm product/gm N).

(2)   Spun concentrated soybean protein product.
          Ingredients: water, soy protein concentrate, corn flour, beef tallow, artificial flavoring, dried egg whites, brown sugar, onion powder, salt, calcium phosphate, caramel, cocoa, ferric pyrophosphate, niacin, sodium lauryl sulfate, riboflavin, vitamin B6 and B12 (33.40 gm product/gm N).

(3)   Wheat gluten-based protein product.
          Ingredients: wheat protein, soy flour, hydrolyzed vegeta-ble protein, salt, yeast extract, dextrose, powdered onion, caramel color, lysine, monosodium glutamate, celery and parsley extractives (30.82 gm product/gm N).

(4)   Ground beef.
          Low-fat ground beef, ground chuck with all visible fat re-moved (28.53 gm product/gm N).

(5)   Dried whole egg.
          Ingredients: dried egg solids, stabilizing syrup (dextrin, dextrose, maltose), cellulose gum and salt (20.96 gm product/gm N).

The human metabolic study was 32 days in length. Nine subjects were fed 4.0 gm N from the test products plus 0.8 gm N from the basal diet.

The results showed that the mean nitrogen balance of subjects fed extruded defatted soybean protein, spun concentrated soybean protein and wheat protein products were: −1.16, 1.31 and 0.99, respectively, as compared to the standard controls beef and egg, which were: −0.42 and −0.34, respectively.

Vitamin/Protein Interrelationships Influencing the Protein Value of TVP

In studying the protein value of a food product, it is customary to supplement diets with optimal amounts of other nutrients to eliminate secondary variables. Earlier studies from this laboratory designed to compare beef and a soy TVP (textured vegetable protein) product used this approach. However, in situations in which the protein intake is so marginal that difference in protein quality between beef and soy makes any real, practical difference, the vitamin environment is most likely to be far from ideal. Furthermore, the processing techniques used in making TVP are likely to be far more damaging to vitamin value than to protein value. Earlier studies from this laboratory indicate that niacin inadequacy results in a decrease in protein nutriture of humans maintained on wheat-protein diets.

The objective of the study was to determine the value of vitamin enrichment of a soy TVP product on its apparent protein value for human adults. In five randomly arranged 5-day periods, 6 human adult subjects were fed beef plus no vitamin supplements, a TVP product resembling beef with no vitamin supplements, a TVP product plus a partial vitamin supplement including niacin, a TVP product plus a "full" vitamin supplement excluding niacin.

Mean nitrogen balances of subjects while receiving these experimental regimens (4.0 gm N per subject per day) were as follows: −0.47, −0.93, −0.72, −0.67, −1.08 gm N/day, respectively. These results suggest that total vitamin nutrition had a positive influence on apparent protein value of the soy TVP product evaluated. Furthermore, niacin supplementation seemed to be particularly important. Data concerning the influence of the various experimental regimens on the niacin nutritional status of subjects are in the process of analysis.

CONCLUSION

Human bioassay evaluations of protein quality of several soy fabricated foods confirm results of earlier animal and chemical evaluations. Namely, these products contain a good quality of protein that can be improved. In general, one does not expect to find great deviations in results using this approach. However, the possibility does exist, and inclusion of human bioassay studies is important.

BIBLIOGRAPHY

BRESSANI, R., VITERL, F., ELLAS, L. G., DEZAGHL, S., ALVARADO, J. and ODELL, A. D. 1967. Protein quality of soybean protein textured food in experimental animals and children. J. Nutr. 93, 349-360.

DORAISWAMY, M. K. 1972. Comparison of the protein nutritional value of several vegetable protein products at equal levels of protein intake for human adults. M.S. Thesis. University of Nebraska, Lincoln.

KIES, C., and FOX, H. M. 1971. Comparison of the protien nutritional value of TVP, methionine enriched TVP, and beef at two levels of intake for human adults. J. Food Sci. 36, 841-845.

KIES, C., and FOX, H. M. 1973A. Vitamin/protein interrelationships influencing the nutritive value of a soy TVP product for humans. Proc. 1973 annual meeting Cereal Chemists (Abstract).

KIES, C., and FOX, H. M. 1973B. Effect of varying the ratio of beef and textured vegetable protein nitrogen on protein nutritive value for humans. J. Food Sci. *38*, 1211-1213.

KORSLUND, M., C. KIES, and H. M. FOX. 1973. Comparison of the protein nutritional value of TVP, methionine-enriched TVP and beef for adolescent boys. J. Food Sci. *38*, 637-638.

TURK, R. E., CORNWELL, P. E., BROOKS, M. D. and BUTTERWORTH, C. E., JR. 1973. Adequacy of spun soy protein containing egg albumin for human nitrition. J. Am. Diet. Assoc. *63*, 519-524.

CHAPTER 15

Daniel Rosenfield

Protein Considerations for Fabricated Foods

Protein considerations for fabricated foods must be closely related to the levels of other nutrients. Evaluation of a fabricated protein food must take into account its total nutritional impact. While this chapter will focus on protein, it should be understood that one must be concerned with content of other nutrients and their relation to the protein sources used in fabricating a new food.

Protein food processing will be described at the beginning in order to illustrate the variety of proteins which may be used in a fabricated food. A discussion in some detail of the Food and Drug Administration's labeling regulations in the context of fabricated protein foods, will follow. Since addition of amino acids to these foods can increase their effective protein content, the impact of the FDA's regulations regarding amino acid fortification will be reviewed. Special emphasis will be given to decisions relating to the use of proteins from different sources and/or adding amino acids to increase the protein impact of fabricated foods. A discussion of the nutritional implications of fabricated foods which contain a variety of protein as well as other ingredients will conclude this chapter.

PROTEIN FOOD PROCESSING

Fig. 15.1 depicts the preparation of fabricated protein foods at Miles Laboratories. Since the majority of Miles products contain fibers in order to have the finished product closely simulate the texture of traditional animal foods, Fig. 15.1 shows a cart containing fiber. As the texture of meat, fish, and poultry is derived mainly from muscle fiber, it is important that fabricated animal food analogs contain some protein fibers. The fact that plant protein fiber is added is not the critical point. Rather, what should be emphasized are the ingredients in the second cart. They are nonfibrous proteins (primarily plant source), binders, flavors, colors, nutrients, and emulsifiers. Examples of proteins which have not been processed into fibers are wheat gluten, oats, soy flour (concentrate and isolate) sodium caseinate, and yeast. The term binder generally refers to a protein ingredient such as egg albumen.

Fabricated foods generally contain protein from more than one source. With reference to the new soy-based fabricated foods, there is a tendency to assume they are almost 100% soy protein with a small amount of colors, flavors, nutrients, seasoning and vegetable fats. The

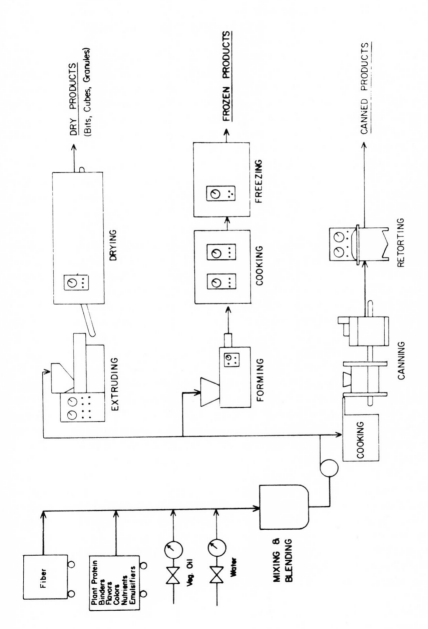

FIG. 15.1. PROTEIN FOOD PROCESSING — MILES LABORATORIES, INC.

following labels from Miles' Morningstar Farms ® Breakfast Links and Breakfast Slices clearly show that these products, as with other types of fabricated foods, contain a wide variety of protein ingredients (Figs. 15.2 and 15.3; Tables 15.1 and 15.2).

Formulations and processes for fabricated foods were originally developed primarily for their organoleptic characteristics. The food technologist learned that it was usually necessary to combine proteins from different sources with vegetable oils and emulsifiers to obtain foods with appealing texture. Methods and conditions of processing, which affect the texture, color, flavor, and appearance of the finished food, are as important as the types and levels of ingredients. In view of the new food labeling regulations of the FDA, increased attention will now be given to the biological value and interrelationships of protein ingredients. Fabricated foods will contain protein from different sources for nutritional reasons as well as for their functional properties.

FOOD LABELING

The Imitation Food Regulation (FDA 1973A) issued by the Food and Drug Administration has significant bearing on the types and levels of protein sources for use in fabricated protein foods. The reasons for this will become apparent after reviewing some key points of the regulation. Section 1.8 defines "nutritional inferiority" as a reduction in any essential vitamin, mineral, or protein. An essential nutrient is one for which there is a U.S. RDA[1] and which is present in a serving of the traditional food at a minimum level of 2%. Thus, if a food resembles a traditional food it must contain at least the same percentage of the U.S. RDA as the traditional food, and must also meet naming requirements in order not to be labeled imitation. In practice, fabricated protein foods are usually analogs of animal protein foods. For analogs not to be labeled imitation, they must contain the same percentage of the U.S. RDA for protein as well as other nutrients for which there is a U.S. RDA. The U.S. RDA for protein is 45 gm if the Protein Efficiency Ratio (PER) is equal to or greater than that of casein, and 65 gm if the PER is less than that of casein (FDA 1973B). If the PER of the protein in the food is less than 20% of casein, then the food has no protein value in the context of the regulation. Since the PER of casein for assay purposes is set at 2.5, the above can be summarized as follows. The U.S. RDA for protein is 45 gm if the protein has a PER of 2.5 or higher; it is 65 gm if the PER is less than 2.5; and below 0.5 PER, the protein has no value with respect to the label.

---

[1] U.S. RDA's (Recommended *Daily* Allowances), which are FDA's terminology for and modifications of Recommended *Dietary* Allowances, are given on page 6960 in the Federal Register of March 14, 1973.

FIG. 15.2. MORNINGSTAR FARMS BREAKFAST LINKS LABEL

Ham-like Flavor / Textured Vegetable Protein

Breakfast Slices

K

SERVING SUGGESTION

NET WT 8 OZ   8 SLICES

Ingredients: Textured soy protein, water, vegetable oils (partially hydrogenated soybean and cotton-seed oil, corn oil), natural and imitation flavors and spices, egg albumen, lactose, salt, sodium caseinate, sugar, modified tapioca starch, sodium phosphates (tripolyphosphate, pyrophosphate, hexameta-phosphate, mono-phosphate), hydrolyzed vegetable protein, carrageenan, niacin, U.S. certified colors, iron (as ferrous sulfate), thiamine (B_1), pyridoxine (B_6), riboflavin (B_2), cyanocobalamin (B_{12}).

Morningstar Farms

NO CHOLESTEROL
NO ANIMAL FAT
PROTEIN RICH

NUTRITIONAL DETAILS ON BACK

Morningstar Farms ™

There is a single exception to protein labeling requirements. Paragraph (e) (Rosenfield 1973) in Section 1.8 states that a food shall not be deemed to be an imitation if it complies with the applicable requirements of a standard of identity, nutritional quality guideline or common or usual name regulation which is currently in effect. Therefore, if standards of identity or nutritional guidelines are developed for specific types of fabricated protein foods such as textured vegetable protein foods, the protein requirements discussed thus far might be modified.

As indicated earlier, many fabricated protein foods contain a number of protein ingredients. While the biological values of the individual protein ingredients are of interest, only the value of the composite protein in the fabricated food has significance. Because of the well-known complementary nutritional effects of protein, many fabricated foods have PER values equivalent to or higher than the 2.5 of milk protein. In these cases, percentages of U.S. RDA per serving would be calculated on a 45-gm basis. For example, a fabricated food with a protein PER of 2.5 and simulating a traditional meat item would have to contain only the same amount of protein as in the traditonal item.

If the PER were below 2.5, the fabricated food could be reformulated to raise the PER by varying the protein components or, as discussed later, by adding amino acids. There is another technique currently possible which is illustrated in Table 15.3. A fabricated food with a PER lower than 2.5 can be made nutritionally equivalent to that of animal products by increasing protein quantity. This is possible in view of the nutritional interrelationships of protein quantity and quality.

Under current regulations, Table 15.3 clearly shows that a food precessor has the option of increasing the protein value of a fabricated food to obtain nutritional equivalency by either increasing PER or increasing protein content. If nutritional guidelines by the FDA are developed, which set quality and quantity minimums, these alternatives might no longer be applicable. For certain classes of fabricated foods such as animal food analogs, a minimum standard of 2.5, equivalent to that of

TABLE 15.1

MORNINGSTAR FARMS® • BREAKFAST LINKS

INGREDIENTS: Vegetable protein (wheat, soy, yeast), water, vegetable oils (corn oil and partially hydrogenated soybean and cottonseed oils), oats, egg albumen, natural and imitation flavors and spices, salt, emulsifier (mono and diglycerides, glyceryl lacto esters of fatty acids), corn starch, sodium phosphates (tripolyphosphate, pyrophosphate, hexameta-phosphate, mono-phosphate), hydrolyzed vegetable protein, carmel color, niacin, iron (as ferrous sulfate), thiamine (B_1), pyridoxine (B_6), riboflavin (B_2), cyanocobalamin (B_{12}).

TABLE 15.2

MORNINGSTAR FARMS ® ● BREAKFAST SLICES

INGREDIENTS: Textured soy protein, water, vegetable oils (partially hydrogenated soybean and cottonseed oil, corn oil), natural and imitation flavors and spices, egg albumen, lactose, salt, sodium caseinate, sugar, modified tapioca starch, sodium phosphates (tripoly-phosphate, pyrophosphate, hexameta-phosphate, mono-phosphate), hydrolyzed vegetable protein, carrageenan, niacin, U.S. certifed colors, iron (as ferrous sulfate), thiamine (B_1), pyridoxine (B_6), riboflavin (B_2), cyanocobalamin (B_{12}).

TABLE 15.3

QUANTITY-QUALITY PROTEIN CONSIDERATIONS

Item	PER	Gm Protein in 100 Gm Serving	U.S. RDA Protein in Gm	Percent U.S. RDA
Animal protein product	2.5	18	45	40
Fabricated analog	2.2	18	65	29
Fabricated analog at higher protein level	2.2	26	65	40

milk protein. could be set. While many animal products have PER's greater than 2.5, a number of processed meats, especially those high in fat, have PER's lower than 2.5. Therefore, a single minimum PER standard of 2.5 with respect to imitation labeling has some inherent inequity. It might be more equitable to have two standards for animal food analogs, namely, 2.0 and 2.5. Between 2.0 and 2.49, nutritional equivalency could be calculated on a 65-gm U.S. RDA, as indicated in Table 15.3; for PER's 2.5 and higher, equivalency could be calculated on a 45-gm U.S. RDA.

UTILIZABLE PROTEIN

This discussion highlights the problems involved in developing food regulations related to protein because of the quantity-quality aspects of protein. The FDA has tried to solve this by using the aforenoted two grouping approach in its food-labeling regulations. An alternative approach could be use of a protein rating system based on the concept of utilizable protein (Rosenfield 1973). Biologically utilizable protein is determined by multiplying crude protein content obtained by chemical analysis by the ratio of the PER of food protein to that of casein. For example, if a food has a protein content of 20 gm per 100 gm of food and a PER of 2.0, its utilizable protein content is obtained by the following formula:

Formula: Utilizable Protein = $\dfrac{\text{Protein in gm per 100 gm food}}{} \times \dfrac{\text{PER of food}}{\text{PER of casein}}$

Example: Utilizable Protein = $20 \times \dfrac{2.0}{2.5} = 16$ gm/100 gm food

The concept does not judge the relative merits of the various protein assay systems such as PER, slope-Ratio, Net Protein Utilization (NPU) and Net Protein Ratio (NPR). It is possible to use any of these in place of PER in the equation. The important point is that utilizable protein combines the results of chemical and biological measurements into one number, the meaning of which is clear to those not versed in the esoteric subtleties of nutrition science.

It is interesting that Canada adopted an official method for determining protein rating of a food in late 1966 (Anon 1966A). An adjusted PER[1] is multiplied by grams protein in a reasonable daily intake of the food. Thus, a food containing 20% protein, an adjusted PER of 2.0 and a reasonable daily intake of 100 gm would have a protein rating of 40. A label or advertisement may state a food is an "excellent source" of protein if the rating is not less than 40; it may say "good source" of protein if the rating is not less than 20 (Anon. 1966B). In a sense, this system is comparable in concept to that of utilizable protein since they both allow for the interaction of quality-quantity factors in assessing biological value.

Perhaps the chief virtue of the utilizable protein concept is that it allows for a continuum of protein values in different foods. The current U.S. approval of 45 and 65 gm RDA related to PER's above and below 2.5 does not make any provision for rating foods in the range 0.5 to 2.49.

There is regulatory precedent in the United States for the concept of utilizable protein. This is found in that part of the Dietary Food Regulations concerning infant foods which the consumer may use as a subsitute for human milk (FDA 1973C). The regulations state, in part, that "if the amount and biological quantity of protein per 100 available kilocalories of such food are such that the quality of protein expressed as a fraction of that of casein multiplied by the amount of protein in grams is less than 1.8", then the statement, "This product should not be used as the sole source of protein in the infant diet" must be used on the label. In other words, an infant food must contain 1.8 gm of utilizable protein per kilocalories for this statement not to be included on the label. The

---

[1]Adjusted PER = PER (test food) × $\dfrac{2.5}{\text{PER of casein as determined}}$

regulations also say the biological quality cannot be less than 70% of that of casein. In concise terms, infant foods resembling human milk must have a minimum PER value of 1.75, and the number obtained by multiplying grams of protein per 100 kilocalories by the ratio of PER of the infant food to the PER of casein must be at least 1.8 for the afore-noted warning statement to be omitted from the label.

AMINO ACID FORTIFICATION

As noted earlier, the biological value of a fabricated food can be increased by adding the limiting amino acid(s). The FDA on July 26, 1973, finalized the regulation concerning the use of amino acids in foods (FDA 1973D). The critical point with respect to amino-acid fortification is that the food must furnish, in a reasonable daily intake, at least 6.5 gm of "naturally occurring primarily intact protein" and the finished food after amino-acid fortification must have a PER of 2.5 or more. On the surface this appears to be a regulatory breakthrough for fabricated protein foods in which the limiting amino acid is methionine. DL-methionine and L-methionine can now be added to foods providing the aforenoted condition is met. In practice, there are taste and odor prob-lems associated with the use of methionine which may not be completely solved. While there are reports that techniques have been developed which will make the human food use of methionine feasible from an organoleptic standpoint, all attempts up to now to verify the claims of these reports have been unsuccessful. It would seem that the only realistic way at present to raise the PER to 2.5 of fabricated foods which are not highly seasoned and are deficient in methionine is to alter the types and quantities of the protein ingredients. On the other hand, if another essential amino acid such as lysine is the limiting one, then it is possible to fortify the food with the amino acid itself.

The FDA will consider exceptions to the 2.5 PER level only for those cases in which amino-acid addition raises the PER to 80% of that of casein, or effectively 2.0. In some fabricated foods the predominant or sole protein source is wheat gluten. Lysine addition raises the PER of these foods from approximately 1.1 to 1.8. It can be calculated that this increases the utilizable protein by 2 to 3 gm per 100 gm of fabricated food. Such fortification is no longer possible, since FDA will not consider exceptions below 2.0. It can be argued that this is not important for a majority of consumers since there is no protein shortage in the United States. However, this aspect of the regulation discriminates against certain segments of our society such as religously or otherwise-motivated vegetarians.

NUTRITIONAL IMPLICATIONS

Fabricated foods are usually formulated from a variety of protein-containing ingredients such as soy, wheat, oats, eggs, yeast, and milk. Ingredient statements for fabricated foods show that most contain a diversity of protein ingredients rather than one or two. Consumption of these protein foods can increase the variety of food in the diet. Perhaps the cardinal principle of applied nutrition education is emphasis on the consumption of a variety or diversity of foods. In this manner each individual can increase the chances of consuming known nutrients as well as any of which we have no knowledge. Thus, it is highly unlikely that a daily diet which contains a wide variety of foods will result in any significant nutrient inadequacies. The greater the knowledge of nutrition the greater the likelihood of wise selection of foods.

The consumption of fabricated protein foods gives the consumer the opportunity to increase variety. This is true not only of protein itself, but also of other nutrients contained in the protein sources. The food industry should broaden, whenever possible, the base of ingredients which go into fabricated foods in order to maximize the nutritional impact of single foods. This will help to assure the public that they are receiving adequate nutrition as life styles change from the three sit-down, multi-course meals of yesterday. Government agencies, not only by regulation and guidelines, but also by attitude, can lead the way in encouraging the industry to increase the nutritional value of new fabricated foods. Parenthetically, government regulations should facilitate the introduction and marketing of nutritious fabricated foods. Recent actions show that government recognizes this responsibility.

Finally, mention should be made that fabricated protein foods can and do have nutritional pluses which are intrinsic rather than deliberate. For example, they may contain fewer calories than a similar animal protein food. Also, cholesterol may be absent and saturated fat content may be negligible. These characteristics are meaningful to people who want to modify their diets as part of a total health program. New fabricated foods have nutritional advantages and disadvantages just as traditional foods have. From a broad overview, the only difference between traditional and fabricated foods is familiarity to the consumer. It is possible to give numerous examples where a traditional food was once a fabricated food. Bread is a particularly obvious example. It could be that the fabricated foods discussed in this book will be considered traditional foods by the next generation.

ACKNOWLEDGEMENT

The author gratefully acknowledges the assistance of Mr. Harvey L. Steinberg in the preparation of this manuscript.

BIBLIOGRAPHY

ANON. 1966A. Official method for the determination of protein rating, FO-40. Canada Food and Drug Laboratories, Ottawa.

ANON 1966B. Official Method for the determination of protein rating, B. 01062 and B. 01063 Regulations under Canadian Food and Drug Act. Ottawa.

FDA. 1973A. Food regulation. Federal Register 38, pg. 20702, August 2. Title 21, Code of Federal Regulations, Section 1.8, Washington, D.C.

FDA. 1973B. Food regulation. Federal Register 38, pg. 6951, March 14. Title 21, Code of Federal Regulations, Section 1.17, Washington, D.C.

FDA. 1973C. Federal Register. Title 21. Code of Federal Regulations, Section 125.5, Washington, D.C.

FDA. 1973D. Federal Register 38, pg. 20036, July 26. Title 21, Code of Federal Regulations, Section 121.1002, Washington, D.C.

ROSENFIELD, D. 1973. Utilizable protein: quality and quantity concepts in assessing food. Food Product Development, 7, No. 3, 57-62.

CHAPTER 16

B. Borenstein | Vitamin and Mineral Fortification

The fact that fabricated foods have a significant place in the American diet and present special nutritional problems has now been recognized by the nutrition community. The Food and Nutrition Board has issued a revised statement on the improvement of nutritive quality of foods (Food and Nutrition Board 1973) which discusses this subject as follows: "New foods can imitate common foods in appearance, texture, flavor and odor. Examples are foods resembling dairy products, fruit juices and meats. Other such foods do not physically resemble conventional foods. Another type of product is produced primarily to serve as a meal replacement. Because these products are replacing foods that make signigicant nutrient contributions, their nutritional value should at least equal the foods replaced. The composition of a new or formulated food becomes especially important when an average serving of the product it imitates or replaces contributes 5% or more of the recommended daily allowance of any essential nutrient or energy . . . ."

In 1973 the Food and Drug Administration (FDA) adopted the Recommended Dietary Allowances (RDA) of the Food and Nutrition Board (in place of the Minimum Daily Requirements established by FDA in 1941) as the official way to express nutrient potency in labeling (Table 16.1). This statement is part of a major policy and rule-making procedure on nutritional labeling of foods issued in several parts by FDA (1973A, 1973B, 1973C). It establishes minimum information which must be supplied if any nutritional claims are made, a mandatory label format for claims, compliance procedures for claims of both fortified and unfortified foods, and reference molecular weights for the vitamins. This last point may seem obvious and unnecessary, yet even here there was an apparent disagreement between experts. The reference compound for vitamin B_1 in the January 1973 proposal was thiamine chloride, M. W. 300.8. In the August 1973 revision (FDA 1973C), the reference compound was changed to thiamine chloride hydrochloride, M. W. 337.3, a substantial difference to anyone calculating the vitamin content of foods. Table 16.2 lists the reference compounds chosen in the final version.

What is a fabricated food? The development of a nutritionally designed baked product with cream filling for school feeding was discussed by Cotton *et al.* (1971) This product is fabricated in every sense of the word. A general review of fortification problems is available (Borenstein 1971), but one of the newest and most important applications,

TABLE 16.1

UNITED STATES RECOMMENDED DAILY ALLOWANCES

Vitamins and Minerals	Unit of Measurement	Infants	Children Under 4 Yr of Age	Adults and Children 4 or More Yr of Age	Pregnant or Lactating Women
Vitamin A	International Units	1,500	2,500	5,000	8,000
8,000					
Vitamin D	International Units	400	400	400	400
400					
Vitamin E	International Units	5	10	30	30
Vitamin C	Milligrams	35	40	60	60
Folic Acid	Milligrams	0.1	0.2	0.4	0.8
Thiamine	Milligrams	0.5	0.7	0.5	1.7
Riboflavin	Milligrams	0.6	0.8	1.7	2.0
Niacin	Milligrams	8	9	20	20
Vitamin B_6	Milligrams	0.4	0.7	2.0	2.5
Vitamin B_{12}	Micrograms	2	2	6	8
Biotin	Milligrams	0.05	0.15	0.30	0.30
Pantothenic Acid	Milligrams	3	3	10	10
Calcium	Grams	0.6	0.8	1.0	1.3
Phosphorus	Grams	0.5	0.8	1.0	1.3
Iodine	Micrograms	45	70	150	150
Iron	Milligrams	15	10	18	18
Magnesium	Milligrams	70	200	400	450
Copper	Milligrams	0.6	1.0	2.0	2.0
Zinc	Milligrams	5	8	15	15

TABLE 16.2

VITAMIN REFERENCE FORMS

Vitamin	Name	Molecular
Vitamin C	L-Ascorbic acid	176.12
Folic acid	Pteroylmono-L-glutamic acid	441.41
Niacin	Nicotinic acid	123.11
Riboflavin	Riboflavin	376.37
Thiamine	Thiamine chloride hydrochloride	337.28
Vitamin B_6	Pyridoxine	169.18
Vitamin B_{12}	Cyanocabalamin	1,355.40
Biotin	D-Biotin	244.31
Panthothénic acid	D-Pantothenic acid	219.23

Source: FDA 1973C.

textured vegetable protein, has received little literature attention and will be emphasized in this chapter.

Textured soy protein has commercially been fortified both before and after granulation or "texturization", primarily as a result of individual preferences among the processors as to production ease and control. The two major concerns are uniformity of distribution of the added micronutrients and compliance with label claims (USDA specifications)

(Table 16.3). As a generalization, the most stable vitamin in this specification is niacin. Riboflavin and vitamin B_6 are somewhat less stable than niacin. Vitamins B_1, B_{12}, and calcium pantothenate present the highest potential losses. A convenient way to monitor fortification and improve physical distribution in soy protein fortification is to premix all the added micronutrients and thus add 50 to 100 mg of premixed ingredients to 100 gm of soy protein instead of adding 0.4 mg of vitamin B_1, for example, one at a time. This premix can then be added directly to the soy flour before granulation by batch mixing or continuous metering, or with the "dough water" if the production process and equipment lends itself to this approach.

Assuming this method is followed, the major concern is stability during processing. In our experience, the short processing time requiring heat, pressure and moisture to texturize does not significantly degrade the more labile vitamins—B_1, B_{12} and pantothenic acid—in this system. Although it is generally advisable (Borenstein 1971) to add micronutrients after processes involving heat stress, in the case of soy protein fortification it does not appear necessary. Some processors prefer to add the micronutrient premix to the finished textured protein via a spray of a suspension in vegetable oil. Little has been published on the effect of specific processing variables such as extrusion on vitamin stability. Beetner et al. (1974) showed the interrelationship of extruder temperature, initial moisture and screw rpm on added vitamins B_1 and B_2 stability during corn grits extrusion. They found vitamin B_1 reten-

TABLE 16.3

TEXTURED VEGETABLE PROTEIN SPECIFICATIONS
FNS 219

	Minimum	Maximum
Protein[1], weight %	50.0	—
Fat, weight %	—	30.0
Magnesium, mg/100 gm	70.0	—
Iron, mg/100 gm	10.0	—
Thiamine, mg/100 gm	0.30	—
Riboflavin, mg/100 gm	0.60	—
Niacin, mg/100 gm	16.0	—
Vitamin B_6, mg/100 gm	1.4	—
Vitamin B_{12}, mcg/100 gm	5.7	—
Pantothenic acid, mg/100 gm	2.0	—

Source: USDA 1971.
[1]Nitrogen times 6.25

All values are expressed on the dry basis and are applicable to dry or hydrated forms of the product. Moisture content of the hydrated forms of the product shall not exceed 65.0%, or be less than 60.0%.

The protein efficiency ratio, PER, of the textured vegetable protein shall be not less than 1.8 on basis of PER = 2.5 for casein. PER of a meat-textured vegetable protein combination shall be not less than 2.5.

tion varied from a low of 19% at 380°F, 16% H_2O, 125 rpm to a high of 90% at 300°F, 13% H_2O, 75 rpm. Vitamin B_2 was much more stable than vitamin B_1 in this study. The authors concluded that "riboflavin shows very significant increased degradation from moisture (21% lower for 1.5% moisture increase)". This is probably due to the high level of vitamin B_2 added, coupled with the low solubility of vitamin B_2 in water—approximately 25 mg per liter at 25°C—compared to the experimental input of 100 mg vitamin B_2 per kg of grits containing at most 160 gm of water.

Regardless of the mechanisms of degradation involved, the Beetner study indicated that we cannot change process variables and assume only minor changes in vitamin stability. Similarly, the stability of both vitamins B_1 and B_{12} are highly pH dependent and a change in formulation which shifts pH from 6.0 to 6.7-7.0 could increase the rate of destruction of vitamin B_1 by 7 to 10 fold.

Since the natural micronutrient content of soy protein is high, it is desirable to determine the levels that can be conservatively calculated to be present and adjust the fortification addition levels accordingly. For example, soy protein products contain well over the 70 mg magnesium per 100 gm required in the USDA specification, so there is not scientific reason to add any magnesium to comply with the specification. Similarly, soy products contain substantial levels of iron, 7 to 13 mg per 100 gm, according to soy processors. It is theoretically necessary, therefore, to add only 3 mg of iron per 100 gm of soy product to ensure compliance with FNS 219. In practice, since available data are probably inadequate to make a statistical assessment, it is more logical to add 5 to 6 mg of iron/100 gm of product and be well over the label claim than to add a marginal amount and run expensive control assays. The problems of mineral bioavailability will be unsolved for a long time. Assuming the iron arguments are ended, the question of zinc bioavailability in soy products is still unanswered.

In all fortification projects an input or overage above the label claim is essential to ensure compliance after processing and storage. Even in the case of the most stable vitamin, niacin, an overage of approximately 10% is required because of imperfect distribution in its addition to most products and inherent analytical errors in assaying the food. In addition, leaching can cause losses of stable vitamins, e.g., home-cooking of pasta products, blanching of vegetables. This is extremely important since processes such as brine-grading can cause extraction losses of most vitamins. In one report, up to 50% added vitamin B_1, 40% of the niacin and 30% of the riboflavin was lost in cooking and draining macaroni.

Niacin and niacinamide have essentially the same molecular weight and biopotency, and both can be used in most food applications. Both are completely stable in stress processes. Niacinamide has better solubility in water but lumps readily in handling and storage at ambient relative humidities. The vasodilator effect of niacin does not occur at food use levels, but can affect workers handling the material.

Suitable market forms of vitamin A palmitate are available for a wide range of applications. These include oil-in-water emulsions, polysorbate-based solution, preisomerized vitamin A palmitate oil, dry water-dispersible beadlets, and powders. A dry, fine particle-size, stabilized form of vitamin A palmitate can be added to conventional flour premixes containing vitamin B_1 vitamin B_2, niacin, and iron and metered continuously into flour streams in the usual way.

Vitamin C is unstable in many stress processes and oxidizes readily at high pH. Technology for fortification of bread and cake with vitamin C does not exist at this time. Bread could be fortified by spraying with a solution of vitamin C. Vitamin C can be successfully added to cake fillings, as in the USDA specification FNS Notice 180, Fortified Baked Product with Creamed Filling. In this specification, the only permitted iron source is ferrous sulfate. Since soluble iron salts catalyze ascorbic oxidation, it is desirable in this type of application to add the iron to the baked component and the vitamin C to the filling. This product is designed as a breakfast food for the school lunch program.

Vitamin E, in the form of d-, l-, or d-alpha-tocopheryl acetate, is quite stable in food processing and can be added to foods in a variety of ways. Alpha-tocopherol is available commercially, but generally should be used as an antioxidant rather than for fortification.

SUMMARY

The technology of fortification requires judicious choice of the best in-process point for additions and selection of the proper market forms of the vitamin and mineral additives. Niacin is stable in almost every type of food-processing operation. Vitamin C is sensitive to oxygen, iron, copper, anthocyanin pigments and fortification with vitamin C requires substantial overages above the label claim in almost all applications to insure label claim for the intended shelf life of the product. Vitamin B_2 has good stability in most applications but is extremely light sensitive. Vitamin B_1 has two potential problems, heat lability and odor. Its heat stability is pH-dependent. In most projects the bulk of stability data should be obtained on vitamins A, B_1, and C.

Fortification with all vitamins requires overages to ensure compliance with label claims, since even stable vitamins have distribution and analytical variations. It is usually not difficult to establish a logical overage for each vitamin in each application.

BIBLIOGRAPHY

BEETNER, G., TSAO, T., FREY, A. and HARPER, J. 1974. Degradation of thiamine and riboflavin during extrusion processing. J. Food Sci. *39*, 207-208.

BORENSTEIN, B. 1971. Rationale and technology of food fortification with vitamins, minerals and amino acids, Crit. Rev. Food Technol. *2*, 171-186.

COTTON, R. H., ALLGAUER, A. J., NELSON, A. W., KOEDDING, D. W., and BALDWIN, R. R. 1971. Astrofood a fortified baked product with creamed filling. Cereal Sci. Today *16*, #6, 188-189.

FDA. 1973A. Food Labeling, Fed. Reg., *38*(13), 2124-2164.

FDA. 1973B. Food Labeling, Fed. Reg., *38*(49), 6950-6975.

FDA. 1973C. Food Labeling, Fed. Reg., *38*(148), 20702-20750.

FOOD AND NUTRITION BOARD. 1973. General policies in regard to improvement of nutritive quality of foods. National Research Council. Washington, D.C.

USDA. 1971. Textured vegetable protein products (B-1) to be used in combination with meat for use in lunches and suppers served under child feeding programs. FNS Notice 219. Feb. 22.

Index